UNREMARRIED WIDOW

A memoir

ARTIS HENDERSON

SIMON & SCHUSTER

New York London Toronto Sydney New Delhi

Simon & Schuster
1230 Avenue of the Americas
New York, NY 10020

First Simon & Schuster hardcover edition January 2014

SIMON & SCHUSTER and colophon are registered trademarks of Simon & Schuster, Inc.

For information about special discounts for bulk purchases, please contact Simon & Schuster Special Sales at 1-866-506-1949 or business@simonandschuster.com.

The Simon & Schuster Speakers Bureau can bring authors to your live event. For more information or to book an event, contact the Simon & Schuster Speakers Bureau at 1-866-248-3049 or visit our website at www.simonspeakers.com.

Designed by Aline C. Pace

Manufactured in the United States of America

10   9   8   7   6   5   4   3   2   1

Library of Congress Cataloging-in-Publication Data

Henderson, Artis.
    Unremarried widow : a memoir / Artis Henderson.
      pages cm
    Includes bibliographical references and index.
    1. Iraq War, 2003–2011—Women—United States—Biography. 2. War widows—United States—Biography. 3. Military spouses—United States—Biography. 4. Husband and wife—United States. 5. Bereavement. 6. Helicopter pilots—Iraq. 7. Iraq War, 2003–2011—Personal narratives, American. I. Title.
    DS79.76.H458 2013
    956.7044'38—dc23   2013008799
    [B]
ISBN 978-1-4516-4928-4
ISBN 978-1-4516-4930-7 (ebook)

For Miles
and
my mother

Author's Note

Parts of this book originally appeared in a Modern Love column first printed in the *New York Times* and later reprinted in *Reader's Digest*. A section has been taken from a piece printed in the online literary journal *Common Ties* and several lines were inspired by an op-ed article written for the *Fort Myers News-Press*.

This is a work of nonfiction. Some of the dialogue has been pulled from written transcripts, some is the product of recorded interviews, and some has been re-created from memory. There are no composite characters, although some names have been changed. The chronology of certain events has been altered. As with all memoirs, this story is seen through a specific lens—mine. I have told everything as accurately as I can, to the best of my ability, and in the most generous way I know how.

Do not mourn me dead;
think I am gone and wait for thee,
for we shall meet again.

—Sullivan Ballou to his wife, Sarah,
from a letter found in his personal effects
after his death at the Battle of Bull Run, 1861

UNREMARRIED
WIDOW

My husband Miles dreamed of his death in the fall of 2005, nine months before he deployed to Iraq. He was twenty-three years old.

He told me about the dream on a Saturday morning as he dressed for work at Fort Hood, and I listened from the bed while he pawed through the BDUs hanging in the closet.

"Our helicopter crashed," he said.

He took a pair of camouflage pants off a metal hanger, shook them out by the waistband, and stepped in one leg at a time.

"John Priestner and me."

Already the Texas day was warm and our air conditioner chugged an unconvincing stream of cool air. I squinted at Miles as he talked, trying to shake the sleep from my brain, while he disappeared back into the closet and returned with the jacket to his uniform.

"We floated above the helicopter," he said, "while it burned to the ground."

He pulled a pair of socks out of the dresser and sat on the edge of the bed. He turned to look at me and I rested my fingers against the side of his face. He covered my hand with his, and we sat for a time without speaking. Then he pulled on his socks, laced up his boots, and walked into the living room. I heard the metallic clink of his dog tags slipping around his neck and the front door opened and a shaft of sunlight spilled in. The door closed and I was alone.

The late-morning sun slanted through the windows when I awoke the second time that day. I pushed back the comforter and swung my feet to the ground, working out the stiffness in my back. In the bathroom, I brushed my teeth and leaned closer to the mirror to get a good look at the bottom row. How is it that despite a lifetime of good orthodontics my teeth could already be sliding together? I inspected where they jostled for space behind my lower lip, then shifted my eyes to the window over the shower where the light streaming in made me blink. I felt old for twenty-four.

The AC unit in the living room cranked and cranked but the sun radiated a heat that was palpable in the small space of the apartment. I felt it on the couch as I spooned cereal into my mouth, felt it in the kitchen as I rinsed my bowl, felt it is as I walked into the shadows of the bedroom to put on real clothes. When I had dressed, I turned on the television and opened the front door. A car cruised past playing Kanye West's "Gold Digger." On the TV a news report from New Orleans gave an update on the wreckage from Hurricane Katrina. I changed the channel until I found Judge Judy lecturing a plaintiff about courtroom manners. The man gripped the edge of the podium and shook his head, and I lay on the couch and wondered what to do with the long hot hours of the day.

In the late afternoon, I stood in the kitchen with my hands on my hips, surveying. I owned four wooden spoons, a complete silicone bakeware set, and—somewhere packed away in the boxes from college—a laminated copy of NOW's feminist manifesto. *Because woman's work is never done,* it began. After a long minute, I pulled down a set of mixing bowls. I stirred together cornmeal and oil and eggs, filled two muffin tins I'd inherited from my grandmother, and slipped the trays in the oven. While I moved through the kitchen, looking for oven mitts, setting the hot pan on the stove, I sensed the air in the room change, a subtle shift I felt first with the fine hairs on my arms. I turned to the open doorway and there was Miles, his hair plastered to his forehead, his rucksack slung over one shoulder. He dropped the bag and stepped into the kitchen. He smiled and I smiled and then he had his arms around me. I breathed him in—the fabric of his Army fatigues, the mechanical grease on his hands, the soap smell still on his neck.

He stepped back. "Are those corn muffins?"

I smiled and my cheeks glowed.

He popped a muffin out of the tin with a knife and took a bite as he headed into the bedroom, shedding his uniform, last night's dream already forgotten.

But I did not forget. I thought of the dream often as the unit counted down to the deployment. In the mornings the sound of artillery from the base rumbled long and low, and I imagined distant thunderheads as I lay beside Miles in the smoke-colored light of dawn. Sometimes I placed a hand on his back while he slept. I faced into his sleeping form and turned the dream over in my head. I took it as a warning, an admonition to care for Miles well. If I loved him enough, I reasoned, he would come home.

Part I

2004

1

Just as I started to worry about the direction my life was taking, Psychic Suzanna came to Tallahassee. It was late January and my breath fogged the interior of my Saturn as I turned on the radio and waited for the engine to warm. The announcer ran through the morning's news—the war in Iraq now in its tenth month, the bird flu outbreak in Asia, the upcoming Olympics in Athens—before shifting tones.

"Up next we have Psychic Suzanna taking your calls," the DJ said.

Another DJ, a woman, spoke. "I understand Psychic Suzanna will be in town next week to give readings."

"That's right," the first DJ said. "Five minutes for five dollars."

I scrambled to find a pen in the console next to the driver's seat. My fingers had stiffened in the cold but I forced them to hold the pen as I wrote down the name of the hotel where Suzanna would appear. A psychic? Ridiculous, I know, but here's the truth: I needed some good news. I was twenty-three, working forty hours a week for a U.S. senator, twenty as a staffer and twenty as an unpaid intern. I was broke, or I felt broke, lonely in a new city where the only people I knew were the married women I worked with and the three college boys whose apartment I shared. I spent my weekends at the library paging through travel guides and back issues of *Food & Wine*, and sometimes in the evenings after work, at a stoplight or stuck in traffic, I cried in my car. As long as I could remember, I wanted to be a writer. I had this Hemingway-inspired fantasy of living overseas and writing, and I imagined a life filled with art and literature and well-traveled friends. But I was slowly finding out that people like me, people from where I'm from, we don't live that life. We don't become writers. We don't move overseas. We grow up to be teachers or nurses or we work in an office somewhere.

My widowed mother, a teacher, took a second job to put me through college. I studied business at Wharton because my fear of being poor outweighed any of my dreams. The idea was that someday I would work on Wall Street, although anyone who knew me—anyone from back home—would have told you that was the most unlikely place for me to end up. Many of my classmates' fathers worked in finance and for the first time I understood what it meant to be middle-class. My clothes were never right. I could never afford the expensive haircuts the other girls wore. I spent all four years living in a dorm. Sometimes I made furtive visits to the writers' house on campus but the students there wore trendy glasses and discussed the finer points of books I'd never heard of. They cited the latest issue of the *New Yorker* and talked about all the talked-about authors. Once a friend of a friend who was briefly in the running for an editorial position at the school's alternative weekly had an idea for a relationship column. A mutual friend suggested my name. I was known on campus as someone with strong opinions on gender politics and women's sexuality, mainly because I was always talking about how women get the short end of the stick. I belonged to one of those groups that handed out condoms on the walk, and I encouraged young women to dictate the terms of their lives. My mother always taught me that a woman makes her own way. The friend of a friend running for editor asked me to write a few sample columns and over lunch at a chic restaurant near campus he said he thought I'd be a good fit. But in the weeks that followed, another candidate beat him for the editorial position and the column idea disappeared.

In the midst of all this I headed to the south of France on a six-month semester-abroad program. The streets of the old French village where I lived smelled like lavender and fresh-baked bread, and fountains gurgled beside the streets on my way to class. The school drew students from across the U.S. and I finally made friends who were like me. We lingered over lunches on the school's terrace and I learned to drink strong black coffee. We traveled together—to Venice, to Fez, to Arles—and I couldn't remember a time when I was so happy.

During my senior year back in Philadelphia, I stayed in contact with those friends and held on to the memories of my time in France. The scent of espresso or lavender could make me weak with nostalgia. I applied to be a teacher in Paris for the fall after I graduated, and I spent the next year living and working in the City of Light. I bought a pair of black leather boots and learned to smile coquettishly at men on the *métro*. I liked that they called me *charmante*. I spent weekends at the Louvre and drank bottles of wine in outdoor cafés with my friends. But I was homesick. And lonely in a way I had trouble explaining. When my teaching contract expired the next May, I decided to come home, to Florida, to take a job in an office somewhere. The senator's office, in fact. But I was certain it would be temporary, that I would soon be back overseas. I even kept my bank account in France open, I was that sure. I still envisioned a life abroad filled with people who had traveled widely, who loved talking about books and gourmet food. I imagined museums and marketplaces, cherries in spring and figs in fall, fields of sunflowers under a blue sky. In all of this, I never saw myself married.

———————

The sun had set by the time I left the senator's office, and as I drove across town the stoplights glowed red against the night. People were already gathered in the hotel lobby by the time I arrived, and they sat silently, anxious and expectant, as if in a physician's waiting room. When my turn came I approached Suzanna's handler, a graying man who took my cash and pointed to a low table in the bar where Suzanna sat across from an empty red chair. She looked exactly how I imagined her: a blond bouffant, wispy at the top, large framed glasses, painted fingernails. When she said hello, I recognized her voice from the radio program, all smoke and ash, the kind of voice that comes from nicotine over many years. I imagined her vocal cords dried and yellowed like tobacco leaves hung in the fields of North Carolina. She pulled out a blank scrap of paper and positioned a ball-point pen over the sheet as I sat.

"How old are you?" she asked.

"I'm twenty-three."

"Then you haven't met your daughter yet."

I was surprised when hot tears came to my eyes; children were not part of my plan.

"You haven't met your son, either."

Her pen scrawled across the page.

"You'll be married when you're twenty-five."

She wrote this down.

"Better pack your cowboy boots, because your life and love will be out west."

At this, I laughed out loud. I had been willing to buy into a certain amount of Psychic Suzanna shtick, but she had gone too far. Out west? I didn't plan on getting married at all, let alone to some cowboy from the far side of the Mississippi. Suzanna's hand stopped moving across the page and she refocused her eyes on the dimly lit hotel lobby. My five minutes were up. I hoped for some last parting wisdom, a promise of a future I could actually believe, but she was already looking toward the next customer.

On the weekends in Tallahassee I often went dancing with my roommates and their friends at a place called Chubby's, just this side of rough. Lights flashed across the dance floor where I let sweaty college boys dance up against me, but I rarely handed out my number. They were too young, too rangy—like colts set loose in a pasture. I wasn't interested in what they had to offer.

One Saturday night we headed instead for Late Night Library, a step above Chubby's, where Florida State's frat boys prowled. It was cold—cold for Florida anyway—and we cranked up the heat in my car. We dashed from the parking lot to the doors of the club, our arms wrapped around ourselves, trying to hold on to our body heat. The mass of sweating bodies inside had warmed the interior and we stepped into a boozy sauna. Our group staked out a strip of territory against an arm rail before making our way to the dance floor. People crushed around us. I danced until sweat soaked my hair and my thighs began to burn. Breathless, I stepped away from the crowd and worked my way back to our railing. I leaned there, catching my breath, and saw a young man out of the corner of my eye. He leaned against the railing, too, with a beer in one hand. I had the distinct feeling he was working his way toward me. Let me say this: I'm not the kind of girl men pick up. I'm not the right kind of pretty, not the right kind of flirty. There's some reluctance in me, an unwillingness to go with their game. While other girls had steady boyfriends, I mostly spent time with boys I didn't take seriously. Or who didn't take me seriously. I could never find anyone who felt just right.

The young man against the rail moved next to me. He was dressed casually in a red baseball cap and a brown T-shirt. He was about my height, built thin and wiry, and I could just make out his face in the dark bar. Handsome with blue eyes that made me think of the Gulf in winter.

"Would you like to dance?" he asked.

"I just came off the dance floor. I'm beat," I said. "But if you ask me again in five minutes, I'll say yes."

He nodded and sauntered off. In five minutes, he came back. This time I let him lead me into the crowd and we danced to the beat from the enormous speakers. He tried to make conversation, but it was impossible in all that musical noise. A few songs later he pulled me to the side.

"My name's Miles," he said.

He stuck out a hand and I shook it.

"Where are you from?" I asked.

"Texas," he said. "How about you?"

"Florida. Are you a student here?"

"I'm in the Army," he said. "A pilot."

I liked that he wasn't in school and that he had a steady job. I liked how he was quick to smile and seemed to listen when I talked. I liked the way he leaned in close to hear me over the music. When we moved back to the dance floor, Miles stepped in to kiss me. I pulled back, shook my head, and rolled my eyes as if to say, *I'm not that kind of girl.* But when he moved to kiss me again a few minutes later, I let him. I am that kind of girl.

At the senator's office on Monday, I tried not to think about the dark-haired boy I met at the Library. I made sympathetic noises to the callers who complained about the state of the economy, the left-wing conspiracy, the war in Iraq. They worried about weapons of mass destruction and asked me to urge the senator to have Terri Schiavo's feeding tube removed.

"The senator's not in right now," I said. "But I'd be happy to pass your message on to him."

I logged correspondence from heartsick newlyweds, men in their sixties trying to convince immigration services that their twenty-something Colombian wives were not scheming for green cards. I filed letters, sent faxes, and shredded documents. Despite myself, I thought about Miles. I thought about the way he laughed, how he took me in when we talked. I thought about his quickness, his brightness. I thought about the way his skin felt beneath my fingertips. I waited for him to call.

Monday came and went. And Tuesday. By Wednesday, I'd entered that place women go when we decide the world has contrived to keep us single for the rest of our lives. When my phone rang that evening, I'd nearly given up on the boy from the club. But there was Miles, and all that worry, all that irrational fear, disappeared.

"I just thought I'd call and see how your week was going," he said.

I had the impression the line was rehearsed, that he had gone through several versions before calling, trying each one out, feeling the heft of them in his mouth.

"It's going all right," I said.

Casual, too, as if I hadn't imagined the conversation from every angle. We worked like that for half an hour, easing into the talk, seeing how we might fit together.

"What are you doing this weekend?" Miles said finally.

My stomach folded in on itself, the way it does when I'm nervous or excited.

"I don't know yet," I said. "What are you up to?"

"We're coming back down to Tallahassee," he said. "Me and some guys from flight school. I was wondering if I could see you again."

I smiled, and I knew he could hear it in my voice.

"That would be great."

Miles came to my apartment the next Saturday afternoon. He carried two long-stemmed roses he had bought at a gas station on the drive down.

"Let me put these in water," I said.

I turned away so he wouldn't see me blush.

We set out across town in his pickup, and I asked about his family.

"My dad's a pilot for Southwest Airlines," he said.

"No kidding? My dad was a pilot too."

"Who'd he fly for?"

"Eastern," I said. "But that was back in the day. He died when I was five."

"I'm sorry to hear that."

I shook my head. "It was a long time ago."

Miles told me about growing up in the Texas Panhandle across the border from Oklahoma. I told him about my half siblings, two brothers and a sister, much older than I am and scattered across the country. He talked about flight school in Alabama where he was learning to fly Apaches, the Army's attack helicopters. I understood only vaguely that he was training for war. We drove to a park north of the city and pulled alongside an empty pavilion. The sun had lowered in the sky by the time we found a footpath that ran through the woods. Dry leaves had fallen across the trail and they crackled beneath our feet as we walked. Miles pushed aside a hanging branch and held it for me as I passed.

"Do you go to church?" he asked.

He let the branch go and caught up to walk beside me.

"I'm a spiritual person," I said, "but I don't go to church."

Miles pressed. "Do you believe in God?"

I could tell it mattered to him what I said, as if this were some minimum requirement.

"Yes," I said. "My mom went to church every Sunday growing up. I was raised in a Christian house."

A hedge, but not a lie. I run more New Age light than biblical. But it must have been enough because on the way back to the truck, Miles took my hand. He slid his fingers between mine as the last light of day seeped through the trees, and he held my hand the entire way home. Later that night, when his breath had evened beside me and he had relaxed into sleep, he held it still.

The next morning I stood at the stove in my kitchen while Miles sat at the breakfast bar. He told me stories about Texas while I fried eggs in a pan. I salted a pot of boiling water for grits, and my roommates joined Miles at the bar. I dished out plates for everyone and all of it—the rowdy boys behind me, the grease popping on the stove, the butter melting in a dish—felt right. It looked nothing like the life I had imagined and yet it was the most natural thing in the world, with Miles there at the center of it.

2

That summer Florida had its worst hurricane season in years. Four storms hit the state, one after the other, knocking down power lines and tearing off roofs. The phone lines at the senator's office never stopped ringing. On the drive home from work I would open the car windows and gulp the fresh air, already counting down the days to the weekend when I would see Miles and we would set off on some new adventure.

On a dense and humid Saturday late in the summer we decided to visit limestone caverns just south of the Alabama line. Water dripped from the rocks overhead as we shuffled along with the group, following a guide, and Miles and I pressed together in the tight space.

"The caverns date back more than thirty-eight million years," the guide said, "to when the state of Florida was covered with a warm shallow sea."

I had the sudden image of salt tides spread over the land, and I stepped closer to Miles to breathe in his sun-warmed smell, like hay in summer. Even in the cold and damp he radiated heat. I still had to catch my breath with him sometimes, the way he made me feel. When I thought of the men who came before him, I thought of weighty materials, of earth and metal, bags filled with sand. I imagined carrying them like a load, being yoked to their desires. They asked too much of me. Miles asked nothing; he took me whole. When I thought of him I thought of water, of running my hand through a clear pool. Even surrounded by him, I could still see myself.

"And these here," the guide said, indicating the rocks that thrust up from the cavern floor, knee-high, thick-headed, with shafts as big as my fist, "are stalagmites. They'll grow a cubic inch every hundred years."

I leaned close to Miles. "Does that look like . . . ?"

He was already smiling. "Sure does."

The caves had a corporeal quality, like cloistered parts of the earth's body, damp and dark and moist, lungs breathing in and out. I pressed against Miles's back and we were a pinpoint of warmth in that vast and humid cavern. The distant dripping of water reached us, a steady *plunk-plunk-plunk* into a hidden pool, and as the group shuffled forward Miles took my hand. He ran his thumb over the fleshy webbing between my thumb and first finger, back and forth, so that the rhythm matched the fall of water. The guide led us farther into the cave and pointed to small ridges in the rock.

"These marks here?" she said. "Made by the retreating tides. Water giving over to dry land."

Miles gave my hand a squeeze and I squeezed back, softly at first, then more urgently. Did we feel the tidal pull of our own lives then? Or were we content to simply lean into each other and let the heat of our bodies build in that cold space?

———

The parking lot emptied quickly after the tour. By the time we arrived at the car, the other visitors had gone. Miles unlocked the passenger side door and held it open for me as I climbed in. I sifted through the glove compartment and retrieved a folded map, and Miles perched on the edge of my seat as I pored over it.

"There's a lake not far from here," I said. "We could go for a swim."

Miles moved his head close to mine to peer at the map. He looked up to see me looking at him and he leaned forward to kiss me, a slow kiss that deepened and lengthened. I reached up and circled his neck with my arms. He pulled back and looked at me, and I smiled at him as he surveyed the parking lot through the windshield.

"Nobody's around," he said. "Parking lot's empty."

"Do you think . . . ?"

"Do you?"

He raised an eyebrow, a question, and I raised mine, an answer.

"I've never—" I said.

"Me neither."

"But maybe we could . . . ?"

The passenger door stood open to the afternoon and the air was hot and damp, an exhaled breath.

"If we were quick," he said.

"If we were quick."

"But how would we—"

"Like this?" I said.

Miles whispered, "Is that—"

"Just like that."

We were all talk until suddenly we stopped talking. The day stilled except for a light breeze at the tops of the trees. They leaned together, talking in whispers. A bird called out. Then silence. Miles's breath echoed in my ear, and I watched a droplet of sweat bead on his fore-head and run down to his ear. It hung there for a second before falling to my chest and sliding beneath my shirt. I kissed him and his mouth tasted like salt water. Beneath us the caves reached down to the earth's molten center, the place where the planet is hottest, and the ground heaved up and collapsed onto itself with a shudder that left fissures in the pavement.

Afterward we drove twenty miles west. I navigated on the folded map and Miles held my hand as he drove. He looked over at me from time to time and smiled. I smiled back. We were like cats licking our paws, slow and content. We found the lake tucked back behind a stand of pines, three hundred yards off the main road. By then the sky had clouded over and a cold wind coursed over the surface of the water. A single family gathered on the man-made beach at the water's edge. In a folding camp chair a heavy woman with oily skin and red splotches high on her cheeks sat surveying the lake. Her hair was short and wispy, the color of old copper. I walked to the edge of the brown water and stood with my hands on my hips. I looked over my shoulder at Miles.

"Do we go in?" I said.

He scanned the dark lake. "I don't know, babe."

The woman in the camp chair leaned forward.

"You all thinking about going swimming?"

"Thinking about it," Miles said.

"Might better wait awhile," the woman said. "My boys seen a water moccasin just a few minutes ago."

I took a step back.

"Here?"

The woman pointed to a spot by my feet.

"Right over there."

I backed out of the water and ducked beneath the sheltering beam of Miles's arm.

"Should we go back?" I said.

Miles surveyed the water and the almost deserted beach. My skin pricked with goose bumps.

"Let's go home," he said.

That was how life felt then, danger lurking in the sweetest days.

On a Friday afternoon a few weeks later I left work early and drove west through Tallahassee and north into Alabama to the outskirts of Fort Rucker. Outside Miles's apartment in the late afternoon I stood on the tips of my toes and felt above the light for his spare key. My fingers came back covered with dust but otherwise empty. I lifted the rug in front of the door and hunted beneath the lip of the step and in the corners, but no key. I checked my watch. Miles wouldn't be home for another hour. I thought about sitting in my car and cranking the AC, but I hated to waste the gas. Instead I fetched a book from the backseat and settled myself on the staircase beside Miles's door. Before long, gravel crunched under tires and gave off the sound of rubber rolling in. I looked up to see not Miles's pickup but another, smaller truck. Jimmy Hyde. He climbed out of the cab of his truck and hoisted a pack over one shoulder, and as he moved up the walkway toward the building I turned back to my book.

"Hey, there," he said.

He stopped in front of me and pushed his sunglasses to the top of his head.

"Hey, Hyde."

"Jimmy," he said. "I hear 'Hyde' all day. You locked out?"

I raised my hands in front of me, palms open.

"Locked out," I said. "Am I in your way?"

"You're fine." He dropped his pack to the ground. "Miles forget to leave you the key?"

I held my place in my book with one finger and closed the front flap.

"Looks like it. He normally hides the key over the light there"—I pointed—"but I can't find it."

Jimmy reached above the light and felt across the flat strip of metal. "Anything?"

"Nothing." He bent down to the doormat. "Did you check under the rug?"

He lifted the mat by the corners and glanced to the left and right, then lowered it back in place.

"Guess you're stuck," he said.

I shrugged. "Miles'll be here in an hour."

Jimmy leaned one shoulder against the side of the building. Sticky heat draped over the apartment complex and shimmered in pools above the pavement.

"How was your drive up?" he said. "Hit traffic on I-10?"

"Just the usual."

I marked the page in my book and set it on the step beside me.

"How's flight school?" I said.

"They work us hard."

"That's what Miles tells me. You're flying Black Hawks?"

He nodded. "UH-60s."

"How do you like it?"

"They're good aircraft."

As a car pulled into the parking lot I looked past Jimmy, hoping to see Miles.. But a woman in cutoff shorts stepped out of a faded El Camino. She hoisted a toddler on her hip and headed for the stairs at the far end of the building.

"How's Tallahassee?" Jimmy said. "Miles told me—you're working for a senator down there? Is that right?"

I nodded.

"How's that going?"

"It's okay."

Heat rolled off the pavement in waves and in the distance rotor blades chopped the air with a steady *thwack-thwack-thwack*. Jimmy stopped leaning against the brick wall and took a seat on the bottom step, near enough that I could smell his end-of-the-day mix of sweat and hydraulic fluid.

"So, how long have you and Miles been dating?"

"About six months now."

"Is that all?"

I laughed. "Seems like a lot to me."

"I shouldn't be talking." Jimmy shook his head. "My longest relationship lasted three months."

"You're kidding. Three months?"

He smirked. "Guess I haven't met the right girl."

I kicked at the dirt under my heel and looked over the empty parking lot. Jimmy watched me from the corners of his eyes.

"Think you'll have to go overseas?" I said after a while. "To Iraq?"

"Or Afghanistan. Looks like I'll be headed that way once I get done here and they assign me to a unit."

I heard tires ground the pavement in the parking lot and saw Miles's truck pull in. Jimmy stood and dusted his hands on his pants.

"Guess I'll be leaving you," he said.

Miles stepped out of his Chevy and waved. I waved back. He came up the concrete pathway with his pack hefted over one shoulder.

"Hey, man," he said. He tapped Jimmy on the back. "How you doing?"

"Good, good," Jimmy said. "Just got home from class."

I stood, smiling.

"Hey, babe," I said.

"Hey." Miles leaned forward to kiss me.

"What are you doing out here?" he said when he stepped back.

"I'm locked out."

"Did I forget to leave you the key?"

"No big deal," I said. "Hyde kept an eye on me."

Miles turned to Jimmy.

"Were you watching her for me?"

"Yes, sir," Jimmy said.

"Well, thanks, man."

"Anytime."

Miles unlocked the front door and I picked my book up off the stoop. Jimmy hoisted his pack and headed up the stairs.

"Dude," he called over his shoulder to Miles, "I love your girlfriend."

That Sunday morning we drove to church on base. At the security checkpoint I handed my driver's license to Miles and he passed it with his military ID through the window. The guard inspected both cards, looked at the military decal on the windshield, and waved us through. The base was deserted, the brisk hum of weekday activity ceased. Normally there were soldiers everywhere, crisscrossing streets in their smart uniforms, hurrying down sidewalks on important errands. I straightened the hem of my skirt and stared anxiously out the truck window.

"Can't you drive any faster?" I said. "We're going to be late."

Miles pointed to a speed limit sign as we passed. "That's as fast as I can go. If I get a ticket and it gets back to my instructors, I'm in big trouble."

"Seriously?" I said.

"Oh, yeah. And you better not get a ticket on base, either."

I looked across the seat at him. "Or what? Don't tell me you'd get in trouble for that, too."

"That's what I've heard. If a wife or girlfriend is caught speeding and it gets back to your commanding officer, then you get a stern talking-to."

"What would they say? 'Control your wife'?"

"Something like that."

"Jesus."

Miles gave me a sharp look, and I clapped a hand over my mouth.

"Sorry," I said as he turned into the church parking lot.

During the service a slick preacher spoke in front of the crowded church while his done-up wife sat in the first pew, holding a baby in her lap. She laughed indulgently when he made jokes at her expense. The praise band took the stage, a mix of boys in their late teens who held their guitars with stiff arms. They were mostly the kind of young men who let the hair on their upper lips grow in thick and dark, whose palms are always clammy, who take on a wistful faraway look when they talk about doing missionary work overseas. The lead singer, though, was pure rock star. He wore a microphone headpiece and ran down the aisle during sets high-fiving parishioners. When the band wasn't playing he sipped water from a bottle and dabbed his forehead with a towel. I made paper airplanes with the church program. When a man came around with plates of wafers and wine for Communion, I declined, and on the church steps afterward I carefully avoided taking the preacher's hand.

In the truck after the service Miles loosened his necktie and cranked up the radio. I lowered my window and let the warm breeze blow in. With church behind us, the day felt suddenly light and limitless.

"Where to now?" I said.

Miles tilted his head as he considered.

"Want to see an Apache?" He pointed to a stretch of grass in the distance. "They're having an exhibition. They've got Black Hawks, a Chinook. One of the guys from class told me he took his wife. You can climb up into it and everything."

I hesitated. When the U.S. invaded Iraq the year before, I was vehemently, vocally against the war. I was angry about the politics of it and angry at the lives lost—on both sides. I understood why Miles had joined the Army. After September 11 he felt like it was his duty. He said he wanted to step up so that someone else would not have to. I respected that and I was proud of him. But I struggled with the realities of the Apache. The Army calls them gunships; the pilots call what they do hunting. I looked at Miles beside me and his face was radiant.

"Let's go," I said.

He pulled into the parking lot alongside the exhibition field, and I followed him across the grass.

"Here she is," he said in front of the helicopter.

I reached out to touch the side the way I might touch a strange animal. The metal had warmed in the sun and I flinched from the heat. The helicopter was wasplike and barbed, frightening, and it was all I could do to keep my feet rooted to the ground.

"You want to sit inside?" Miles asked.

I thought for a moment that I might not want to know the inside of the Apache, that I might not want to have a memory of its tight spaces or the narrow view through the glass. But instead I said, "The back seat or the front?"

"I usually sit in the front," Miles said.

I pulled myself up the side and lowered my frame into the seat. The upholstery was rough beneath my hands. I slipped the straps of the seat belt over each of my shoulders and had the feeling not so much of strapping myself in as strapping the Apache on. Through the front windows I saw the nose of the aircraft and the grass below. I took hold of the cyclic that rose between my legs and imagined what it felt like to sit in that seat, to shoot the guns, to fire the rockets. How to understand that the man I was falling in love with—a man who almost never cussed, who went to church every Sunday, who pressed his nose to the back of my neck as we slept—would kill other men? I released the cyclic and stripped off the seat belt. I stood in the open door and Miles peered up at me from the ground, smiling.

"What do you think?" he said.

I held out a hand so he could help me down.

"I think this is a dangerous piece of machinery."

"I know," he said as he reached up for me. "Isn't it great?"

1985

3

The aborigines say we live a spiral life, that our narratives curl around like smoke, the events of one moment rhyming with the events of previous moments so that in a single lifetime we live the same story many times. Before my father died, my family had a farm in the Appalachian foothills. We lived in northeast Georgia, red-earth country, and when my father ran a tiller auburn clods of dirt turned toward the blue sky. He had a lean frame although he carried a thickness around his waist that had come with age, and he kept his dark hair and mustache short. He drove an American-made pickup, hung a shotgun in the back, and wore a bear claw on a chain around his neck. He was funny, I'm told, and in photos his smile seems to just stifle a laugh. I'm sure his first wife had her own stories about him— about infidelity, certainly—but my mother says he was a great man. I like to think it took a particular kind of woman to catch and hold my father's attention, and my mother was that woman. She was nine years younger than my father, born two months and a day before the first bomb fell on Japan in the summer of 1945. Her family scraped by on a farm in central Florida where she learned to ride horses bareback and scuffle with the neighborhood boys. She hated dolls and dresses, nearly failed home economics, and never made a casserole in her life.

"I'm no lady," she said.

But my mother was beautiful. She was tall for a woman and her skin tanned a deep brown. She wore her dark hair long and parted down the middle like the Seminole women on her mother's side. I imagine she created a stir at the University of Miami, where she earned her teaching degree, and afterward when she took a job at a high school in one of Miami's toughest neighborhoods. During her first year teaching she caught a student in the hallway after the bell had rung.

"You need to get to class," she told him.

The boy was built tall and strong, and he stepped close to my mother with his fist cocked as if he meant to hit her in the face.

"Go ahead," my mother said. "I'll give you one shot. After that, I'm going to wipe your ass all over this floor."

The boy froze, then dropped his fist and moved off down the hall.

By the time my mother met my father in 1971, they each had a marriage behind them. He showed up at a mutual friend's house for dinner carrying a pineapple.

"Everybody brings flowers," he said.

To hear my mother tell it, their relationship was special from the beginning.

"Sometimes it was like, could this really be happening?" my mother said. "Because when something feels too good, you're sure something bad's going to happen."

Beside our house in Georgia, my father kept a runway where the hills sloped into flat land. He parked a single-engine Piper Cub in a hangar by our house. The plane had seats upholstered in red leather, cracked in places, and windows that slid open in the back. A layer of dust coated the instruments in the console. My father took my mother and me flying the way some families go for a drive, and a week after my fifth birthday he pushed the plane out of the hangar for an afternoon flight. It was mid-June and warm and the backs of my thighs stuck to the seat as my mother belted me in. She stood in the open door of the airplane and pulled the seat belt tight across the tops of my legs until the fabric pinched my skin.

"It's too tight," I said.

"Leave it."

"You sure you don't want to come?" my father asked her.

She shook her head. "No, Lamar."

"Come on," he said. "Get in."

"I've got too much to do."

She stepped across the wheel of the plane and moved to shut the door but she stopped, turned back to me, and pulled the seat belt tighter.

"It hurts," I said.

"Leave it," she said again.

She stepped away from the plane and closed the door, and my father cranked the engine. The propeller swung in an arc and the blades disappeared in a blur of whirling metal. The grass whipped the tires as we motored down the runway, and the frame of the plane vibrated so that my bones buzzed like hornets beneath my skin. My father pulled back on the throttle and the plane surged forward, picking up speed until we lifted into the air. He pulled higher into the summer sky and then he banked, circling the farm from above. I pressed my face to the window and looked down at the trees that parted for the creek that ran beside the house.

"How you doing back there, A.J.?" my father asked.

He turned his head slightly so I could see the side of his face, the metal frame of his sunglasses, his radio headset. I smiled at him and he turned back to the controls. Not long after, the engine fell silent. The buzzing stilled. My father must have said something—*Oh, shit*—he must have jerked the yoke, because I leaned close to him.

"Daddy, are we going to crash?"

"No, baby," he said. "Sit back down."

My father almost brought the plane in. He angled for the open space of the runway and we nearly made the clearing, but the tail caught on a tree at the last second. The body pitched forward and the nose slammed into the ground. I have no memory of the impact, no recollection of the jolt that crushed my spine or the strike to the head that left a shallow indent on my skull. My father was thrown against his seat belt and the force separated his veins from his organs. They call this bleeding out. He was dead before anyone reached the plane.

My mother's parents were staying at the guesthouse on the farm for the summer and they had come out to watch us take off. They followed the plane with their eyes as it cruised across the sky. They watched as we fell. They were the first ones at the crash site and my grandfather pulled me free.

"I know I shouldn't have moved her," he told my mother later, "but I smelled gasoline. I thought it was going to blow."

My grandfather stayed beside the plane and looked to my father while my grandmother carried me to the ambulance that was already turning down the dirt road. The freshness of morning had given over to thick afternoon heat, and as I looked back at the plane I saw everything through a film of stirred yellow dust.

At our house my mother was in the kitchen when her mother-in-law, who lived up the mountain, called.

"There's been an accident," she said.

"What?"

"An accident."

"Is it the plane?" my mother said.

"You need to come down here."

My mother didn't even put on shoes. She ran to the car barefoot and drove to the county road that traveled parallel to the farm. She followed the blacktop until she could see the crash site in the distance, threw the car in park, and dashed across the field. My grandfather met her at the plane.

"Where's A.J.?" she said.

"In the ambulance. They need to take her now."

"Where's Lamar?"

"In the plane."

"I need to see him."

"He's bad," my grandfather said. "There's nothing you can do for him."

"I need to see him," my mother insisted.

She made her way to the plane, to where my father hung from his seat, his neck all wrong, blood on his hands. She reached out and took his wrist and searched for a pulse.

"Come away," my grandfather said. "You need to come away from there. You need to get in the ambulance. They're waiting on you."

My mother let him lead her away and put her in the back of the ambulance, where I was strapped to a backboard but conscious.

"Hi, Mommy," I said.

"Hi, baby."

"Mommy, I'm scared."

"I know, baby."

"I'm hurt."

"I know, baby," she said. "I know."

At the hospital, my mother sat in the room with me as people filtered in. My grandparents. My half brother and his wife. My uncle, who brought my mother steaming cups of coffee one after the other.

"I need to see my husband," my mother said to anyone who would listen.

Finally, a nurse stepped into the room.

"He's arrived," she said. "I'll escort you to the morgue."

My mother followed the nurse through the hospital hallways, her bare feet against the cool floor.

"You are about the strongest person I've ever seen," the nurse said as they walked together. "You're not even crying."

In the morgue my father lay beneath a white sheet. There were cuts on his cheeks and stains of blood on his hands. His body had started to swell from the trauma and his skin stretched tight across his face. His eyes were open.

"I'll be right here," the nurse said off to the side. "Take as long as you want."

My mother laid her hand on my father's shoulder and on his arm— already he felt cold to her touch—and she looked at him. She looked and looked until she had seen enough.

"You know you're going to have to tell A.J.," my grandmother said when my mother came back to the room. "You have to be the one to tell her. About Lamar."

"I know," my mother said.

Three days later, when I was fully conscious for the first time since the crash, the people who had crowded into the room made their way out, leaving my mother and me alone.

"Do you know where you are?" she said.

"I'm in the hospital."

"Do you know why?"

"Daddy crashed the plane."

"Yes, he did," my mother said.

"Daddy's dead," I said. "I saw him hanging upside down."

My mother took a long, quiet breath.

"He lied to me," I said. "He said we weren't going to crash. He told me to hold on really tight and that everything would be okay."

My mother cried softly then, the way people will when they have been crying for a long time.

Doctors spent more than six weeks repairing my broken spine. They soldered a rod to my backbone, looped hooks through my vertebrae, and pinned my skeleton in place. When they finished they stitched the skin together, a neat job that left a straight scar running down the middle of my back. A doctor plastered a cast around my middle that drove me mad with itching, and for weeks afterward I had to take a bath standing up in a bucket. I often dreamed of planes crashing, reliving in the night what I could not remember during the day.

In the months that followed, my father's presence in our life remained untouched. My mother kept the sheets he had slept in on their bed. His toothbrush stayed by the bathroom sink. His comb and electric razor lay where he had left them. His clothes hung in the closet and his pictures stayed fixed to the wall. His chair at the head of the table remained empty, and no one—not me, not my mother, not the friends or neighbors who passed through—sat in my father's seat while the table remained in the house.

But two years after the plane crash my mother performed an impossible feat: she made my father disappear. She decided to move us to Florida, near what she considered home, and in coming home she erased my father from our lives. She donated his clothes to the Salvation Army and she threw out the toothbrush and the toothpaste that had sat for so long beside the bathroom sink. She sold all the furniture in the house, including the table where my father had once sat at the head, and she kept almost nothing that belonged to him but a wool winter coat, his Eastern Airlines cap, the bear claw necklace, his shotgun, and two bottles of his cologne.

We moved first to my grandmother's house in Clewiston, then one hundred miles west to the shrimping community where my mother had spent her summers growing up. She found a job teaching at the local elementary school and she planted papaya trees and yellow hibiscus bushes in the front yard of our house. If she missed the acres of farmland in north Georgia, she never said as much. Except for the scar on my back and the shallow dent at my hairline, little evidence of the crash remained. My mother kept my father's pictures in the study, where she would not have to look at them every day. She stored his coat in the back of her closet and put the bear claw necklace in a safety-deposit box at the bank along with both their wedding rings. She wrapped the shotgun in a towel that she hid on the top shelf of my closet. She stored the cologne in the cabinet by her bed.

By silent agreement, we never talked about my father. More than anything I wanted to protect my mother, and I knew that to ask about him would hurt her. So I pretended like he never existed. I let him fade from my memory until I could not remember him at all. I could not have told you if he smelled like lemon or leather or smoke, if his hair grew in thick or fine, if his hands were rough or smooth. I could not have described the sound of his voice.

And yet, the first time I brought Miles home to meet my mother, she put her hand to her chest, shook her head, and smiled.

"He's so much like your father," she said.

·

2005

4

When Miles and I decided to move in together, I asked him if his mother, Terry, would be upset. We sat at the beat-up kitchen table in his apartment near Fort Rucker while the warm fall evening pressed against the sliding glass doors. Miles would graduate from flight school in December and the Army would be sending him to Fort Bragg, North Carolina. The senator was set to retire and the office in Tallahassee would be closing around the same time. The move felt right to both of us.

"Don't worry about it," he said. He leaned back in his wooden chair and propped a foot against the leg of the table. "She'll probably want to send us a housewarming gift. Go ahead and think of something."

I thought place mats would be nice.

While Southeast Asia reeled from the tsunami that had washed ashore Christmas Eve and Iraq prepared for its first free Parliamentary elections in almost fifty years, Miles and I left for Fort Bragg. A cold front had worked its way across lower Alabama in the night and heavy clouds hung above the cotton fields. We slipped on roads patched with ice as we headed east but the front stayed behind us as we made our way north. We pulled into the flatlands of central North Carolina and I nervously held my breath as we followed the exit to Fayetteville, wondering how I would weather Army life.

The cold front caught up to us by the time we signed a lease on a house. We unloaded our U-Haul beneath a rain that fell without pause and my knuckles were rubbed raw in the chill and damp as we toted in our combined life: kitchen utensils and bed linens, spices in glass jars, jugs of olive oil turned cloudy in the cold. The house had yellow paneling and hardwood floors scuffed with age. The rooms filled with a heavy animal smell when we ran the gas heater, and I imagined geological strata of dog fur collected beneath the vents. My mother had given us her old washer and we stuck it in the kitchen. We paid fifty dollars for a secondhand dryer at the flea market in Dunn. At a thrift store in Fayetteville we bought a gold brocade couch, a battered coffee table, and a bureau with a rough paint job. By all accounts our place was shoddy—but I loved it. I loved having a house of our own, furniture that belonged to us, a backyard surrounded by trees that leaned together in the wind.

Miles's mother came for a visit three weeks after we moved in. She did not bring place mats. She was tense and unsettled and she refused to stay in our guest bedroom. She stayed in a hotel across town instead. In our home Terry was cordial. She cooked dinner, churning out Miles's favorites, like burnt-steak stew, meals with a history that reached back to their hometown in Texas. She made the sugar cookies Miles liked, the kind I could never get right, and she talked about home and church and family.

On the second day of her visit, after Miles had put on his uniform and left for the base, Terry suggested we drive to the mall in Raleigh. Spring unfolds slowly in North Carolina, and the air was cool and damp even as the first daffodils pushed through the wet earth. We climbed into her rental car and drove through Fayetteville where rhododendrons bloomed pink against the gray morning. The rain started when we reached the interstate and Terry launched into the reason for her visit.

"You know Brad and I don't approve of you living together," she said, referring to Miles's father. She called it living in sin. Her hands gripped the steering wheel and outside it poured and poured. "When Miles has sex with you, he's disrespecting you."

I thought about telling her that he sometimes disrespected me on the couch. Once in the kitchen. But I said nothing.

She talked for an hour and a half without pause, without my input, but when we reached the shopping center in Raleigh the space between us seemed somehow lighter. We spent the afternoon shopping, inspecting sales racks, and eating Chinese takeout in the food court. At the Macy's makeup counter, Terry tried on lavender eye shadow.

"That looks nice on you," I said.

She smiled shyly into the hand mirror, and when the saleswoman asked if she'd like her to wrap up the makeup, Terry nodded. She was strangely tentative about the exchange, as if she wasn't used to buying nice things for herself.

The drive home was easier, and I imagined a time when Terry and I might be close.

I quickly found out that the city of Fayetteville lived and breathed Fort Bragg. Most of the businesses in town catered to a military lifestyle. Barbers, laundromats, boot repair shops. Storage units where men locked away their lives while they headed overseas to fight in battles whose political under layers they could not always explain. Strip clubs with names like Victoria's Cabaret and Bottom's Up. There were used-car joints, too, where a hundred dollars gets you riding, and pawnshops for the end of the month when the money runs out. But on the base itself, none of this existed. No pawnshops, no titty bars, no used-car hucksters. Everything was neat and organized, the grass cut short, the streets clean. Even the soldiers themselves looked fresh with their trimmed hair and polished boots. There was such vitality about them, it was easy to forget they trade in war.

Clouds covered the sky for days, and a smell like burning rubber or wet animal fur, unidentifiable and vaguely sinister, hung over Fayetteville. People said it came from the tire factory outside town. Others pointed to the chicken processing plant. Either way, the smell filled my nose and clung to my skin. I needed a job: my savings were running low and I was obstinate about splitting everything. Miles offered to pick up the rent, to pay for utilities, to cover groceries, but my mother had always warned me about depending on a man. I was afraid that if he paid my share, I would owe more than I wanted to give.

At an interview at a call center for a major cell phone company, more than twenty of us looked to fill a handful of spots. A woman thumbed my résumé and asked, "Don't you think you're a little over-qualified for this job?"

I looked at her squarely.

"Are you hiring for other positions?" I said. "Because I didn't see any advertised."

Most jobs in Fayetteville didn't require a college degree. I applied to be a secretary, a bank teller, a receptionist—but it was always the same response. My savings disappeared, and when I saw an ad in the paper for a waitress at a nightclub, I slipped on my Parisian boots and headed to the seedy downtown district. The club appeared stark and dingy in the daylight as I waited for my turn to speak to the manager. He looked me over as we sat on a pair of low chairs in the bar.

"Do you have a problem working in an all-black nightclub?" he asked.

"Do you have a problem hiring me?" I said.

The manager smiled, stood, and shook my hand. I never heard back, which was all the answer I needed.

I spent my mornings in bed and my afternoons at the public library. I checked out books and drove home to read on the back porch until the light faded into evening. I began to worry about what it would mean to be tied to the military. How would I navigate this life for the long haul? Where would my own dreams and ambitions fit in? When the brightness had disappeared from the day, I turned on the porch light and sat in the yellow glow, waiting for Miles to come home.

On a Saturday afternoon Miles and I drove across town, up Bragg Boulevard and out the other side to the small communities that bordered the base. We pulled off the main road into a subdivision tucked behind a copse of pines.

"We're here to see the Priestmans," Miles said to the guard at the gate.

The guard flipped through a sheaf of papers tacked to his clipboard. "The Priestners?"

Miles knitted his eyebrows together, considering. "It could be the Priestners."

The guard waved us through.

"Follow the road around the lake to your left," he said. "Take the first road on your right."

We pulled past the guardhouse and onto the road that wound toward the water.

"The Priestmans?" I said.

Miles laughed. "I thought it was Priestman."

"Who is this guy?"

"Another pilot. A CW4. His wife's Alpha Company's FRG leader."

FRG: family readiness group. For the wives of the soldiers in the unit—not for the girlfriends like me. When we'd first gotten to Bragg, Miles had handed me a sheet of paper with the emergency contact information for the wives.

"In case something happens," he said.

I looked over the printout. "Would you mind giving whoever's in charge of this list my number?"

Miles said he would. But later he told me the FRG refused to add me to the list, even as a courtesy. Unless we were married, I was discovering, I had no status in the unit.

We followed the lake into the subdivision. Wood frame houses lined the street and leafless dogwoods waited for spring in yards laid with pale yellow grass. In the driveway at the end of a cul-de-sac, Miles nosed his truck between the pickups already parked alongside the road. When we rang the doorbell we heard the scratching of nails from the other side and an excited yipping.

"You get back," a woman's voice called.

Miles and I looked at each other. The door opened and a woman shooed away a miniature collie.

"That's Captain," she said. "Don't worry about him. He's just happy to see you. Aren't you, Cappy?"

The dog pranced in the doorway, looking from the woman to me to Miles.

"I'm Teresa." She stuck out a hand. "John's wife."

"Nice to meet you," Miles said.

"John's told me all about you. The new CW2."

"That's right. Straight out of Fort Rucker. Trying to get the hang of things."

"Don't worry. John will show you the ropes," Teresa said. "Come on downstairs. Everyone's around the pool table."

We followed her to the first floor where sliding glass doors looked out on the lake.

"Glad you guys could make it," John said.

He pulled two beers out of the fridge behind the bar and handed one to each of us. To me, Teresa pointed out the men in the unit and introduced me to their wives. I shook their hands and smiled politely, but as I tried to follow the conversation I realized I did not have the vocabulary for this language of Army wives.

"They'll be going to Hood in July."

"I heard August."

"Who'd you hear that from?"

"A wife in Bravo Company."

"The commander's wife? I thought they got divorced."

"Didn't you hear—"

"I saw them at the commissary—"

At the pool table, the men talked about flying. Miles ate guacamole out of a bowl and followed the conversation with his eyes. Our knees bumped and he looked at me and we gave each other half smiles. Teresa was talking about the military bases where John had been stationed, the cross-country drives she made alone, and how many months he'd been gone on his two previous deployments. It struck me how lonely that life must have been for her. She talked about their two daughters, their seventeenth wedding anniversary in January, and their plans for John's retirement.

"We're going to buy a boat," John said. "Bigger than the one we have now."

He traced the route on an imaginary map while Teresa stood beside him and nodded.

"We'll cruise down the Mississippi. Go across the Gulf of Mexico. Head back up the Atlantic."

"The girls will be old enough to take care of themselves by then," Teresa said. "But we'll bring Captain. Or our next dog."

I sipped my beer and thought of days spent on the water, the sun beating down, a succession of collies nosing into the wind.

Spring gave way to early summer. The clouds disappeared but the humidity stayed so that Fayetteville was suddenly hot and muggy like the inside of a mouth. Our neighbor sent over bags of cucumbers and tomatoes from her garden and I baked loaves of zucchini bread that Miles ate standing up in the kitchen, still in his uniform. He told me about the guys in the unit and the funny things they said during the day. One of them claimed that seventy-five percent of all warrant officers have two of three things: a pickup, a boat, and an ex-wife. We laughed and ran through the pilots in the unit and, sure enough, the statistic held true. We agreed that the military must be hell on marriage.

That summer theaters showed Tom Cruise's *War of the Worlds,* every radio seemed to be playing "Mr. Brightside," and the cover of *Time* explained "Why we're going gaga over real estate." I was hired in the marketing department at the local sports arena and they gave me free tickets to hockey games and dirt bike shows. I decided to close my bank account in France. Miles and I were invited to pool parties and backyard barbecues with the other families in the unit, and I finally met Scott Delancey, the company commander.

"Captain Delancey!" Miles yelled when the captain showed up.

Everyone looked to the far end of the deck where the captain stood. He was tall and broad shouldered, a bear of a man. Recently divorced, I'd heard. From the way Miles talked about him, I could tell he genuinely liked and respected him.

"I want you to meet my girlfriend," Miles said.

I stuck out a hand as the captain walked over.

"I've heard a lot about you," I said.

"Oh, yeah?"

The captain took my hand briefly, but he was already turning away to clap Miles on the shoulder.

"Let's get you another beer," he said.

Miles put in an application for SERE C, a three-week survival and evasion course staged on the outer reaches of Fort Bragg. The one-week intro version, SERE B, had been required in flight school in Alabama. The soldiers killed rabbits and navigated by compass, went without food and forded a lake at night. The experience left Miles thin and hollow, and he didn't speak much about what happened during those hungry nights in the woods. SERE C was the next level. Three weeks of survivalist conditions, an evasive maneuver where the soldiers always got caught, and time in a simulated POW camp. The physical abuse, he was told, would not be simulated.

"Why did you apply for this course?" I asked Miles before he left.

"I want to be ready," he said, "in case we go down."

I knew that the survival rate of an Apache crash is very low.

"Ready for what?"

"Just ready."

Miles's application was approved at the beginning of May, and he packed his gear and prepared to set out for the North Carolina woods. On the morning he was scheduled to leave, he called me at work.

"Can I take you out to lunch?" he said. "Our departure got pushed back to this afternoon."

I met him at a restaurant near the arena. Miles was ashen over lunch and we tried not to talk about the rough days ahead.

"Make sure you keep the doors locked when you're at home," he said as we walked to the parking lot. "Don't let anyone in."

"I won't," I promised.

We stopped and I leaned against my car. The sun was bright overhead and heat rolled off the asphalt. I could see fine beads of sweat spread across Miles's forehead and I reached out to touch his cheek. I wanted to hold on to the moment but already it was slipping away, running like sand through my fingers.

"And you have plans?" Miles was saying. "You'll stay busy on the weekends?"

I nodded and squeezed his hand. He kissed me the way he used to kiss me at the end of his visits to Tallahassee.

"Be safe," I said.

"I'll see you in three weeks."

For the next twenty-one days, I worked during the day and read in the evenings. Sometimes I rented a movie. I drove to Greensboro one Saturday and to the coast to visit family the next. Time opened up, wide and empty as an airfield, and the weeks that stretched in front of me were airless and oppressive, time spent holding my breath.

The day Miles was scheduled to return, I heard the front door open while I was in the shower. I wrapped myself in a towel and stepped out of the bathroom. He stood in the living room with his rucksack at his feet, thin and pale, bruised in places, but wholly himself. He sat on the couch and I sat beside him touching his face, his hands, his knees. I ran my fingers over the fabric of his uniform, still cool from the morning air, and traced his jaw and the tops of his cheeks. I imagined this was how he would look returning from war, and for a moment I let myself consider that distant future date when he would deploy. The three-week stint had felt like an eternity. Later we would ask ourselves how we would ever survive the fifteen months he'd be gone to Iraq.

"Can I get you something to eat?" I said.

He leaned his head against the couch and closed his eyes.

"That would be wonderful," he said.

Miles told me over time some of what happened, bits and pieces that came out during dinner, late nights while we watched TV, on long drives across the state. But he never told me all of it. Just stories, brief peeks into the experience, like peering through a window covered by venetian blinds. A breeze would blow and a panel would shift to show what lay beneath, then the gust would die down, the blind would drop, and that part of Miles would seal off again. He told me they had been made to strip down when they first arrived at the POW camp and they were hosed off and forced to roll on the ground. Miles laughed when he talked about the cold water and biting gravel. They made him remove the laces from his boots and the chafing left raw welts on his heels. He went for days without food. Once he banged on the door to his cell and yelled until his throat went raw.

"I want some peanuts," he said, "and a Pepsi."

He yelled and banged until they brought him peanuts and a cup of soda.

"I want some for the guy next to me too," he said.

They brought more peanuts and another cup of soda for the soldier next to him.

Miles wanted me to believe it was one grand adventure, a three-week camping trip with the guys from work. But he told me later about a soldier from an earlier group who ran into one of the SERE instructors afterward. The soldier almost killed the instructor in the middle of a restaurant in Fayetteville, the effects of the course were that enduring. Miles just shrugged his shoulders and laughed. SERE C was no big deal.

But in the night he would thrash in his sleep and I would have to lay a hand on his chest.

"Miles," I'd say.

He would open his eyes and look at me and I would feel his confusion in the dark room. Then he would remember and relax back into sleep.

By the time we settled into Fayetteville, it was time to move again. Only six months after we arrived, the unit received orders to Fort Hood, in Texas, to train for the coming deployment. Most of the soldiers would go to Hood alone, without their families. What was the alternative? Pull their kids out of school, uproot the lives they had built, only to do it all again in nine months? I was learning that there were no good options.

Miles and I had a yard sale and sold most of what we owned for less than three hundred dollars. What remained we packed into boxes. A summer storm raged the night before we left and thunder cracked as Miles loaded the boxes into his truck. He came in soaked after each round, water coursing down his neck and collecting in the collar of his shirt, while I swept around his wet footprints, erasing any trace that we had ever lived there.

5

The morning we left for Fort Hood dawned cool and gray, and we pulled out of town before the sun had a chance to burn off the clouds. We wound through the mountains of western North Carolina, along roads shaded by towering trees, with steep rock embankments that dropped to the green forest floor below. We cruised past Hickory and Asheville, through the Great Smoky Mountains and onto the sun-covered plains of Tennessee. We drove through Knoxville and Memphis before crossing the churning blue-gray waters of the Mississippi. Then it was west to Arkansas, humid and crowded with mosquitoes. We reached Oklahoma and continued through the pointing finger of the panhandle until we hit north Texas, where Miles's family owned three hundred and twenty acres. We pulled off the highway on an afternoon in late July, the heat so intense it sucked the air out of my lungs. Acres of scrub brush stretched across the dry land, and a plume of dust rose behind the truck as we rattled over the dirt road. Cows grazed alongside a barbed-wire fence, their coats ruffling in the breeze. I was finally out west, as Psychic Suzanna had predicted the year before.

Miles spent the days of our visit outside under the big Texas sky. He rode horses and worked the ranch with his father while I stayed inside with Terry. She showed me how to make her meat loaf and wrote the recipe for her sugar cookies on an index card for me to take to Fort Hood. She talked endlessly, hardly pausing for breath, as if she wasn't used to having an audience and needed to unload the things she carried in her heart. Mostly she talked about Miles—about how long it took to conceive him, about the miscarriages that came after. She numbered her lost babies among her children. She talked about breast-feeding, sleepless nights, and Miles's sweet baby smile. She cornered me once about the move to Texas, but before she could get to the sinful parts, Brad and Miles tromped into the kitchen.

We stayed just a couple of days before heading south to Fort Hood. The night had only begun to give over to dawn when we left the panhandle. The sun sent up angry red fingers that turned the sky a mottled pink like a bruise. Blue filtered in as we drove southward, and by mid-afternoon the light had hardened, all sharp edges that made me wince as I stared through the windshield. By the time we hit I–20 the day had given way to pale twilight. A violet light split the air, smoky and flint-tipped like Indian arrowheads. I thought of ambushes in that vast and craggy country. We parked at a rest stop overlooking a valley fringed in red rock and sat beside each other in moody silence.

"What's the matter with you?" I said after a time.

Miles scowled. "Me? What's the matter with *you*?"

"I'm not the one in a bad mood."

"You've been a pill all day. Ever since we left this morning."

I stared across the cliffs without answering, and the wind picked up and scattered the leaves at our feet.

"I'm just worried," I said.

"About what?"

"That Fort Hood will be like Fort Bragg. That I won't be able to find a job, that I'll be sitting there every day waiting for you to come home. That you'll always be gone."

"Don't make this my fault."

"I'm not saying it's your fault."

"Then what are you saying?"

"I don't know."

Miles stood. "Then how can I fix it?"

"I don't know," I said again. "But later, when this is all done, I want to have a say in what we do, in where we go."

"Of course. What do you think? That I'm not going to take what you want into consideration?"

I turned the dirt with the toe of my shoe.

"I've seen how some guys in the unit are. It doesn't matter what their wives want."

"Well, that's not me."

"I know, but I worry—"

"Stop worrying, babe. We'll make it through Hood together. We'll make it through the deployment. When I get back, we can talk about what base we want to go to next."

"But what if all the bases are the same?"

———————

The city of Killeen crouched at the edge of Fort Hood the way Fayetteville loitered outside Fort Bragg. Its streets smelled of hot concrete and old grease, and the city was pocked with fast-food joints and pawnshops. Plastic bags blew through empty parking lots and roaches crawled across the sidewalks at night. Killeen had a high murder rate and hookers on the corner of Rancier and Second Avenue, where Miles and I found an apartment. It was cheap and convenient and already furnished. Anyway, we told ourselves, we'd only be there nine months. I found a job at an elementary school as a second-grade teaching assistant making less than eight hundred dollars a month. Every Monday I prayed my old Saturn would limp through anther week.

Our first month at Fort Hood, Miles trained every day. At night he only wanted to eat dinner and go to bed. He laughed less; he was always exhausted. Even on the weekends, the unit worked. I'd sit by the pool and read until my eyes ached. I'd move inside and watch news reports from New Orleans, where Hurricane Katrina had recently passed through, pulverizing the city. By the time Miles came home I would have the restless, irritable feeling that comes with unfilled days. One Saturday morning, as I scooped cat food onto the sidewalk in front of our apartment for the strays who lived in the complex, I had a sudden thought. I stood and dusted my hands on my shorts.

"You know what?" I said to the scattered cats. "I don't have to stay here today."

I traced the route from Killeen to Austin on a map. I showered, brushed my hair, and dressed in my nice clothes. The morning was clear and fresh, and I cracked the windows of my car on the drive to let the air blow through. In Austin, I parked downtown and walked the empty streets. I ate lunch in a small Korean café and listened to the sound of my footsteps echo off the marble floors of the capitol building. It was lonely in a way, but I'd forgotten the joys of discovering a place on my own.

Miles called as I headed back to the car.

"Hey," I said. I smiled into the phone. "How's your day going?"

Miles sounded angry. "Where are you?"

"I'm in Austin," I said brightly. "Where are you?"

"I just got home from class."

I looked at my watch. "Already?"

"We got done early," Miles said. "I thought we would spend the rest of the day together. But I guess that's not what you want to do."

"I'll come back right now."

Miles sulked. "No, no. Take your time."

"I'll be home in an hour," I said, the day suddenly spoiled.

———————

At school one afternoon during cafeteria duty, I sidled up to another aide, Kelley, who wore her red apron over tailored clothes. She had just turned forty, sported an athletic build and perfectly highlighted hair, and was in every way the kind of woman who makes other women say, *I hope I look like that when I'm forty.*

"Ready for this day to be over?" she said.

"Been ready."

Three tables away, a hand shot up in the air.

"I got this one," I said.

A girl lifted a milk carton and I pulled out the snub-nosed scissors I carried in my apron pocket. After I cut open the cardboard and passed the milk down to her, I walked the length of the table. Small hands reached out to pat me on the way by, leaving sticky handprints on my pants. When I got back to Kelley, she started up the story she'd been telling me all day. We talked like that, in fits and starts, picking up threads where we could. Her husband had come home from Iraq over the summer, she told me.

"And do you know what that bastard did?"

I scanned the cafeteria, trying to look busy.

"He told me he was leaving me."

I looked at her, all pretense of work gone.

"He did what?"

"He told me he'd met someone else."

"In Iraq?"

"One of his soldiers. A young woman."

"Shit."

"Guess how old she is."

"Tell me."

"She's twenty-five."

"Jesus."

On the far side of the room, Ms. Walker ushered her second grad-ers through the line and waved at me across the cafeteria.

"How are you doing?" she yelled.

I gave her a thumbs-up.

"You coming by my classroom later?"

"This afternoon," I said.

"Good. I got a bulletin board I need you to hang."

In the opposite line, a tall girl with her hair in braids whacked the boy behind her with a tray. He leaned forward and karate-chopped the girl in the stomach.

"Second grade!" Kelley shouted across the cafeteria as she strode toward the pair. "Cut that out."

I circulated through the back tables and she eventually worked her way over.

"She's pregnant," she picked up.

"The soldier?"

"She got pregnant while they were over there."

I shook my head. "Kelley, that's unbelievable."

We stood side by side, our backs to the painted cinder-block wall, surveying the open space of the cafeteria.

"You know the worst part?" Kelley said.

I looked away from the racket and directly at her.

"I went to college. I studied art history. I had plans for my own life, but I gave them up for him. In the military, you know, his career would always come first."

She pushed her hair behind her ears and tucked her hands into the front pocket of her apron.

"Now look at me."

I did. She was beautiful and smart, overeducated and working a dead-end job. She turned and laid a hand on my arm.

"Don't let this happen to you," she said.

———————

A new soldier came to the unit—Troy, a CW2 straight out of Rucker—and he brought his wife, Crystal. She had black curly hair and beautiful skin and she peppered her conversation with Spanish words from her Panamanian mother. We were the same age, neither of us had children, and Crystal knew less about the unit than I did. In the ways that counted in Army life, we were practically the same person.

When the unit went into the field and Miles and Troy were gone for weeks, I called Crystal on the weekends and we drove down to Austin together. Sometimes we played tennis at the courts on base. When Crystal sprained her ankle, I was the one who drove her to the emergency room. When my car broke down, she was the one I called for a lift to the mechanic. We took a country-western dance class together at the local community college and Crystal turned out to be a graceful dancer. She picked up the two-step in one night, and because the class was always short of men, sometimes the teacher paired us together. She led and I followed, spinning around the dance floor, both of us laughing. I thought of the other wives from the unit, the ones who had stayed at Bragg, and I realized why they were so close. With the men gone, we would only have each other to rely on.

On a Friday evening I sat on the bed in our apartment, still in the house clothes I'd changed into after work.

"I don't see why we have to go," I said. "They can't tell you what to do when you're not on the clock."

Miles slipped the top half of his BDUs over his head and started unbuttoning his pants.

"You don't have to go," he said. "But I do."

I crossed my arms over my chest. "They can order you to go to a bar?"

He stepped into the bathroom and I could hear the faucet on the shower crank on.

"It's mandatory fun," he said over the pounding of the water.

I followed him into the bathroom and lowered the seat on the toilet. I raised my voice to be heard over the shower.

"But I'm tired, babe," I said. "I was hoping we could just go to dinner. Maybe that Thai place? Or the good Mexican restaurant you were talking about?"

Miles pulled back the edge of the curtain to look at me, and steam billowed over his head.

"I'm tired, too," he said. "You think I don't want to stay home? Look, this is how it is. I have to go. If you want to come, you need to hurry up."

I almost managed to wipe the sour expression off my face by the time we made it to the officers' club on base. The inside felt like any bar— varnished tabletops, two pool tables in the back, a dartboard by the door—except that there were almost no women. Not that anyone at the O club seemed to mind. The soldiers drank and joked, and you'd have thought this was the way things ought to be. The way they'd like them to be, anyway. I followed Miles out the back door to the fenced-in patio where the guys from Alpha Company sat on plastic chairs. They yelled out a greeting to Miles and he grinned. Captain Delancey came around with a pitcher of beer.

"Where's your glass?" he said to Miles.

"Just got here, sir."

"Well, don't fucking stand there. Find a glass."

Miles looked at me and smiled sheepishly.

"I'll grab us some chairs," I said.

I saw Crystal across the patio and pulled an empty chair beside her.

"Friday night at the O club," I said.

"I know, right?"

She stuck out her lips in this funny, pouty way she had.

"Think we'll go out later?" I said.

"I heard some of the guys were talking about going to Wild Country."

"That place is so trashy."

"I know."

When she stood up to find the bathroom a little later, one of the soldiers from the unit—a guy Miles didn't particularly like—came and sat beside me.

"How's it going?" he said. "Miles dragged you to this thing?"

I rolled my eyes. "Didn't have much of a choice."

We sat there talking while Miles made the rounds. By the time he came out, he was on his third glass of beer.

"Here's your chair, man," the guy said, standing.

"No, stay," Miles said. "I'm going to say hello to the captain."

I watched him walk across the terrace and give Captain Delancey a light punch on the arm. The captain turned and draped one of his big arms across Miles's shoulders.

"Finish that beer," the captain said.

Miles raised the glass to his mouth and downed the beer in one long swallow. The captain refilled his cup and Miles made his way back to drop into the empty chair beside me.

"Having fun?" I said.

He closed his eyes and a smile spread across his face.

"This is great," he said.

On the far side of the patio, the colonel stood to speak. When the chatter didn't die down, he said in a loud voice, "All the wives out there, shut the fuck up."

Everyone laughed. He said it every week.

The drinking picked up as the sun slipped from the sky. A gray twilight fell and lingered. Someone brought out a guitar, and a drunken camaraderie settled over the bar. Miles left to play a round of pool, but not long afterward one of the guys from the unit found me on the patio.

"I think Miles needs to go home," he said, laughing.

I looked at my watch. It wasn't even ten o'clock.

"Is he that bad?" I said.

"He's puking in the bushes out front."

By the time I got to the door, three of the soldiers had wrangled Miles into the parking lot. He laughed and tried to fight them off.

"I'm not going to take him home like that," I said.

One of the soldiers stepped back and looked at me.

"You have to."

"Not like that."

"He's your responsibility."

I crossed my arms over my chest and we glared at each other.

"Well, help me get him in the truck," I said.

I climbed behind the wheel and one of the guys pulled Miles into the truck. The soldier sat beside me and cinched his arms around Miles's waist. I locked the three of us in. Miles kicked at the window until his shoe slipped off and then he kicked again and left a dirty footprint on the glass.

"Dammit, Miles," I said. "Stop it."

He laughed and kicked the window again.

"I'm serious. Cut that shit out."

"Just drive," the soldier said.

I backed the truck out of the parking space while Miles flailed. At a stoplight he tried to wrench the door open, but the soldier grabbed his arm and held it tight.

"Jesus Christ, Miles," I yelled. "Stop it!"

"Hurry up," the soldier said.

At our apartment building I angled into a space. I ran ahead to unlock the door and the soldier dragged Miles out of the truck. They maneuvered together through the front door and all of the fight seemed to fade out of him. Miles slumped against the soldier's shoulder and half walked, half fell into the bedroom. The soldier laid him on the bed, closed the door, and stepped into the living room, where I waited.

"What the fuck?" I said.

"Don't get mad," the soldier said. "He's just blowing off steam. Everybody's pretty stressed-out right now."

"But he's never like this. He was out of control tonight."

"Well, maybe if you hadn't been flirting, he wouldn't have gotten so drunk."

"Flirting?" I said. "With who?"

He said the name of the soldier Miles didn't like.

"Wait," I said. "You're saying this is my fault?"

"I'm just saying maybe you shouldn't have been flirting."

"We had a fucking conversation."

"That's not what it looked like."

"This is unbelievable."

The soldier shrugged and walked out the door.

———————

The ghostly outline of Miles's foot was still on the window of the truck when we went out to dinner with a group of pilots from the unit not long afterward. On the way to the parking lot at the end of the evening, they talked about dust-offs and night landings and the flying conditions in Iraq. I must have stiffened or a look must have shadowed my face, because one of the pilots called out to me as he unlocked his pick-up, "Don't worry, we'll bring your boy home."

"You better," I called back.

In Miles's truck, the two of us looked at the clock on the dash. It was still early.

"What should we do now?" Miles asked.

"I don't know," I said. "It's too late for a movie. Too soon to go home."

Miles gave me a sly look. "Want to go parking?"

I giggled. "Where?"

"I'm sure we can find something around here," Miles said as he put the truck in reverse.

We found a deserted construction site on a strip of back road where the streetlights did not reach. Miles cut the engine and we faced out on a rare bit of darkness. In the distance, lights cut the horizon in two, a line drawn between the earth and night sky. Overhead, the stars glowed faintly and cast their light over the stalled front loaders and bulldozers. We scooted to the middle of the seat and Miles reached over to take my hand. We did not speak for a time, just let the place where our sides touched warm each other in the cooling cab of the truck.

"I'm sorry about the other night," Miles said when a long space of silence had passed.

I shrugged. "It was no big deal."

"It won't happen again."

"I know."

I laid my head against his shoulder and looked out over the black expanse, conscious of the world's impartial turning and how we can be terrifyingly alone in it all. But Miles was there beside me, and I was not afraid.

At school on Monday I climbed the outdoor ramp to Mr. Ball's portable classroom. His students were in the music room, but I knew he'd let me stay to staple artwork to the bulletin board or organize his bookshelves.

"How are you doing, Mr. Ball?" I said.

He sat behind his desk with a stack of homework assignments at hand, leafing through the pages and making marks with a red pen.

"Doing okay," he said.

He set the packet on the corrected pile and picked up the next in the stack.

"Can I help you with anything?" I asked.

"You can look over that pile of geography assignments. The answer key's on top."

I grabbed the worksheets and sat behind the low horseshoe table pushed against the side wall. Mr. Ball had the radio going and we listened to the music for a few minutes without talking.

"How's your baby doing?" I said.

He looked up and laughed.

"He never sleeps. Sometimes I'm like, 'Kid, take it easy.'"

He shook his head.

"And these little people in here. Daniel's been giving me crap all week."

I skimmed the page in front of me for wrong answers.

"Did you have to ride him?"

"I sat on him all morning," he joked.

I marked a red X through Australia, mistakenly labeled as Antarctica.

"Did you know his dad's in Iraq?" Mr. Ball said. "I think that's part of his problem. Why he's acting out. Sometimes when I take him aside—not to yell at him, but just to talk—he gets all teary-eyed. Like he just needs a man to talk to him."

I nodded. "I can see that."

On the radio the music switched from a rock song to a car dealership commercial and I looked at the clock on the wall. Ten minutes before I had to head to PE.

"Let me ask you something," Mr. Ball said.

I scanned the map of the world printed on the worksheet in front of me.

"Sure."

"Did you go to college?

"I did."

"Where'd you go?"

"Penn."

"That's a good school."

"It's not bad."

"So tell me something."

I looked up from the page in my hand and saw that Mr. Ball had stopped marking the paper on his desk and leaned forward, as if to make sure he heard my answer. I raised my eyebrows.

"What are you doing here?" he said.

I started to laugh but I realized he was serious. I thought for a second to tell him about Miles—the way he spoke, the way he listened, the way I felt around him—but I stopped myself. How could I tell him that Miles was what I had been looking for my entire life? That the great lonely space inside me, deep and wide as a canyon, shrank to nothing when Miles stepped into the room? That even in that shitty job in that god-awful town, I still considered myself a lucky, lucky girl? Instead I shrugged my shoulders.

"I ask myself that every day," I said.

6

I try to imagine the sacrifices my mother made to mold her life to my father's. I think of her days in the mountains of north Georgia, where clouds covered the sun much of the time, and the winters—nothing like blue-skied south Florida winters—hung heavy and gray for months. I know she quit teaching when they left Miami and I try to understand how she filled her time on the farm. She must have cooked for my father. I remember the table set with pork chops, okra, and collard greens. She must have washed his jeans and folded his shirts, even the white ones that had yellowed under the arms. She must have stripped the sheets from the bed and thrown them in the wash with the other dirty laundry, the unsaid things. She must have lived this life and still loved my father, because after he died she never remarried.

"What's that old saying?" she said. " 'If you've had the best, you know you never can replace that'?"

Cavender's Boot City is in Temple, Texas, twenty-seven miles outside Fort Hood and thirty-six miles from Waco, where David Koresh and his Branch Davidians once lived. I wanted to point this out to Miles on the drive there, to take a jab at that land of holy-rolling crazies, but he was a fiercely proud Texan, the kind who lived by the slogan "American by birth, Texan by the grace of God." So I let it pass.

In the store I followed him to the back, to the shelves of simple work boots, the strong Texan boots, not the showy versions tourists bought in Austin to take back to New York.

"Dime-store cowboys," he called them.

On a shelf in the back half of the store I found a pair of riding boots in rich sorrel leather. They were hand-worked with stitching running up the shaft, and I traced the thread with one finger, following the dips and knots the color of straw. They were undeniably beautiful but I worried if they were right for me.

For that matter, was Miles? Here was a man who voted Republican, who drove a pickup and owned a shotgun, who could ride a horse and rope a cow. He went to church most Sundays, with or without me. More without than with as time went on. He tithed from every paycheck. He prayed before meals, even in restaurants, and we became the sort of couple—hands held, heads bowed over our plates in public—that used to dismay me. When my roommate in Tallahassee said in the first month Miles and I were dating "You two are going to get married," I laughed.

"No way," I said. "He's way too country for me."

But one day, after a game of tennis on the cracked courts of Fort Rucker, Miles looked across the bed of his truck and said, "When I'm with you, no matter what we're doing—tennis or whatever—I want it to go on forever." Until that moment I had always said I would never get married because I could not imagine loving someone enough to be with them forever. But really I could not imagine someone loving me that much.

In Cavender's I handed Miles the boots.

"What do you think?"

He turned them over to inspect the heel and ran his fingers down the leather shaft.

"Looks good," he said.

I sat on a wooden bench and slipped the leg of my jeans up to my knee. I stuck one foot down into the boot and worked the heel until my ankle slipped in.

"Try walking around," Miles said. "How do they feel?"

"They feel good."

"A little tight?"

"A little. In the ankles."

"That'll stretch out."

I walked the length of the store while Miles watched from the bench. When I sat down beside him, he leaned over to whisper in my ear.

"Those boots look good on you," he said.

I extended one foot and tilted the boot to both sides.

Did they?

I called my mother on a weekend afternoon while Miles was in the field. The day was overcast and humid, brooding weather.

"I don't know what I'm doing here," I said when she picked up. "I feel like I'm wasting my life."

My mother was quiet on her end of the phone.

"I have a crappy job," I said. "We live in this shitty apartment. My car's on its last leg. I don't know what to do."

The weak sun cast a pale light through the kitchen window. People passed in front of the door on their way to the laundry room, and their shadows cut the light that seeped under the frame.

"What am I supposed to do?" I asked, and when my mother was silent: "Should I leave?"

"I don't think that's the solution," she said.

I sat at the breakfast bar and looked over our tiny kitchen—at the loaf of bread stacked on top of the refrigerator, the yellow box of off-brand cookies on the counter.

"Then what do I do?"

My mother breathed a long slow breath. "Do you love him?"

I closed my eyes for a moment, and when I opened them I took in the pot holders by the stove, the calendar tacked to the wall, the weekly menu I'd written. A shopping list was pinned to the corkboard beside a note in Miles's handwriting. I saw how all those bits of domesticity formed the working fabric of our relationship and I realized that this was how people built a life together. Not in the plans or schemes or worries or fears but in the day-to-day. The dish soap, the spoon rest, the coupons.

"I love him more than anything," I said.

Perhaps my mother considered her own life then. The mountains of north Georgia, the red earth and the daffodils in spring, my father on his tractor waving at the house.

"Then you stay," she said.

———

In late November Miles and I drove to Austin for the weekend. He booked us a room in a fancy hotel and we ate venison and wild boar at an expensive restaurant. I wore my good dress. When we came back to the room, Miles got down on one knee. I cried and he cried and the next thing I knew, he was slipping a ring on my finger.

But in the night I got up to use the bathroom and stood for a long time in front of the mirror. People say we always think we look like

ourselves, even as we age, even as we put on weight, even as we're cra-
tered with uncertainty. I turned my face from side to side, trying to
determine if I resembled the woman I had once been.

At school on Monday the other aides fussed over my ring. I blushed as I
held out my hand and the diamonds glinted in the glare from the fluorescent lights. Later in the week Ms. Walker stopped me in the hallway.

"You coming to the party tonight?" she said.

Her second-grade class trailed after her in a line and slumped
against the wall as we talked.

"Is that tonight?" I said.

"You got other plans?"

"Miles is in the field."

"Then come over."

I pulled into her driveway a little after eight, and when I knocked on
the front door a woman answered. She was curved like Ms. Walker—
not heavy exactly but full-figured. Pretty with good hair.

"Come on in," she said.

I followed her through the coatroom and into the living room,
where people milled. Some of the teachers from school were there but
mostly it was women I didn't know. I saw a plate of cheese cubes on a
side table next to a bowl of spinach dip and I headed there.

"Girl, there you are." Ms. Walker gave me a hug. "Glad you could
come."

"You look great," I said.

She did. She had on dark red lip gloss and tight brown pants.

"Let me get you something to drink," she said. "Can I get you some
wine?"

"Wine would be great."

She filled a glass with chardonnay from a gallon-size bottle, the kind you buy at Walmart for $8.99. The doorbell rang and she handed me the glass.

"Let me go get that," she said.

I took a sip and started in on the cheese. I ate cube after cube of orange squares. When women began moving to the couch, I filled a paper plate and followed them to the sectional. The cushions sank as I sat. Ms. Walker flipped on the big flat-screen TV at the center of the room and scanned the channels until she found an Oprah rerun.

"Did you see the episode where she—"

"And that time when she—"

"That outfit she wore when—"

I sipped my chardonnay and shifted on the couch. If someone looked in my direction, I smiled.

"Let's play that game," the friend who had answered the door said. "The game with the questions."

Ms. Walker turned from the kitchen counter.

"The paper's right there on the table."

The friend picked up squares of blank paper and a handful of pens.

"Pay attention now," she said.

The hum of conversation died down.

"We thought we'd play a little game so everybody can get to know one another," she said. "Here's how this is going to work. I'm going to hand out these pieces of paper. You write down a question for the group—don't put your name on it—and fold it up and put it in this jar I'm going to pass around."

The conversations started up again, louder.

The woman on my left turned to me. "We put our name on it?"

I shook my head. "Just your question."

A woman standing in the kitchen raised her hand. "I've got a question."

"Girl, we're not in school," the pretty friend said. "You don't have to raise your hand."

"Well, what kind of question are we asking?"

"Anything you want."

I looked at the blank scrap of paper in my hand. Anything? I thought about something dirty, something funny, something crazy. But I didn't know these women or how it would go over. Something I already knew the answer to? The women on either side of me scrawled on the paper they pressed against their thighs. The pretty friend folded up her piece of paper and dropped it into a ceramic jar on the table next to the cheese.

"I'm going to start passing this around," she said. "Just drop your question in."

Should I ask about sex? About school? About books? I discarded every question that came to mind while the jar worked its way around the couch.

"You want us to fold it up?" a woman three cushions over asked. She balanced the jar on her round knees. "Or just drop it in?"

"Do whatever you want," the friend said.

The woman crumpled the paper into a ball the size of a marble. I needed a question. Any question. So I wrote what I worried about every day. I wrote the question that I thought about when I woke up in the morning and that pressed me into sleep at night.

What if you love someone with all your heart but you're afraid that being with him means giving up the life you imagined for yourself?

I folded the slip of paper just as the jar reached me and dropped my question in. The container finished making its way around the room and already the pockets of conversation were starting up again. I clutched my paper plate in my hand, crimping the cardboard edges.

Please don't pick mine, I thought. *Please pick another question.*

The pretty friend held the jar over her head.

"I'm going to choose now," she said.

The room grew quieter but not quiet. Ms. Walker leaned against the counter and talked to another teacher. Three women at the far end of the couch ate tiny meatballs and talked in low voices. One burst out with a loud laugh.

"Hush," Ms. Walker's friend said.

The woman with the meatballs covered her mouth with her hand and one of the other women slapped her knee. They all three laughed.

The pretty friend stirred the jar dramatically.

"Come on, pick one!" Ms. Walker shouted from the kitchen.

"I'm getting there," the friend said. She gave her hand a final swirl and then with her perfectly manicured nails lifted a folded slip of paper.

Not mine, I prayed.

She unfolded the paper and skimmed the question. She cleared her throat and the room waited.

"What if you love someone," she paraphrased, "but being with them means giving up your own life?"

There was a lull as people considered the question. I looked at the floor. The meatball women started talking again in low voices, their feet pushed close together.

"And I said, 'If you're not going to bother to treat me like a lady, then don't bother—'"

The woman next to her nodded vigorously. A woman at the end of the couch stood up to fix herself another plate of cheese, and I thought the moment might pass. But Ms. Walker stepped out of the kitchen and leaned over her friend's shoulder to read the paper. She looked pointedly in my direction.

"You figure out how to make it work," she said. "That's what marriage is."

On a clear day at the end of the year, Miles and I drove through the hills that surround Killeen. The day was cool enough that we rolled down the windows and let the dry air blow into the car. Thistle bushes grew beside the road and mesquite trees crouched back from the shoulder. Sunlight filtered through the open sunroof and the wind flowed into the car and back out, taking with it the air we exhaled and the evaporating sweat from our bodies. We drove until we spotted a vegetable stand beside the highway.

"Should we stop?" Miles asked.

"Sure," I said.

Inside the wood frame of the market stall, heat radiated from the corrugated tin roof. Rays of sunlight angled into the shed and illuminated the motes of dust that rose in our wake. Miles pointed to the clear plastic bags of water hanging from the rafters.

"Keeps the flies off," the man behind the counter said.

He laughed a dry, old man's laugh.

"You in the military?" he asked Miles.

"Yes, sir."

"Thought so. Always can tell by the hair."

He leaned back and propped his hands on the wooden countertop.

"Used to be in the military myself."

I worked my way around the stand while the man talked to Miles about the Army, bases they both knew, tours overseas. I put a jar of honey on the counter beside a pound of tomatoes. The man poked at the keys of a large cash register while he talked, and Miles pulled bills from his wallet and passed them across the counter.

"You all take care," the man said as we walked back to the car, and to Miles: "Watch out for yourself over there."

"I will," Miles said.

The tires kicked up dust as we pulled back onto the asphalt and the low hum of the road worked its way through the undercarriage.

"Are you going to sell vegetables out of the back of your pickup when you get done with the Army?"

Miles laughed.

"Nah," he said. "I think I'll be a teacher. Maybe coach football."

I looked through the windshield and nodded thoughtfully.

"They have this Troops to Teachers program," he said. "The Army'll pay for you to go back to college and get your degree. When you're done, you teach in a public school somewhere."

"That sounds all right," I said.

Miles looked at me. "Yeah?"

I took his hand and held it over the console.

"Yeah."

He drove for a few minutes without speaking, then asked, "How about you? What do you want to do when this Army business is over?"

I shrugged my shoulders. "I don't know."

Miles squeezed my hand.

"Seriously," he said. "What do you want?"

"Anything?"

"Anything."

"I want to be a writer."

Miles held the steering wheel and I could feel him considering.

"What would you write? Books?"

"Books, articles—I don't know. I'd like to travel too. To write from overseas."

Miles was quiet for a time. Finally he said, "I like that idea."

"You do?"

"It feels right."

I smiled to myself and watched the road wind through the hills. Anything seemed possible in that land bare of everything but rye grass and barbed wire, and it was easy to imagine a future where our plans would come to pass. We followed the dashed line dividing the asphalt until the road spit us out at the foot of a rise where a stoplight blinked. Miles slowed and I pointed to a hand-lettered sign in the grass.

"'House for Sale,'" I read. "Want to give it a try?"

Miles followed my finger to the sign, to the path that turned off the main highway, and to the low hills beyond.

"Let's do it," he said.

He put on his blinker and we watched for cardboard arrows planted in the ground.

"This it?" he said in front of a leaning mailbox.

I craned my neck to read the sign staked into the ground.

"I think so."

The driveway sloped upward to a small house at the top of the hill. I say *house* loosely. It was a trailer. A double-wide, but still. Pale grasshoppers skittered from beneath my feet as I stepped out of the car and a breeze combed through the knee-high weeds. The property was nothing special—open space and untamed grass buffeted by wind and sun—but it possessed a certain quality that brought to mind the word *homestead*. For a brief moment we let ourselves believe in the possibility of a settled life. Miles looked toward the base of the property and the road we drove in on. His sunglasses hid his eyes, but I guessed what he was thinking. I was thinking the same.

"We could live here," he said.

I surveyed the property, nodding. "We could."

On the front porch I pressed my face against the dusty sliding glass door. Inside, the trailer was empty. Thin carpet covered the floors and a fan sagged from the ceiling. I could see straight through to the back window that looked out on the hills beyond. The wooden planks of the porch creaked with our steps as we jumped down and pushed a path through the grass before circling around to the car.

"Do you think we should call the number on the sign?" he said.

"Let's give it a try."

Miles called the real estate agent but got the agent's voice mail instead. He left a message before we drove back to Killeen. We both had work on Monday, and then it was the middle of the week, and soon it was the next weekend. The agent never called back. In the weeks that followed I would find grass seeds stuck to the clothes we wore that day. Sometimes Miles would mention the place. But over time we forgot.

Much later—in the wake of the war—I would dream of that house. Flat plains stretched behind the property, wide-open and empty, and in the distance sand hills rose up like dunes. In the dream I was lost. I tried to find my way through that vast stretch of sameness, a land without discernible pathways, and all the while I felt the house pressing at my back, its solidness there just over the rise.

2006

7

In early March, Miles and I phoned home, first to my mother, then to Miles's parents. I sat at the breakfast counter with my arms folded nervously in my lap and watched Miles as he spoke.

"Hello, Dad," Miles said. "Is Mom there?"

He stood beside my chair and reached a hand over to touch my arm.

"Good, good," he said. "Glad I got both of you there."

I gave him a small smile.

"Listen, we wanted to call and see if it would be all right if—if we—if we went ahead and got married. Before the wedding, I mean."

There was a long silence and I reached out to Miles.

"We were thinking, you know, to go ahead and get the administrative details out of the way. Get Artis her military ID. Get her on Tricare. We don't want to have to mess with all that while I'm deployed."

I ran my thumb over the rough skin around his fingernail and inspected the folds of his knuckle. I was afraid to look at his face. But when he started to talk again, I could hear the smile in his voice. I looked up and he nodded his head.

"Sure, sure," he said. "She's right here. I'll put her on."

I covered the mouthpiece with my hand. "Is everything okay?"

"No worries," he said.

I held the phone to my ear. "Hello?"

Terry was on the other end.

"Hey, girl," she said. "This is great news. We're so happy for you."

"Really?" I said. "You guys are okay with this?"

"Sweetie, we just want you married."

Three months before our real wedding, Miles and I drove to the courthouse in Killeen, a squat building in red brick that was bland in the way of government offices everywhere. Miles came straight from the base, still in his uniform, and I wore jeans and my cowboy boots. When we approached the administrative window, the clerk behind the glass slid out a paper form.

"You'll both need to sign this," she said. "We'll need thirty-two dollars for the ceremony and sixty-seven for the marriage license. No personal checks."

I looked over the form and signed with a pen tethered to the counter. I passed the page to Miles and he placed his signature next to mine. He slid the paper through the slot along with a money order. The clerk ran her eyes over the page.

"Have a seat," she said.

We sat in plastic chairs bolted to the floor as the lights overhead reflected off the linoleum that ran the length of the hallway. After a time a door opened to the judicial office and a secretary in a pink sweater stepped out.

"Henderson?" she said.

Miles looked at me. I gave him a nervous smile.

"That's us," he said.

"You all can follow me back."

We walked through the lobby with its Texas seal on the wall, over beige carpeting that absorbed the sound of our footsteps. I hooked a finger in the collar of my shirt and pulled, trying to vent my neck as the secretary led us into the courtroom chambers.

"The judge will be right in," she said.

I leaned into Miles and he placed his hand on the small of my back the way he did when I was scared. The judge stepped into the room. He had traded his judicial robes for a pair of stonewashed jeans and low-heeled cowboy boots. He was a large man with round cheeks that were red, as if someone had just pinched them. I could see the appeal. He had a thick drawl and I imagined he kept a Stetson hanging on the back of his office door.

"How you all doing?" he said. "Ready to get this done?"

We nodded.

"Good. I can see you all are holding hands. That's a good sign. Sometimes we get people in here and one of them looks like they might bolt out the door. It's good to hold on to each other. Keeps you both here."

Miles gave my hand a squeeze.

"You all want to go ahead and face one another," the judge said. "I'm going to run through this. It'll be quick. You got rings?"

"No, sir," Miles said.

"That's all right. Don't need them anyhow."

The judge covered all the bases and asked if we agreed to the terms.

"Yes," I said in a tight voice.

"Yes," Miles echoed.

"Then by the power vested in me by the state of Texas, I now pronounce you husband and wife. Go on and kiss now."

We gave each other a chaste peck and the judge shook both our hands. We walked out the way we had come in and the secretary handed us our marriage certificate. We left the carpeted office and followed the linoleum back to the front entrance, walking without speaking, dazed as if we had just survived a wreck. On the steps to the courthouse we stopped and looked at each other.

"Holy shit," I said. "We're married."

Miles pulled a camera out of his uniform pocket and stopped a man walking into the building.

"Would you mind taking a picture for us?"

We stood together in front of the courthouse wall and the man took a close-up shot as we smiled big brave smiles into the camera. When the newspapers ask for a photo of Miles, this is the one I send. They crop me out so that Miles is alone, looking unaccountably happy on the courthouse steps.

———————

Spring gave way to early summer and we were suddenly, finally done with Fort Hood. We loaded Miles's truck and hitched my car to the back in a drill we were starting to perfect. I sat beside Miles in the cab of the pickup and we both felt free. Free of Killeen, free of Fort Hood. Yes, we were headed back to Fort Bragg and all the coarseness of that place, but in the interim—in the liminal space between one base and the next where the future was stacked with limitless possibilities—we were free. Or I was free. And Miles beside me with his uncomplicated air and easy laugh, I think he was free too.

Our second time at Fort Bragg, we stayed out of Fayetteville. We rented a trailer north of the base off a dirt road that ran beside a cornfield. The earth had been newly planted when we arrived and young seedlings pushed out of the dirt in neat rows. Insects hummed in the fields during the early afternoons when the heat set in and the trailer baked beneath the sun. Our place had brown carpet that had once been plush, old furniture that had seen generations of tenants, and pink toilet seat covers that made me think somebody's grandma had once lived there. We unloaded the boxes we had packed in Killeen; the Crock-Pot made its way onto the counter and the dish towels went into a side drawer. I pulled out my rolling pin, our salt and pepper shakers, the green ceramic mugs. Miles carted armloads into the spare bedroom: his extra uniforms, a second set of desert boots, the Gore-Tex jacket in green camo. In that way we set up house—again.

There was a sweetness to the time Miles and I spent in the trailer next to the cornfield, even as the deployment loomed. The unit was scheduled to ship out in three months, in late July, but we pretended not to notice. The air was soft and clear as if all the turbulence of the previous season had blown over. Miles and I slept in the back bedroom in a white-framed double bed. We held hands in the night. One morning I woke with my nose pressed against his neck, my face tucked into the space beneath his chin, and blinked in the feathered light of early day.

"You're sweaty," I said.

"*You're* sweaty."

I pulled away from his pillow and rolled onto my back, and he rolled onto his and reached across the bed for my sweaty hand.

Once a storm blew through in the night and I woke with an inexplicable fear inside me. Rain roared against the walls of the trailer and wind shook the oaks in the front yard. Their branches dragged across the roof like the tines of a rake, and I lay beside Miles filled with a nameless dread. In the morning we walked the rutted dirt road that ran beside the trailer. Stalks of corn shot into the sky, hopped up on rain and fertilizer. The gravel that pocked the road crunched under Miles's boots as we debated the question that hung over everything: what to do with me while he was gone.

"You could go to my folks' place in Texas," Miles said. He walked with his hands shoved down in the front pockets of his jeans.

"Why would I do that?"

"I don't know. To be close to family."

"My mom is my family."

"Maybe you should go home to live with your mom, then."

We continued in silence for a bit, both of us turning over the idea.

"I could go back overseas," I said unconvincingly. "Teach English somewhere."

I had already given up on the idea of that life, but it felt wrong not to say it, to pretend like it wasn't even an option. But Miles shook his head.

"You don't want to be that far away. Not while I'm gone. Not in case something happens."

"Nothing's going to happen," I said. "But if I lived with my mom, we could save some money. You'll be earning hazard pay and I'll get a job. We could put a lot of money in the bank and maybe when you get back we could buy a house."

"It would be nice to have a place of our own," Miles said.

"Plus my friends are in Florida. It might be okay to be back there."

"It might." He smiled slyly. "You could always stay here."

I gave him a push with my elbow. "What would I do here?"

"Hang out with the other wives. Get tangled up in the FRG drama."

"That's my worst nightmare," I said. I shook my head as I imagined the infighting, the backstabbing, the rampant gossip. It never occurred to me that those women might be a source of support while Miles was gone, that they might comfort me if the worst happened.

"No, send me home," I said. "Get me away from the military. Let me live with my mom. That way, when you get back, we can buy our own place."

"And if something happens—"

"Nothing's going to happen."

"But if something happens," he said, "you'll have everybody there."

On the first day of July, three weeks before Miles deployed, we held our wedding at my mother's beach house in Florida. My best friends were there, Heather and Annabelle and Stacy, young women I had known all my life. They joined me in my bedroom as I nervously dressed and fixed my makeup. My mother stepped into the bathroom, tugging at her hair. She still wore it long and parted down the middle, like the day she met my father. Like the day he died. Though her hair had gone gray in places, its weighty power remained unchanged.

"How do I look?" she said to Annabelle.

"You look nice," Annabelle said, moving into the bathroom to look her over. "Maybe a flower?"

She chose a rose from a stack on the bathroom counter, snapped off the stem, and worked the bud into the long loop of hair my mother had pulled over her right shoulder.

"That looks better," Annabelle said.

My mother eyed herself in the mirror as I leaned forward to dab gloss on my lips.

"You look beautiful, Mommy," I said.

"Really?"

I twisted the cap back on the tube and looked at my mother. People say I look like her but mostly they are talking about our hair. Mine is long too. It never feels long enough. I smiled and she dabbed at her eyes with a balled-up piece of toilet paper.

"I'm so happy for you," she said.

The tip of my nose went red and I wiped at my eyes with my fingers.

"Don't get me started," I said. "I'm already a mess."

My mother checked herself over one last time before heading downstairs.

"Five minutes," Annabelle said.

"Shit," I said. "I'm not ready."

I smoothed my dress to my body. It was floor-length silk, off-white, bought at J.Crew. I didn't wear shoes. A pearl on a silver chain hung around my neck and small diamond earrings dangled from my ears, both gifts from Miles. Somewhere downstairs he waited in a blue button-up oxford shirt from the Gap and green chinos he had rolled to his ankles. He wore flip-flops. When we decided to get married, I said I didn't want tulle or a reception hall or plates of salmon served by waiters in black ties. I wanted a moment where our friends and family could eat good food—we had arroz con pollo, black beans and rice, sweet plantains—and dance to my favorite songs. If people told me I was glowing, I didn't want it to be because I had my hair done at a salon or makeup spray painted over my skin, but because I was young and happy and in love.

I turned to Heather and Stacy, who sat on the bed, and it struck me what beautiful young women my friends had become. They were all three lithe and long-haired, well-spoken and well-read; they had good jobs and stable lives.

"What do you think?" I said.

Heather stretched her feet to the floor, hopped off the bed, and fitted her toes into her high heels. "I think it's time to go. Let's get this party started."

The day had been clear and hot, the Gulf green and flat, but a storm rolled in as Miles and I said our vows. The water went gray and the petals in my hair trembled. The storm broke after the kiss and people dashed for cover as rain came down in fat warm drops. After dinner and cake, people made their way to the dance floor. The Priestners had driven in from Fort Bragg and Captain Scott Delancey came too. In the half-light of torches stuck in the sand, Miles and I watched John and Teresa sway to Marvin Gaye.

"Check out the captain," he said.

In a dark corner, Captain Delancey danced close to Heather.

I laughed. "Same old, same old."

The rain had left standing puddles of water that caught the light from the torches, and the damp air soaked up the scent of lilies from the side yard. I could hardly make out Miles's face in the dark, but I could feel him there beside me. My worries from the last few months seemed small and distant and a tender gratitude welled in me. I felt a sense of homecoming not because of the salt air or the pounding tides but because of Miles, a man of gentleness and courage whose goodness emanated from him like heat. His strength would protect us, I was sure, and I let myself believe we were safe.

8

The night before Miles left for Iraq, two tough bins sat open on our living room floor. I watched Miles race around the trailer, pulling clothes out of closets, sorting through important papers.

"Don't worry," I said from the couch. "You'll get everything."

He stopped long enough to give me a look.

I laughed. "Maybe we should have done this a week ago."

When Miles moved into the bedroom around midnight, I followed. I climbed into bed and opened a book in my lap while he pulled another shirt out of the closet and threw it in a pile on the floor.

"That's for R & R," he said. "You'll keep them at your mom's place?"

"I'll have them waiting for you."

He picked up his bottle of cologne and set it in the R & R pile. "This too."

My eyelids were heavy as I sat on the bed, and when Miles left the room they drifted shut. I lifted them when he walked back in.

"You're going to feel bad if something happens to me over there and you spent our last night together sleeping."

"I know," I said and fell asleep.

The next morning we were both up early. I lay in bed while Miles showered and talked to him as he moved through the room. He dressed in his uniform and laced up his boots. Outside, the damp heat of July was already building and pressing against the sides of the trailer. I wished that a breeze might sweep down and blow the cornstalks in the fields, that a wind might stir the leaves and send up clouds of black dirt. But the air remained without moving, saturated and suffocating, hard to breathe.

I showered and dressed in time to hear Miles's parents pull into the driveway. The four of us hugged, spoke some, then stood in the front yard to snap photos. The ground was uneven and the roots of the old oaks rose up and fell back under the soil in waves. We balanced the camera on the back of Miles's truck so we could take a picture of the four of us together. When we finished, Miles and I climbed into his pickup. He cranked the engine and we rumbled up the driveway, rolling over the knobby roots, driving past the corn standing stiff in the fields. Miles stuck a hand out his window and his parents raised theirs in return.

At the hangar on base, Miles dropped off his tough bins and loaded his rucksack while I leaned against the truck. People from the unit milled around the parking lot and I watched the wives whose husbands had been on previous deployments. They had learned to be still and wait. I saw Crystal across the parking lot and waved.

"How's it going?" she said when she came over.

I shrugged and we stood beside each other for a long minute without talking. Across the parking lot Troy called out to her.

"I better go," she said. "I'll come find you when the buses leave."

Miles came back to the truck and I followed him into the hangar. The helicopters were already gone, sent on a boat halfway across the world. Miles and I sat facing each other on the cool concrete and I tried not to watch the other families. I saw the men hold small children and touch the shoulders of their wives beside them. They sat in tight groups, wagons circled against the night. Miles and I formed our own circle. He ran his fingers along my arm in a way that made me shiver and I rested my hand on his knee. We hardly spoke.

When the buses rolled up outside, Miles stood and I stood with him. We made our way back into the parking lot. I wrapped my arms around his neck and felt his body beneath my hands, the muscles of his back, the hardness in his shoulders, and realized this would be the last time I would touch him for a long while. Fear filled me then, hot and raw, and swept through my body, leaving me shaken and hollowed. Miles held me close before he turned and stepped onto the bus. He took a seat near the back beside a window while I waited on the ground outside. Crystal stood to my right. With the men gone, the wives had regrouped. Miles waved to me from his seat and I waved back, waved the entire time the bus rumbled away. When it had disappeared around the corner I thought to myself, *Not all of them will come home.* I hoped it would not be anyone I knew.

In the month after the unit deployed, buyers everywhere paid too much for property they couldn't afford. Police arrested Mel Gibson in California and readers cried over *Marley & Me.* An article in the *Atlantic* discussed the possible pullout of troops from Iraq and the death toll reached more than two thousand. I did not hear from Miles for more than two weeks, and then one afternoon my phone rang with a number I did not recognize. My mother was driving us down Daniels Parkway, a strip of land that once was scrub brush and palmetto hammocks but like most of south Florida had given over to strip malls and subdivisions.

"Hello?" I said.

"Hello, babe?"

"Oh, my God."

My mother looked at me, at the road, back at me, and she was already slowing down and putting on her blinker. She turned into a new housing complex, past the ornamental landscaping at the entrance, and put the car in park. I pointed to the phone and mouthed *I'm sorry* but she shook her head and waved me out of the car. *Go.*

"How are you?" I asked Miles as I opened the door.

"Doing all right," he said.

I sat on the smooth lip of the concrete curb and watched waves of heat roll off the asphalt. There were plumbago bushes at my back, their tiny purple flowers vibrant, and red blossoms on the ixora plant. Round-bottomed clouds billowed across the blue sky.

"How was your trip over?" I said. "Did everything go okay?"

"Everything was smooth. No problems getting here."

"And now you're there? In Iraq?"

"We're here."

"Where are you staying?"

"They have us in barracks. Two to a room."

"Who are you rooming with?"

"Troy."

I laughed. "No kidding."

"Chow's pretty good."

"What are they feeding you?"

"The normal stuff. We had pecan pie the other night."

"Not bad," I said. "How's the weather?"

"Pretty hot. But listen, babe, tell me about things there. How are you doing?"

"Me?" I said. "I'm fine. Missing you."

"I miss you too."

The phone line lagged and we were both quiet, waiting for the other person to speak.

"Did you—"

"How are—"

We laughed and the phone went silent again.

"You talk," Miles said. "I want to hear what's going on with you. How are things going with your mom?"

I glanced at the car, where my mother flipped through a newspaper. It was ninety-five degrees and she had the engine off but kept the windows rolled up to give me space.

"Great," I said. "We're doing great. It's been surprisingly easy to be back home."

"Good, good."

A line of ants marched out of the cracks in the pavement and into the recently laid mulch. One crawled over my painted toenails and tickled the skin there. The traffic on Daniels hummed past and I pressed my ear to the phone. If I closed my eyes and shallowed my breath so that the damp air didn't come too close, if I ignored the fragrance from the narrow-throated flowers at my back and the acrid pinch of the tar in the pavement—if I focused just on the phone in my hand, not on the road, not on the plants, not on the thunderheads gathering in the east, just the phone—it was almost as if Miles and I were together.

The phone line stuttered and cracked.

"Miles?"

"I'm here but I have to go."

"Already?"

"My time's up."

"I love you," I said.

"I love you too."

"Be safe."

"I will."

A car pulled into the subdivision and turned into the loop where my mother had parked. She waved the driver around but he honked his horn and she had to put the car in gear and pull forward. She gave him the finger as he drove past. The fronds of the cabbage palm behind me hung limp and a gnat hovered close to my face. I held the receiver for a full minute before realizing the line was dead in my hand.

———

Not long afterward I applied for a PR position at a research farm north of town. It was a good job, with decent pay and nice people. I'd handle the tours of the property, scheduling the groups of students and international aid workers who came to examine the tropical agriculture grown on the farm. The place had chaya and Moringa and jicama, pomelos twice the size of grapefruits, and a staff that had traveled the world. My office would have a window that looked out on a pond stocked with tilapia, and in the high season I could take home bags of mangoes and avocados. They told me I could even drive the golf cart.

Another month passed. The Dow Jones hit stratospheric levels; it turned out war was good for business. The housing boom started to look like it might go on forever. I got the job. Miles called to tell me, laughing breathlessly into the phone, about a jog he had taken around base.

"I wanted to get in a quick run before we went to the chow hall," he said, "and everything started out all right. But then as I was coming in for the last leg, I saw this other guy running ahead of me."

I could hear him smiling across the ocean between us.

"He looked back over his shoulder at me and stepped up his pace.

By now he's sprinting. He looked back again with this scared look in his eyes and I'm thinking, *I'm going to nail this guy.*"

I laughed into the phone.

"So we ran like that for another twenty yards and I started closing in. The guy looked back two more times and every time he had this worried expression."

Miles laughed to himself on the other end of the line.

"By now people were gathered at the barracks watching us come in," he said. "It was like *Chariots of Fire.* I put on an extra burst of speed and *bam!* I surged past him at the finish. Everybody's high-fiving me and slapping me on the back. Then I turn around to shake this guy's hand and I stopped."

His voice dropped to a whisper.

"It was like nothing I've ever seen. A wall of sand."

A sandstorm had come up during the last leg of the race and the men from the unit had come outside to see the squall move in. They saw Miles and the other runner heading to camp at a breakneck pace.

"I thought they were all out there to see me," Miles said, and I could hear him shake his head. "But they thought I was running for my life."

The soldiers had a few seconds of openmouthed wonder before the fury of the storm overtook the camp, obliterating the sun and pushing red dust into every crevice. Miles and his crew hustled inside as the first abrasive blast shook their hovel.

"It was great," he said to me over the phone. "I outran a sandstorm."

When we couldn't speak on the phone, we talked in letters. I told him about leading tours, managing docents, and growing food in the tropics. I sent him photos of me behind the wheel of a golf cart. He wrote back:

*Everything is going alright over here. We had some rockets shot
into the airfield the other day, but they were so far away we could
not even hear them. I am so excited that power bars and pump-
kin pie are being served in the chow hall now. I have already
gathered tons of snacks for my room. I bet I have already stored
up fifteen power bars, two travel bowls of cereal, and one package
of oatmeal raisin cookies. If we come under siege, I want to be
ready. Not much real news to talk about. Nothing new, anyway. I
guess that is a good thing. Just the same old crap as always, con-
tinuous commo problems, trouble getting parts, mission planning,
and of course flying is keeping everyone busy.*

I sent packages once a week. I figured out how to make a video of
myself—sitting on my bed, monologuing for five minutes—and burned
the short clip to a CD that I mailed with a bad batch of cookies. I wrote:

*Just a quick note to tell you how very much I love you and miss
you. You are the light of my life; if I were a redneck town, you
would be my Gun and Knife show. You are my free t-shirt thrown
into the crowd. Enjoy the goodies. The cookies are terrible. The
first batch, the few crackly ones on top, are good, but the rest are
terrible. I threw some of them away, but I wanted you to know I
baked for you, so I just wrapped them up and sent them anyway.
My mom actually suggested I stopped baking, and said she'd
throw in $5 so I could buy cookies. We got down a world map
today and looked at Korea. I think there are great possibilities for
adventures if you are assigned there next.*

He wrote back:

*I received an awesome package in the mail today that included a
most wonderful video message. How did you do it? I would love to*

send you one. By the way, I tried the ginger snaps on both the top
and bottom of the bag and I thought they all tasted very, very good.

From his letters it was hard to tell he was fighting a war. But I often wondered what he did during his missions over the desert cities. And afterward? Did he count his kills like scalps after an Indian raid? Did he weep softly in his bunk at night?

In early October, his letters began to change:

Today was kind of rough. All of us are doing just fine, but today
was long and rough. Please remember us in your prayers, babe.
Especially remember the ground guys. Remember them, babe. I
love you and can hardly wait to be home with you again.

And in another:

We made it through one more flight here. I hate night flights, and
I always will.

During Saturday brunch at Annabelle's house, French toast sat on the table next to strawberries in a bowl and a casserole dish with grits and cheese and bacon. Annabelle stood at the kitchen counter juicing oranges while I worried the pulp might get stuck in her engagement ring. Stacy wore an engagement ring too. We were like that, all of us getting engaged at the same time, our weddings just six months apart.

Heather sat across the table from me and fished a strawberry out of the bowl.

"You guys are lucky to have bought this place before the prices got crazy," she said to Annabelle. "It has to be worth twice what you paid for it."

Annabelle sliced an orange on the cutting board. "We got a good deal."

She carried two glasses of juice to the table, took a seat at the head, and passed plates down the line. Stacy leaned forward and propped her elbows on the table.

"Everybody says real estate is a good investment right now."

"People keep telling me property values will never go down," I said.

I speared a slice of French toast with my fork and lifted it onto my plate. Across the table, Heather twisted the cap off a bottle of maple syrup and doused her plate.

"Are you and Miles going to buy a house in North Carolina when he gets back?" she said.

"I wish we could buy a place down here."

"Down here?" Heather said.

They stopped eating and looked at me.

"I don't know. With Miles gone so much—"

I let the thought hang as I reached for my glass of orange juice.

"Well, I would love it if you were down here," Heather said.

Annabelle held her knife and fork motionless and looked at me as she spoke.

"What would you do with the house when he gets back?" she said.

I chewed for a few moments, thinking. "Rent it out?"

Annabelle nodded thoughtfully.

"It's just—" I considered. "It's so nice here. Nice to be around all of you, nice to be near my mom. Nice to be away from the Army."

"But don't you miss Miles?" Heather said.

"Of course."

"So, how would you have a house down here?"

"I don't know. I'm still trying to figure all this out," I said, waving my fork to take everything in: marriage, real estate, the military.

When Miles called in mid-October, south Florida had settled into fall. Sunlight poured through the jalousie windows of my bedroom and the Gulf below stretched flat and smooth to the horizon.

"How are things over there?" I asked.

"I'm pretty beat," Miles said. "They have us flying all the time. Not much time to rest."

I worked a length of my hair around my index finger and twisted it tight against my skull. The phone line hummed.

"Listen, Miles," I said. "I have something I want to talk to you about."

"All right," Miles said.

"I think maybe we should buy a house here."

"A house?"

"I was just thinking." I twisted the lock of hair tighter. "My friends are here. My mom's here. I'm really happy here."

A breeze blew through the open window and lifted the curtains before setting them carefully back down.

"I mean, I'm not happy," I said. "Because I don't have you."

I took a deep breath.

"That came out wrong."

I waited for Miles to speak, and when he didn't I continued.

"I mean, I want you here. I want to live with you. But you're going to be gone for a year. Maybe more."

"Definitely more."

"Okay. So you're going to be gone for more than a year. And when you come home, you'll only be home for another year or so until you deploy again. Right?"

"Right."

"So maybe it makes sense to buy a house down here."

"I just don't know if it's the right decision for us right now," Miles said.

I looked out to the beach, where women in sorbet-colored bathing suits called out to children grouped on the sand. They answered in tiny, shrill voices. I could feel the quality of the sunlight changing as the day headed toward noon and the light pushed through the screens like honey through a comb.

"But we're both working now," I said. "Together we make good money."

"But what happens when I come home?"

"We rent out the house. Or—"

"Or what, babe?"

"Maybe I just stay here."

"Stay there?" Miles said. "What do you mean, stay there? Like, after I come home?"

"Listen, it's just . . . I've been thinking. You've got, what? Six more years in the Army? Five after you get done with this tour? You're going to be deployed most of the time. Look at the other guys from flight school. They've been home one year the last three."

"So, what are you saying? That you want to live in Florida and not where I am?"

"That's not what I'm saying." I closed my eyes and took a deep breath. "I'm just saying it's been hard. All those towns we lived in. All those jobs I worked. Always moving."

"You think it wasn't hard for me? I didn't like those towns, either.

But at least we were together. That's what got me through. And if that's
not enough for you—"

"It is. It *is* enough."

"Doesn't sound like it."

"I just thought—"

"I have to go."

"Already?"

"My time is up."

"When will I get to talk to you again?"

"I'll try to call next week."

"Miles?" I said. "I'm sorry."

I bit my bottom lip and listened as he took an uneven breath.

"It's okay," he said.

Teresa Priestner called not long after.

"Hey, there. How are you doing?" she said when I answered.

"Great," I said. "Really great."

"Oh, yeah?"

"Yeah. I got a great job. I'm working now."

"Oh, yeah? That's good news. Do you see your girlfriends, the ones
who were at the wedding? What were their names? Heather? Annabelle?"

"I just saw them on Saturday. Annabelle's getting married in March.
We went bridesmaid dress shopping."

"That's good."

Teresa was quiet for a long while and I starting raking the cat fur on
the counter into a pile.

"But how are you doing?" I said. "I haven't talked to you in forever.
Have you heard from John?"

"I spoke to him last night. That's why I'm calling."

I stopped raking the counter.

"Is everything okay?"

"He told me he's been talking to Miles."

I started on the pile again, slower this time, pulling grains of sand with long strokes across the Corian.

"Miles said you guys have been having a tough time."

"Excuse me?"

"He confided in John and I thought I should give you a call."

I let out an exasperated breath.

"Honey, they are in hell over there," Teresa said. "They get shot at all the time. John found bullet holes in his aircraft yesterday."

I traced the clear space that surrounded the pile with the tip of one finger.

"I'm just saying," Teresa said. "He doesn't need any extra stress right now, you know? Things are really hard over there and he doesn't need to be worried about you."

I picked up a crumb between my thumb and index finger and dropped it on top of the pile.

"Okay? I don't mean to yell at you. I don't want you to think I'm mad at you. I wish you were up here at Fort Bragg. We could keep your mind off stuff."

You could keep me in line, I thought.

"I just want you to do what you can for Miles while our boys are over there," she said, and paused for me to answer. I held the phone in my hand and stared at the white countertop.

"All right, honey," she said after a while. "You hang in there. How's your mom?"

"She's fine."

"Tell her I said hello."

"Okay."

"Take care, sweetie."

I hung up the phone and looked up to see my mother coming down the stairs.

"You are not going to believe who I just got off the phone with," I said.

She stopped walking and put her hands on her hips. "Who?"

"Teresa Priestner."

My mother's eyebrows pulled together and the muscles along her jaw tightened.

"Is everything okay?"

"No, no. Nothing like that. She called to yell at me."

I waved an indignant hand, incensed at the meddling of Army wives, blind to how hard it must have been for Teresa to make that call.

"Yell at you?" my mother said. "About what?"

"About not being a good wife."

My mother stood quietly and looked away, toward the sliding glass doors and the beach beyond.

"Can you believe that?" I said. "Like I'm not supposed to talk to my husband? Like, since he's in Iraq I have to be sweet to him all the time?"

"Do you think maybe—"

"It's bullshit," I said. "Right?"

"I don't know," my mother said.

"But to call me like that? To reprimand me?"

I waved my hands angrily in front of my face.

"She thinks because her husband outranks Miles that she can boss me around. No one but me seems to realize that I am not in the military."

My mother stayed with her hands on her hips, and when I could tell she wasn't going to say anything, I turned and stomped to the back room.

"It's bullshit," I said again over my shoulder.

That night I sat down to write Miles an angry letter, a piece of mail that would sum up how I felt, how I was right, how it *was* bullshit. But I thought back to something we had said months ago when we were both new to Army life: the military is hell on marriage. I realized how hard the other wives worked to keep their relationships going. Teresa—who had already seen John through two deployments—knew exactly what to do. So instead of my angry letter, I wrote a love letter in its place. I put down all the things I loved about Miles. The freckles across his shoulders, the way his skin smelled after a shower, the calluses on his hands, how we talked before falling asleep at night, his breath in my face in the mornings. I stopped bringing up the house. Teresa was right. He was in hell.

Miles wrote back:

I find myself dreaming about your hair. How I love to touch it and run my fingers through it. How, when you sit beside me in bed and bend your head down to kiss me and your hair falls around me to where the only thing I can see is your face. Your hair acts as curtains blocking out the world so that all I can see is you, and all you can see is me. I wish that we could wrap your hair around both of us and block out all of this.

Afterward there was a long silence from him and then:

The internet has been down for a few days. It sounds like you know why. His name was Spc. Timothy Adam Fulkerson. He was hit by a landmine while providing security for the rest of us in the entire base. I didn't know him personally. Just knew who he was, the guidon bearer for D Co. Most of our enlisted knew him though; some were good friends. It really sucks to see these men hurting, and I can only imagine what Spc. Fulkerson's family is going through right now. Also keep in your prayers the family of Cpt. Matthew Mattingly. He was the 58 driver that was shot and killed a few weeks ago. Both of these men were among the finest in the Task Force from what I understand and from what their peers say. We had Fulkerson's memorial service today. I hope it looked nice for his family's sake. We taped it to send to them. Throughout the service I just kept getting the feeling that this young man has given the absolute sacrifice, and his family deserved so much more, much more. But a stupid ceremony is all we have to offer in place of a promising future and a wonderful son and friend.

Later he wrote to tell me about the death of another soldier:

I hate telling you this kind of stuff, babe. I don't tell you these things to try to scare you or make sure you know things are rough over here. On the contrary, I really try my best to protect you from all of the cruelty and ugliness that goes on over here. I attempt to make all news sound positive at best and uneventful at worst. I just sometimes can't hide everything. Some things have to be told, ugly or not. I am here to protect you and all our friends and family from all this crap, and I wish you did not have to see or hear anything about what is going on over here. I honestly do not know if what we are doing over here is helping or hurting, but I know that if I wasn't here then someone else would have to be. I can't think about that now though. I just try to focus on the good things, like you, and home, and our bright future that I know is ahead of us.

At the beginning of November he wrote:

No real news here. Just keeping on keeping on.

And:

*I tried the video thing today. I think it worked. I did not burn it
to the CD yet in case I make another video before I go to the post
office again.*

And:

I love you.

It was his last letter home.

Part II

9

Women would tell me later that they knew. *Just knew.* They knew the minute they woke up. They knew as they cleaned their houses in fits of clairvoyant anticipation. They knew as they dressed and waited on the couch for the soldiers to come.

Did I know?

At Fort Rucker, Miles once took me into the equipment room to try out a pair of night-vision goggles. He turned out the lights and we stood in unbroken darkness.

"Can you see that?" he said.

I felt his fingers brush the air in front of my face.

"Nothing."

"Put these on."

He placed the goggles in my hand and showed me the strap with his fingers, guiding me as if I were blind, and I strapped the bulky headset over my face.

"Holy shit," I said.

I could see everything. The countertop, the shelving units, Miles next to me. The room glowed in shades of incandescent green as if someone had flipped the switch on a powerful floodlight. I saw in emerald tones what had been there all along.

Looking back to the notification—and even earlier, to the time of impact—I recognize this knowing that the other women describe. As Miles was making a hard left bank over the sands of northeastern Iraq, I threw my car in reverse and ran straight into the bed of a parked pickup.

"Damn it," I said.

I gritted my teeth and climbed out to check the bumper. A three-inch puncture cut into the black rubber. The car was brand-new, our first big purchase together, bought the week after the wedding. I ran my finger over the gash.

"Shit," I said.

I checked the truck for damage—none—and drove home angry. That night I couldn't sleep, and the next morning arrived fogged over with feelings of guilt and anger and—there it is, in vibrant green—foreboding.

At work I called a docent about coming in early. I scheduled a group tour for the following Thursday. I had promised to make crêpes the week before and I had brought in sugar, flour, and eggs, but the plan seemed more interesting than the execution or I was too busy or I forgot, and at five o'clock I put all the ingredients back into my tote bag and lugged it out to the car. I drove home with the seed of unease stuck like a stone in the back of my throat. The lights in the garage were turned off when I pulled in and the feeling was deeper there, thicker, murky like the waters of a slow-moving river. I made my way up the stairs with my purse in one hand and the heavy tote bag in the other. I set the sack of ingredients on the top step and put my key in the dead bolt, but the door was already unlocked. I pushed it open with my free hand.

A doctor friend once spoke about a diagnostic technique used during his medical school days in the 1960s. A resident would walk past a patient's open door and try to make a diagnosis from those brief moments of passage—the time it took to step from one doorjamb to the next. The doctor said the residents were often successful at diagnosing an ailment in those few seconds. They could even tell you the likelihood of survival.

"It's true," the doctor had told me. "You'd be surprised at how quickly you can assess a situation."

I swept my eyes across the room: my mother in a dining chair in the middle of the living room, nowhere near where it should be; the living room lights turned off; two soldiers in dress uniform filling the space. I felt a drawing in at my navel, a great coming together of all the esoteric parts of me that are neither flesh nor blood nor skin. A silver cord slipped free, pulling from that central place, the part that keeps me whole. I imagined my soul draining out of me like liquid mercury, disappearing into the ether of my suddenly intangible existence. I hesitated on the top step and thought about turning and walking back down to the garage. If I stayed on the far side of the door, the soldiers could not tell me what they had come there to say. If they didn't say it, it wouldn't be true. But I am too rational, too predictable. I am a rule follower. I opened the door wider. I stepped in.

In the living room I went first to where my mother sat and bent stiffly down to put my arms around her.

"Everything will be okay," I said.

I straightened and the soldiers were beside me. One, a chaplain. The non-chaplain said, "On behalf of the President of the United States, I regret to inform you that your husband, Miles Henderson, has been killed in Iraq."

I looked at him numbly. This was not the way it was supposed to happen. Every military wife imagines this scenario, and in my visions the soldiers always came during the day. I would be in the kitchen and

I could see them through the sliding glass doors. The sky would be deep summer blue, the Gulf green at their backs. I would be wearing my house clothes and I would duck down on the opposite side of the breakfast bar, embarrassed that they might see me that way. I would hide until they left. But this was an ambush. I never imagined the soldiers there after dark, already in the house, where I could not hide, could not turn them away.

I asked the non-chaplain if he knew what had happened.

"We don't have many details," he said.

"Did he crash?"

"Yes, ma'am. That's what we're hearing."

"Was he shot down?"

"We heard maybe weather."

"Weather?"

"A sandstorm may have brought them down."

I crossed my arms over my chest as if to shield myself from this information, already understanding that there were some details I would not want to know.

"Who was the second pilot?" I said.

"The second pilot?"

"In the helicopter. Who else was killed?"

"We're not at liberty to say."

"Do you know?"

"No, ma'am."

I faced the soldiers for a long moment. No one spoke.

"Would you like us to stay?" the chaplain said.

"No. Thank you."

When the door shut behind them, I turned to the dark living room. Neighbors, a husband and wife, stepped in off the porch. I realized they must have seen the soldiers when they first arrived and they had been sitting with my mother all that time, waiting.

"Do you want to sit down?" the wife asked.

"Yes," I said. "Outside."

Waves folded against the sand and the salted humidity of the sea pushed against my skin as we sat on the deck. I turned my eyes upward to the night sky, where clouds scudded across the knit darkness, and then dropped my face into my hands. A wail worked its way up from my belly and pushed past my lips, sweeping back in waves across my chest and down my legs. The tender parts of me that are soft and unprotected like the flesh of a crab met the night air. I was all hurt.

"What do I do?" I said to the wife. "Do I take down his photos? Do I give his stuff away?"

She patted my hand. "You don't have to think about that right now."

I turned to my mother, who has a road map for this grief, who might have shown me the way, but she looked at her lap and said nothing. Much later my mother would say about this time, "You were so angry. At me. At the world." She was right. I was suddenly furious at everyone. The soldiers in Miles's unit, the ones who had survived; the government, whose political decision makers ordered men overseas but would never send their own sons to die; the American public whose SUPPORT OUR TROOPS bumper stickers faded and peeled while everyone turned their faces from the war and forgot. Saddam Hussein; Osama bin Laden; George W. Bush, who years later would hold my fingers between his soft damp hands and when my escort told him of Miles's death would say, "That's disappointing," who wouldn't even have the gumption to say, "I'm sorry." I was angry at all of them. But more than anyone I was angry at my mother. My mother, who knew exactly how I was feeling. Who had also lost a husband. Who I rarely saw cry after my father's death and who had done such an effective job of erasing him from our lives, from the reality that he had been lost to me. My mother, who never remarried. Who was permanently, unpardonably alone. Who I had tried my entire life not to become and whose fate, despite my best efforts, I now shared.

Amidst all this anger, I clung to a single idea—that another wife was suffering the same way I was. I needed to know the name of the second pilot. From the back room I called Amy McNish, the company FRG leader.

"What do you know, Amy?" I said when she answered the phone.

"We don't know much. What have you heard?"

I realized that she did not yet have the names of the pilots, that she did not know Miles was one of them. The Army waits until the next of kin has been notified before releasing the names of those killed. The other wives in the unit had heard about the crash on the news, they knew an Apache had gone down, but they did not know who had been lost.

"They came to my door today," I said.

Amy was silent as she sat down hard, the phone still in her hand.

"I need to know the name of the second pilot."

"I'll find out," Amy said. "I'll call you back as soon as I know."

The next day people poured into my mother's house. My half brother from D.C. My uncle from Virginia. Heather. Annabelle. Stacy. If my mother stepped close to speak a kind word or touch my hand, I turned away. The only private moments I had were in the bathroom, where I would sit on the toilet with my eyes closed, bow my head, and speak to Miles.

"I miss you," I said. "I miss you so much."

They seemed like the only words that mattered.

Outside, the sky hung low and gray. Florida had entered the dry season, a period of blue skies and flat water, but a rare autumn storm had moved in overnight. The Gulf churned in the wind as I sat on the deck with Heather and Annabelle. Stray gusts lifted our hair and we were mostly quiet as we watched the waves. The collapse of the offshore rig Deepwater Horizon was still four years away, but I see now what an apt image that is for those first hours after the notification. I remember watching the news as the underwater well pumped oil into the Gulf and how it seemed arterial, as if the earth itself should collapse from the loss. But the well continued to gush with no sign of stopping. In the same way hurt pumped out of me, slick and black as oil. I imagine it covering the deck, dripping down the pilings, pouring onto the beach as the tide rolled in. I hurt and I hurt and I hurt and still there was more, a limitless tonnage. I knew I could bleed hurt forever.

In the early afternoon another soldier arrived, my casualty assistance officer.

"Your CAO," he said.

Already we were talking in military shorthand.

I offered him a seat at the dining room table and he placed a stack of papers between us. He took a pair of wire-rimmed glasses out of his shirt pocket and placed them on his nose.

"My wife says these make me look more intelligent," he said.

I smiled, amazed at my politeness.

"I'll be helping you with the administrative details."

He handed me a heavy black binder stuffed with notebook paper.

"In case you want to take notes."

I didn't. I left the unopened binder on the table in front of me.

"Of course, you know you'll be receiving the death gratuity," he said. The payout from the military if a soldier is killed overseas. Miles had mentioned it once in passing.

"Don't let them try to give you the twelve thousand," he said. "If I die over there, make sure they give you the full hundred thousand."

To the casualty assistance officer I said, "Don't let them give me the twelve thousand."

He laughed.

"No," he said. "You'll get the full one hundred thousand."

I learned that I'd have health insurance for another three years. Dental too. I'd also receive half of the Servicemembers Group Life Insurance policy every soldier buys into. Miles had called it winning the SGLI lottery. His parents and sister would receive the other half. Later I discovered that many widows call the SGLI payout "blood money." They tuck the cash into low-yield savings accounts and pride themselves on never tapping into it.

"I haven't touched that money," these widows will tell me.

They smile as they say this and their cheeks flush, their meaning clear: they will not be bought off. But I felt none of their resentment. I saw the survivor's benefits as continued marks of Miles's generosity. I was strangely grateful to the military and I saw what people meant when they said the Army takes care of its own.

The casualty assistance officer slid a sheet of paper across the dining table. He removed his glasses and polished them with a cloth he pulled from his pocket.

"I'll need you to sign this for me," he said.

I looked at the form without touching the paper. "What is it?"

"It asks if you'd like to receive partial remains."

"Partial remains?"

"If they find anything after the funeral."

He put his glasses back on.

"Body parts. That sort of thing."

I imagined a tooth, a sliver of bone, bits of Miles trickling in over time. I wondered if it would be worse to lose him that way, in pieces.

I declined.

The casualty assistance officer filed the form in his binder, stood, and shook my hand.

"I'll be in touch," he said.

More people arrived the next day. The mother of a soldier in the unit who lived in Tampa. A soldier from the unit's rear detachment. Friends.

Neighbors. I thought often of the second pilot. Who had been with Miles at the end? When Amy McNish finally called, I crept away to the back room.

"I have the name of the other pilot," she said.

"Is he alive?"

Amy was quiet. "No."

I thought of all the soldiers in the unit. I wondered who would hurt the most.

"Are you ready?" she said.

"Tell me."

"It's John Priestner."

I was standing when she called but then I was on my knees. The rough fibers of the carpet rubbed my skin raw and a wail escaped from me. How was this possible? John was one of the most experienced pilots in the unit. He had fifteen hundred flight hours and two deployments behind him. John should have kept Miles safe.

"Do you want me to tell Teresa?" Amy said.

"Yes," I said. "Please tell her. Tell her to call me."

Teresa called the night we drove to the airport to pick up another close friend.

"How are you doing?" Teresa said when I answered.

"I'm okay." I didn't know what else to say.

"Did you hear anything about the crash?" she asked.

"Not really," I said. "I heard maybe weather."

"Did you hear they were trapped inside?"

I shook my head but could not speak. *Please stop talking,* I thought. *Please stop telling me this.*

"The helicopter caught on fire," Teresa said. "They were burned. Our boys were burned."

It shouldn't have mattered, shouldn't have made a difference, but it did. It was unimaginable. So I didn't imagine it. I tried to let it go, let the information pour through me, no filtration, nothing to stop it. I was a sieve, wide-wired. If I could prevent myself from knowing, from letting that knowledge lodge in my brain, then I could keep myself sane. But if I listened to Teresa, if I took in what she was saying, then the magnitude of what had happened would destroy me.

At the airport my friend folded his tall frame into the backseat while Teresa talked on the phone about what came next. I wasn't listening. Or I was listening but it was flowing through me so that I held on to none of it. Nothing but the image of Miles burned to dust.

10

The week after the notification I flew to Washington, D.C., for John's funeral at Arlington.

"You don't have to come," Teresa said on the phone.

I stopped her before she could finish.

"Of course I'm coming."

I drove straight to the wake from the airport and stopped on the steps of the funeral home when a girl looked up at me with John's face.

"Megan," I said.

She smiled. "My mom's inside."

I pushed open the glass doors to a dark entryway that was mostly empty and waded through the pools of light cast by lamps until I reached the chapel where everyone had gathered. I stepped in and the low murmur stopped. A man whispered to the woman next to him.

"That's the other pilot's wife," he said.

The silence stretched out while I tried to settle my eyes on someone I knew and then there came a sudden rush. Soldiers stepped forward, pushed past one another, and scooped me into their arms. These were men from the unit, men who had known Miles. I pressed my face against the green cloth of their uniforms and everything about them reminded me of him—the shape of their frames, the low pitch of their voices. It was impossible to be next to those men and not think of Miles. Impossible that they should be there and he should be dead. The soldiers passed me from embrace to embrace until Teresa had her arms around me and there was nothing to do but stand together in our great sadness. When we stepped apart I saw the coffin at the front of the room. Closed. Of course. Teresa took me by the hand and led me to it. She knelt in front of the casket and I knelt beside her. When she raised her hand to lay her palm against the flag draped over the coffin, I held my hand at my side as long as I could. I hated to touch the metal, hated to imagine what lay inside. When I managed to reach out and touch the coffin with the tips of my fingers, I shook with the horror of it. I squeezed my eyes shut and took a deep breath and when I raised my head, Teresa looked at me.

"You okay, honey?" she said.

I nodded.

We stood and I circulated through the room to speak to the soldiers I knew. One squeezed me close before stepping back to hold me at arm's length.

"I'm glad to see you," he said.

I could feel the heat that radiated from him and I wanted to step away, but I did not know how. Instead I let him hold my hands and stroke my hair, conscious that I had become porous and malleable, easily breached.

The morning of John's funeral was already soaked with rain by the time I arrived at the chapel. The space inside the cathedral was viscous with humidity as I found a seat in a pew near the back. I took shallow breaths of air that smelled of damp cloth and incense while I half-listened to the service. Mostly I was bracing myself. I knew the Mass was only a prelude to the real event, the interment, the part where the earth would open up and swallow John whole. My body stiffened with the weight of my anxiety, and when the service ended I moved with the current that flowed out of the chapel, pulling in mourners like branches beside a swollen river. We swept behind John's coffin and spilled into the parking lot, then drove through the rain to a plot of fresh earth in Section 60 where the combatants of the wars in Iraq and Afghanistan are buried. There are female soldiers there, though the majority are men, husbands and fathers and brothers and sons, each laid to rest in that crowded field, their lives come down to a plot not much bigger than a man. I realized that somewhere—elsewhere—there were lovers and wives and children whose minds were thick with those men as Teresa's mind was thick with John and as my mind was thick with Miles. The memories of those men existed even though their bodies lay beneath the autumn fog, and it occurred to me that one day when the details have faded, when I can no longer recall if it rained the day we buried John or what shoes I wore or the color of my coat, Miles's memory will still be in me, fresh and alive and fully formed. I thought of my mother, to whom I had imagined my father was forgotten, and I knew in a way I had never known that she must still carry his memory tucked inside her, just beneath the skin, beating with the rhythms of her own heart.

They buried John with full military honors. The sound of rain pinged off the white tent stretched over our heads, and I shook as the guns fired the final salute. Teresa stood by the coffin, her arms around her daughters, and I watched closely so that I might know how to behave when my turn came.

The first time I flew into the Amarillo airport, the smell of manure hit me at the gate. I followed Miles to the baggage claim, trying to breathe through my mouth.

"What is that smell?" I asked his aunt on the way to the car.

"That," she said, "is the smell of money."

It was there again when I arrived for the funeral—the smell of money: fresh and green and processed through the gut of a cow. I met my mother, Heather, and Annabelle in Dallas, and when we reached Amarillo Miles's mother hugged all of us. She hugged me last and longest, as if we were two unlikely members of the same team. I was silent on the drive away from the airport and up the Texas Panhandle, too stunned by my sorrow to speak. In the distance I saw the lights from oil rigs that pump all night. They flashed on and off, signaling in the dark, as we followed the route Miles's casket had taken earlier in the week, carried in the back of the Hendersons' pickup. People had lined the highway along the route, waiting in the cold autumn night for the coffin to pass so that they might welcome their Texas son home.

The day before the funeral a neighbor who rode in the rodeo circuit brought horses to the Hendersons' ranch to take us riding. He hoisted Heather into the saddle first.

"I hope I don't fall off this thing," she said.

He gave Annabelle a boost and then heaved me up. When we all sat squarely in our saddles, he led us through the pasture and across the far hills. I surprised myself at the easy way I sat in the saddle. I had always been a nervous rider; I clung tightly to the saddle horn and jerked the reins. I kept my legs stiff and my back too straight.

"Just relax," Miles told me the first time we rode together. "Show the

horse where you want to go. Here"—he kicked back with his heels—
"and here." He gently tugged the reins.

But that day before the funeral I was fearless. I worked the reins
deftly. When the horse beneath me wanted to gallop, I let him open
up. The ground pounded under his feet and I tipped my head back
and tilted my face to the sky. I felt Miles everywhere, in the wind that
streamed past, in the grass that bent below the hooves. He was there
in the alfalfa smell of the horses and the smooth leather of the reins.
He was in the open land and the wide expanse of the sky. I turned and
faced into him like a wildflower following the sun.

"There were times that week when you weren't there," Annabelle
said later. "Like that day we went riding. I looked over at you and
thought, 'She's not even here.'"

I was nowhere. And everywhere. I was disappearing, becoming
part of the landscape, blowing into the yucca and mesquite and sage.
If I rode hard enough, I thought, if I just kept moving, I might vanish
into the air.

But I never managed it. I was never fast enough. Because the day ended
and the night passed and the next day dawned, and I was still there. I
rose early, showered, and brushed my hair. I dressed in front of the mirror, watching myself, and tried to memorize every moment of the day.
Years later I would attend an art exhibit in New York where an entire
room was dedicated to paintings of the artist's lover on her deathbed. I
would immediately recognize the impulse—not to chronicle the grim-
ness of the lover's death, as the exhibit implied, but to hold tight to her,
not to let her go.

Though, in a way, I had already let Miles go. I had given the funeral
home permission to cremate his remains before I arrived, and by the

time I made it to Texas he was gone. I told myself it was better that way, not to have to touch his coffin as I had touched John's, knowing what was inside.

On the morning of the funeral, we followed the procession to a low spot beneath the trees on the Hendersons' property. I walked to my seat numbly and watched the sky blown clear of clouds as a pastor stood on a platform made of cypress wood and talked about God. I wanted none of it—none of his smooth words, his easy eulogies, the facile balm of his faith. When he finished, we stood and moved to an assembly of chairs facing a flagpole. The honor guard—young soldiers mostly, their faces like boys'—lowered the flag and folded it at right angles. They handed it to a colonel in white gloves who knelt at my feet. He presented the flag that had draped Miles's coffin all the way from Iraq and I took the folded fabric in my hands. My hurt welled in me and threatened to stain the cloth. I cradled the flag in my lap as a bugler played taps, the notes rising high and clear in the morning air. Someone behind me pressed steadying fingers into my shoulders; I didn't know who but I reached up and held on. From over the ridge a bagpiper played "Amazing Grace" and Miles's old horse rode down to the trees, his master's boots backward in the stirrups.

"That's how we do a cowboy burial," Miles's mother said when it was all over.

Afterward we gathered at the Hendersons' home to eat brisket and drink lemonade, these strange rituals of death, and a woman with white hair and liver-spotted hands stopped me in the kitchen. She patted my arm as she spoke.

"Don't worry," she said. "You'll get married again."

I smiled at her the way I smiled at everyone then and I turned politely away so she would not see how her words had sliced me open, a fish knife to the belly. The woman's husband doddered in the kitchen, a paper plate clutched in his hand, and I knew she could not understand.

The Hendersons' casualty assistance officer took me aside.

"These are for you," he said.

He pulled a black velvet pouch out of his pocket and placed it in my hand.

"What is it?"

"They're Miles's dog tags."

When he had stepped away, I unknotted the black cord and poured them into my hand, rolling the disks over to feel the lightness of the thin metal. They were not burned. They were smooth, clean, polished. In a part of my mind I was not yet ready to acknowledge, I knew that the dog tags came by way of Miles's body. For me to hold them in my palm, they must have been lifted from around his neck. Someone would have had to clean them up before sending them home.

The day wore down and peopled trickled out. Someone fixed me a plate of barbecue and beans. Miles's young cousin pointed to me and asked his mother why my face was so red.

"Sometimes when people are very sad," she said, "they cry for a long time."

In a quiet moment I escaped with Annabelle and Heather to Miles's old bedroom. A soldier who had known Miles at Fort Rucker followed us and we spread out across the room. We talked about Miles and flight school, and after a time the soldier told us the story of his own helicopter crash. He'd been in the back of a Black Hawk, he said, and there had been fog. The pilot had pulled too far back on the cyclic and the nose of the helicopter rose. The Black Hawk dipped forward and rocked back, and the soldier knew they were going down. Often in Black Hawk crashes the transom, the middle part of the aircraft that supports the rotors, will fall and crush the crew in the back. The soldier knew this; he was sure he was going to die.

"And you know what I thought of in those last seconds?" he said. "I thought of my wife."

The fields had gone brown with drought and the dry grass crunched under our feet as our small group made our way across the pasture the next morning. The wind turned our cheeks red and carried the whinny of horses from across the corral. We headed for a low space of land where cottonwoods grew, and when we reached the trees we stopped.

"Here, do you think?" Terry asked.

I had ridden there with Miles the first time I visited the ranch; the last time he rode with his family he brought them to the same place. Miles had snapped a few photos. They would come home with his things from Iraq.

"This is right," I said.

The dry edges of the cottonwood leaves rubbed together in the breeze and sunlight filtered through the branches. Miles's father took a few steps away from the group with the bag containing the ashes and placed himself downwind. He opened the bag and I closed my eyes. The ashes made a whooshing sound of sand being poured from a bucket and I looked back in time to see the lighter bits catch in a current of air. They blew like dust across the high grass and it was easy to imagine Miles had simply disappeared into the wind.

11

The military has a term for everything that comes after a traumatic incident: *right of the boom*, the boom being the moment of the incident itself—an IED blast, a sniper shot, a helicopter crash. This is how I began to think of my life—right of the boom—as all the parts of military protocol fell into place.

My casualty assistance officer called in early December.

"I got the shipment in," he said. "Your husband's things from Iraq. I'm going to need to bring these over to you."

He pulled into my garage on a windy afternoon with the two tough bins loaded into his car. He lifted the smaller of the two bins from his trunk and set it on the concrete floor. He needed my help with the second, and together we maneuvered the plastic container out of the backseat.

"Where do you want these?" he said.

"Over here."

I pointed to an empty space by the stairs and we dragged the containers across the floor, their rough bottoms grinding against the concrete, and pushed them against the base of the stairs, where they sat untouched for weeks. They collected dust and bits of beach sand while I refused to acknowledge them. I knew what they contained, proof that Miles was gone. If I opened them, if I looked inside, then I would have to admit he was never coming home.

But I worked up my courage late in the month and on a Friday afternoon I left work early, pulled into the garage, and before I could lose my nerve I moved a chair beside the larger of the two bins. One of my mother's cats sniffed the edge of the box and rubbed his whiskered face against one corner. I lowered a hand to his back and he raised his tail in greeting. The light had an unsteady quality that put me in mind of grain alcohol. I wished I were drunk on it. But I was sober as I stared down at the latched boxes, sober as I snapped open the first clasp, sober as I lifted the lid and ran my eyes over the contents. There was everything Miles had taken when he deployed, neatly stacked and covered with a fine dusting of Iraqi sand. I quickly realized there would be no surprises in the tough bins, just a perfect ordinariness—Miles's folded undershirts, his socks rolled into balls, his uniforms arranged in ordered stacks. I pulled a T-shirt from the top of the pile and pressed the fabric to my face, but when I breathed deeply the scent was all wrong. They had laundered his clothes before sending them home. I saw that some of the items had come back in black velvet pouches: a pair of sunglasses, a yellow rubber bracelet, the mechanical pencils he used to mark flight charts, his metal nail clippers, a flat-head screwdriver, a key wrench. I pulled open the black drawstrings on each bag and let the items slip into my hand. I held them and felt Miles in every piece. I thought of him using them and wearing them. He kept the pencils tucked into a pocket on the sleeve of his uniform. He stashed the tools in a different Velcroed compartment. He kept the nail clippers in his right front pocket. I looked over the pieces and ran through Miles's routine, and I realized that these were the items taken from his body. These were the possessions he had on him at the time of the crash. I cradled the sunglasses in my hand. They were unharmed. I thought of Miles, bruised and broken, and his sunglasses coming through without a scratch. The world is without reason.

I put each of the items back in their black velvet bags and set the pile to the side. I pulled out more from the trunk. A yellow reflector belt, a set of metal handcuffs, a DVD of *Dr. Strangelove*, past issues of *Men's Health*, two cigars, a newsletter from Miles's church in Texas, an empty ditty bag, his patrol cap, boot blousers, a carabiner. Near the bottom of the tough bin I found the wooden box Miles once kept on the nightstand beside our bed. Inside were tucked his wallet and his wedding ring. I picked up the band, slipped it onto my right ring finger, and cradled my hand in my lap.

"Miles," I called out to the empty garage. "Why aren't you here?"

A yawning ache opened in me. It would have hurt less if I had been cleaved in two. I set the wooden box on the ground next to the velvet bags and I continued to search until I found a Ziploc bag filled with miscellaneous items: paper clips, pens, pieces of notebook paper. I pulled out one of the papers and read the list printed in Miles's handwriting. *Send Nana a birthday card*, it said. *Study*. He had crossed off some of the items, the completed tasks, but others were left undone, lost in the vast and open space of anticipated life, the days he imagined he had left to live.

"Damn it," I said. "Damn it, damn it."

I placed the list back in the bag and pulled out a letter handwritten on notebook paper. I read the first line. *My Dearest Artis*. My heart seized. A breeze blew through the garage and caught the back side of the page so that the paper bowed out like a sail. I pressed the letter flat against my leg as I read:

My Dearest Artis,

I love you. I love you so very much! Oh Babe, I don't think that I could ever convey just how much I love you and how blessed I felt to be with you, no matter how much I wrote. You are the love of my life. It was such a privilege and pleasure to be your "Super Friend," your teammate and especially your husband. The joy you brought into my life was immeasurable and the adventures that we shared were beyond my wildest imagination. The few years that we were able to spend together were absolutely the best of my life, and I owe that all to you. Despite a job as a soldier that was so demanding on both of us, despite living in places that left much to be desired, and despite some of our adventures turning into near catastrophes (mostly due to me, and most turned out to be fun anyway), being with you made it worth it all and kept me looking forward to every day.

I greatly regret that I had to go so soon when I know that we would have continued to grow together and share our lives with each other everyday, enjoying adventures like only the two of us can.

I died doing something that I believe is very honorable, worthwhile, and necessary. I pray that in my life and death I saved others' lives and kept a few from ever having to experience this war. I just regret that it had to come at the price of causing you any pain. The last thing I ever wanted to do was hurt you in any way.

Please do not feel angry or ask questions about why, instead rely on God for comfort and strength always. Live your life to the fullest, and know that I will be looking upon you always and doing everything I can to smooth your way. You are the most gorgeous, talented and smart young woman I know. I always felt so privileged and honored to be with you wherever we were. I hope I was able to make you feel safe and special whenever we were together. Please forgive me for the times when I fell short of this goal. Know that I am infinitely sorry for any pain that I have ever caused you. Your joy was my number one priority.

Live your life on earth to the max. You have so many options with what to do with your life. Pursue your dreams wisely, with all your heart, with honor, and with decency.

I will love you forever, look on you always, and see you soon.

I love you,

No worries!

Miles Henderson

I held the page between both hands, careful not to damage the paper, as I bowed my head and closed my eyes, feeling for Miles. His voice was in me, vibrant, alive in the way I was alive.

"Miles," I said again, this time in a whisper.

I opened my eyes and saw his things lying next to the trunk, propped there, waiting to be repacked. I raised my face to the garage walls and the rough concrete pilings and the empty ceiling overhead. The light had taken on a brightness that made my eyes hurt. Was life cruel that Miles was gone or generous that I should have this letter? I held the page to my chest for a moment, then folded the paper and put the letter in the wooden box that held Miles's wedding band. I bent over the tough bin again until I found his laptop, then replaced the items I had removed, closed the latch, and took the computer upstairs.

The house was quiet, the air-conditioning resting in a down cycle, as I plugged in the computer behind the couch. I held my breath as it booted up.

"Please," I said as the computer worked its slow way through the warm-up. "Please let the video be here. Please."

I begged until my throat was tight with it.

"Please," I said. "Please."

And there: a file created on November 4, two days before the crash. I held myself with both arms and opened the file. There was Miles seated in his bunk. I pressed one hand over my mouth as the video began to play.

"Hey, babe. It's me," he said. "I hope this is working."

He laughed, and I smiled on the couch in the living room. Whereas the letter had been written from a place of fear and worry—only to be read should the worst happen—the video was full of life, of expectations for the future.

"All right, well. This will be a short test video to see if I can figure out how to make all this happen. I hope you enjoy it. I know I really enjoyed the video that you sent to me."

He looked down at the keyboard and then up, as if he were thinking of what to say next. I smiled despite myself. Here was Miles, alive.

"Not much is happening around here. Sometimes lots of things happen. Sometimes nothing happens. But it's nothing to be worried about either way. Everybody's doing just fine."

He thought for another second.

"I guess three days ago our chow hall caught on fire. They have one of those temporary mess tents now. We go by and get something to eat and take it back to our CPR hooch. It's not too bad. They have good cookies."

I let the video wash over me and it wasn't hard to believe Miles was still out there in the desert somewhere.

"But speaking of cookies. Oh, my goodness. Those last ones you sent were awesome. Those ginger snaps were like the first cookies that anybody has brought in that have stayed soft throughout the entire trip. I don't know how you did it. Nobody really does. But, man, I ate like half those things and the other half I took to share and, man, everybody was so impressed. Even Troy."

Troy, who volunteered to pack Miles's tough bins after the crash, who made neat inventories of his gear, who lifted his wedding ring off the nail beside his bed and slipped it into the wooden box.

"Even Troy was, like, 'Man, man these cookies are dang good, man. These are, like, these are, like, awesome. I can't get over it. Your wife baked these, man? You are a lucky man. These are some good cookies.'"

I laughed, my fingers still pressed to my face.

"My hair I think is actually a little thicker over here. I don't know why. I can't tell you. I don't know if you can tell but it's longer I think than it has been in a long time."

He stretched a piece of hair down over his forehead.

"Anyway, it's shaggy for military speaking and I like it. I really like it."

He turned his face to both sides. Even in the dim light I could see the hollow outlines of his cheeks.

"My sideburns are like relatively long and thick. Thick as far as I can get them and long as far as the military will let me push it. So I guess there are some wonderful benefits to being over here. Which I guess is okay."

I laughed again, one hand held tightly in my lap.

"I can't wait to see you again," he said. "I can hardly wait until we can go on adventures together again. And I dream about adventures we can do all the time. Big ones, small ones. I think about being together and I think about you."

He was quiet as he said this and tears coursed down my face. There is no greater hurt than knowing you have been loved and the source of that love disappearing. I looked at the counter on the screen. We had just two minutes left.

"Really, I can't think of anything else," he said. "Flying here honestly at times is kind of scary. But at other times it's been really fun."

I reached out and touched the screen the way I had once touched his face.

"Please don't go," I said. "Please stay with me."

"I love you," he said. "I miss you. Remember that throughout these next couple of months. We've got, like, three down now. Three months down. We're working on number four. Every day is a day closer. Just keep on keeping on."

He laughed, and I knew this would be the last I heard from him.

"We'll see each other again soon, babe," he said. "Tell everybody hi back there for me."

His hand hovered over the keyboard.

"I love you very much," he said, and his image froze on the screen.

2007

12

After a soldier is killed in combat, the Army performs an official death investigation and the report of the findings is presented to the soldier's next of kin in a formal military briefing. I asked that Teresa and I might have our briefings together given the circumstances of our husbands' deaths—also together—and in the spring I flew to Fort Bragg for the presentation. Teresa drove us to the base the morning of the briefing and I was relieved to have her with me, in the way Miles must have been relieved every time he flew with John.

When we stopped at the security checkpoint, I handed over my military ID, the new one I had to carry after Miles's death. My status read URW. Unremarried widow. I smiled in the picture, a big smile that looked genuine. My casualty assistance officer had shuttled me to Mac-Dill Air Force Base in Tampa for the new ID. I sat in a metal desk chair while a clerk entered my information and tapped the camera beside her with a long fingernail.

"Look right here," she said.

I turned to my CAO.

"Should I smile?" I asked him.

He shrugged his shoulders and looked away.

I smiled wide, almost laughing. I didn't want people to think I couldn't handle my grief.

The 1st of the 82nd Division was headquartered in a low brick building that was nowhere near as imposing as I'd hoped. Miles's parents had arrived early and were already inside as Teresa and I entered. She spoke to the soldiers in the office and they smiled at her with tight-lipped smiles and gave each other significant looks as she turned away. I mostly hung back, wanting to disappear into the walls, to shield myself from what was to come.

Before the briefing, I had been careful to protect myself from the details of Miles's death. When Teresa would start in on it, I would make her stop. No talk of burning, no talk of the bodies. When Miles's death certificate arrived in the mail I opened the envelope and scanned the page to make sure it was the right form, but I refused to absorb any of the information printed there. I briefly saw the box labeled CAUSE OF DEATH and before I could stop myself I read *Multiple blunt force trauma*. I flicked my eyes away and slid the sheet back into the envelope. It seemed a great injustice that my memories of Miles should be clouded with the circumstances of his death so that even now when I think of his face I must ask myself what approximation of him came home.

A colonel led us into a conference room outfitted with a polished wooden table, chairs on wheels, and a projector for the PowerPoint presentation. I had the sense that the military trains for these things. Everything would be by the book. But here's what was not by the book: the brownies on the table. They were home-baked, from a mix, but still, someone took the time to make them. I saw a female soldier in the office when I first came in and I thought perhaps it was her. Or maybe the wife of the colonel giving the briefing. Sexist, I know, but I was probably right. Either way, it was a touching gesture.

We took seats around the table. Teresa and me on one side, Miles's parents on the other, three men and one woman in uniform beside Terry and Brad. The colonel sat next to the projector and the laptop. We were talking pleasantries—my flight from Florida, the spring weather, the drought in Texas—and my mind wandered. I was nine years old and on a roller coaster at an amusement park in Maryland. My half brother sat beside me. He'd persuaded me to go on the ride not because I like roller coasters but because I'm easily convinced. We sat side by side in the chair while the metal lap guard descended. When we were secure the line of cars pulled forward with a jerk and then crept out of the boarding area to climb the first steep hill. The track made a ticking noise beneath the cars and I was suddenly terrified.

"This is not so bad," my brother said to reassure me.

I believed him as the car ticked up the tracks.

The first few slides of the PowerPoint covered broad military information. Who was on duty the night of the crash, where the helicopters were headed. The slides had the unit's emblem in the corners, a wolf's head for the Wolfpack, and much of the information—base names, Army units, cities—was written in military shorthand as if to name them in full might dangerously bridge the distance between the war and everyday life. It was not so bad. But as the colonel continued to talk, I had the growing sense that we were balancing on the edge of a steep drop.

In my mind I was in my bedroom in Tallahassee. Miles was there. It was a Sunday evening and he had to leave soon to drive back to Fort Rucker. We lay on my bed and I leaned over him, my hair in his face, over his chest, on his arms. It was early in our relationship, before we moved to North Carolina, before he had said *I love you*. I could feel it welling up in him. I could feel that he felt it, that he wanted to say it. The light in the bedroom was silver and outside the sun had set. Time pressed on us and we both knew he had to go but we stayed like that a moment longer.

In the conference room we were suddenly at the crash. Time of impact: 12:31 a.m. The colonel showed a photo of the crash site taken from above so that we could see the path the helicopter cut through a lemon orchard. The gash was wide and brutal, the kind of damage caused by something hurtling very fast.

My stomach dropped as we fell over the edge.

––––––––––

On the night of November 6, 2006, the midnight sky stretched wide to the horizon, unraveling blackly toward Syria in the west and Iran in the east. A full moon shone overhead and illuminated the palm groves and the black waters of the Tigris, and the blades of the Apaches hummed as soldiers came out to gas up the birds. Warhorse was tight: two concrete landing pads with just enough space for two helicopters. Most dropped in, fueled up, and pulled out, never powering down their engines or shutting off their blades. The rotors from the two helicopters beat in tandem, so close they almost seemed to touch. Miles and John were in the trail aircraft of a two-helicopter team and John was the pilot in charge of the mission. He sat in the backseat of the Apache, behind and slightly above Miles in the front seat. A small round mirror sat to the left of Miles's shoulder so that the forward pilot could see the pilot in the rear, but the Apache's interior was too dark to see much. The only light came from the faint glow of the computer screens on the instrument panel. The helicopters had stopped to refuel after a night mission and would press on, first twenty-five miles west toward the forward operating base near Balad and then fifty miles north to their home base at Speicher outside Tikrit. John let Miles fly the helicopter into Warhorse with its tricky approach and cramped landing space, coaching him on how to pilot the bird in. It was not Miles's best parking job. The soldiers on the ground struggled to maneuver the fuel line over to the Apache.

"Let's see," John had said to Miles over the aircraft intercom system. "He came up. I think they got it hooked up but now there's nobody to give the wave."

"Give the signal," Miles said.

"They're going, 'Miles Henderson, huh?'"

"He's causing trouble in FARPs everywhere."

John laughed. "I think what we'll do is we'll continue to march. Visibility is ten miles here. We'll continue to march toward Balad and we'll take a look at how it is."

"Okay," Miles said.

"The only thing would be—" John stopped and chuckled. "It probably wouldn't happen, but if you call in and the weather was below visibility minimums, that would be bad."

"That would be really bad," Miles said. But he laughed too.

The ground crew connected the gas line to the helicopter and began fueling.

"We're getting gas now," John said.

"See. It all worked out."

"Yeah, it worked out. It took, like, three people twenty minutes of pulling and shoving."

"You want everything easy."

John radioed to the second aircraft. "Hey, One-Six, this is Zero-Eight."

"This is One-Six, Zero-Eight," the second helicopter radioed back. "Did they actually get you gas?"

"Yeah, Mr. Henderson really made it tough for them."

"Awesome. What do you want to do? Do you want to try to push it, see if we can get home? Or do you want to hit the pad here?"

"Well, the message I have says visibility is less than five hundred feet from Balad north," John said. "What I know is that they really, really stink at forecasting the weather. So what I'd just as soon do, if everybody is comfortable, is we know visibility here is, like, ten miles anyway coming in here, let's head out toward Balad. We'll turn the corner and we'll head up. We'll listen for anybody that is out that way, and if the weather gets bad, we'll just head back to Balad and call it a day. What do you think?"

"I say we press to get home," the pilot of the second helicopter said.

"Roger. And the reason I'm saying that is because the weather reporting is so bad here that, you know, it could be a lot better than they think it is."

"I agree. The FLIR might be able to see through it, on top of that. It might blow out, and we've got nothing but good weather behind us. So, yeah, I'll go with that. I'll give you a call when we're REDCON one and we'll push out."

"Roger. I'll do that," John said.

Then he had said to Miles, "Okay. Power levers shift to fly."

The colonel showed us the scene of the crash up close: the torn and bent rotor blades, an engine flung off to the side, fragments of the aircraft strewn around a crater in the earth. I had been well-behaved until that moment. I watched the presentation with tears leaking from my eyes and I politely wiped at my dripping nose. I hardly spoke. Yet seeing the crash ripped a sob from me. Miles's mother moved to stand behind my chair and she pressed her small hands into my shoulders. With my own hands, I held tight to Teresa. We cried together in great heaving gasps. The colonel paused and in that moment I wanted him to cry too. I mentally dared him to show that he was hurting behind the ordered military procedures. I wanted to see from him some of the unruliness of grief that Teresa and I were spilling all over his sanitized conference room. But the colonel did not flinch.

When we had quieted, he started again. The next slide showed where they had recovered the bodies and an *X* marked where each man was found. Miles's seat had come unhinged with the force of the impact and he and it were thrown from the cockpit. He was not burned. I tried not to imagine him slammed through the front window and into the ground, but of course I did.

The *X* for John marked where his seat had been in the helicopter. Only charred fragments of the cockpit remained.

Teresa turned to me.

"What did I bury?" she asked.

"Nothing," I said.

———————

The helicopters lifted out of Warhorse at 12:06 a.m. They would head toward Balad and then fly north along MSR Tampa—the main supply route that connects U.S. bases in a north–south line from Kuwait through Baghdad and beyond. John gave Miles the controls.

"You have the controls," he said.

"I have the controls," Miles responded.

The helicopters cruised at four hundred feet above the ground and the pilots saw through the dark, like cats.

"Man, nobody's out tonight," Miles said. "Air, ground—nowhere."

"Everybody else knows the weather blows."

The second helicopter radioed. "Did you guys just get that message?"

From Scott Delancey, the battle captain.

"Negative," John said. "What's it say?"

"That weather is less than one mile around Balad. Five hundred meters at Speicher."

"I'm estimating our visibility is six miles," John said. "What do you think?"

The second aircraft radioed back. "I think we can make it home through this."

As we neared the end of the presentation, I steadily worked my way through the plate of brownies. I told another widow this story later and she half jokingly diagnosed me as a nervous eater. I didn't think to call myself that then but I knew my blood sugar kept dropping so that I was shaky and fluttery and faint. I washed down the brownies with glass after glass of water, and we had to stop the briefing three times so I could pee. I was still in the habit of talking to Miles in bathrooms, and in the stall at unit headquarters I pressed my hands together.

"Please help me," I said. "Please help me make it through this."

At 12:30 a.m. the sandstorm was moving northeast to southwest. The helicopters had flown into the middle of the tempest. What had appeared at first like haze on the horizon became a blinding rage of gritty sand. Visibility was less than one mile. John ordered both aircraft to turn around.

"Hey, One-Six, turn it around please," John said. "Make a left turn."

"Coming left," the second helicopter responded.

"Okay. See him?" John asked Miles.

"I got him."

With the bad weather and poor visibility, John took over flying.

"I have the controls," he said.

"You have the controls," Miles answered.

The second aircraft radioed. "Do you want to go back to Warhorse? Because Balad doesn't look any better."

"Okay," John said. "What's—"

Then: "Oh, shit."

Then, to Miles: "What's going on? Talk to me."

A warning sounded in the aircraft. *Altitude low.*

"Pull up," Miles said. "Pull up, pull up, pull up, pull up."

Until the colonel let us read the last forty seconds of the transcript from the in-flight audio, I had clung to the idea that the helicopter had fallen so quickly that it hit the ground before either John or Miles realized there was a problem. I had hoped there was no time to be afraid, no moment to imagine the bludgeoning or burning that was to come. If I could not spare Miles from disfigurement, at least I could spare him from fear. The force of my not knowing would keep it from being real.

My throat was hoarse when I spoke to the colonel.

"Do you think—" I said.

My voice caught and I had to start again.

"Do you think Miles said 'Pull up' because he knew from the instruments that they were headed down? Or do you think he said it because he saw the ground?"

The colonel looked apologetic but did not hesitate. "I would imagine, based on the audio and what we know about the flight, that he said it because he saw the ground."

If he saw the ground, then he knew they were going to crash.

"Did you listen to the audio?" I asked the colonel.

"Yes," he said.

"Did you hear Miles at the end?"

The colonel nodded.

"Did he sound afraid?"

This time the colonel was slow to respond.

"No," he said finally, and I knew he was lying.

I often wonder how long it takes to fall four hundred feet. It took thirteen seconds from the time John assumed the controls to the time the helicopter hit the earth. It took five seconds from the time he realized something was wrong to the time the helicopter made impact. It took only one second for Miles to say "Pull up" five times. In that final second, did he glance reflexively into the mirror over his shoulder, trying for a last reassuring look at John?

The colonel reached the final slide, headed INVESTIGATION FINDINGS.

"What they're telling us," he said, "what the investigators are saying, is that the sandstorm decreased visibility for the helicopter and Mr. Priestner became spatially disoriented. Instead of turning left, he turned left and down."

In the chair next to me, Teresa wiped at her eyes with a crumpled tissue. I squeezed her other hand between mine.

"Mr. Henderson was overconfident in Mr. Priestner," the colonel continued. "He didn't catch the error."

Error. The word resonated in the room as the findings glowed on the projector screen. PILOT ERROR. According to the official report, John and Miles had flown the Apache into the ground.

In the Buick after the briefing, Teresa's face looked red and swollen. I flipped down the visor and looked in the mirror. Mine was red too. I licked the tip of my finger and scrubbed at the corner of one eye where the mascara had smudged onto my skin.

"Can you believe that?" Teresa said. "They're lying. I know they're lying."

I licked my finger again and tugged at the other eye. The skin was thin and tender.

"There is no way those men crashed that helicopter," Teresa said. "It's just not possible."

She put on her blinker and turned onto Gruber Road. We passed through the security checkpoint and drove slowly away from the base.

"I'm going to put in a request for the full report," she said. "The full accident investigation."

The asphalt thrummed beneath the tires and the yellow line in the middle of the road ticked past. I wondered what it would be like to be inside Teresa's skin, to wrestle with the blame she doles out—to the military, to John, to herself. I thought of how each of us nurses our secret shames. Here's my secret: in the hours before I knew the name of the second pilot, I selfishly hoped the man who died with Miles had been one of the unit's best. I wanted it to be someone who would have made Miles feel safe through the last seconds of the flight, someone who would have made him think there was a chance they would survive even as they crashed into the ground. I hoped it was John Priestner.

The broad-leafed trees gave over to tall pines, and the dirt beside the road grew sandy as the trees thinned and the land rolled in low hills. Teresa held the steering wheel with both hands. Tears carved tracks in the foundation on her cheeks, and I could see the pale skin underneath. A drop reached her chin and hung suspended above the thin weave of her sweater. Her mascara had also run and we had matching circles under our eyes, as if we had been in the same fight.

"I'm just so afraid you hate me," she said, "for what John did."

I watched the highway unspool and disappear at a distant point. The road sloped upward and the grass out the side window rolled past in a smooth green carpet. A current of air blew through the vents on the dashboard and the inside of the car smelled like lilies. I took a deep breath.

"They're gone," I said. "It doesn't matter how it happened."

13

In the spring of 2007, the stock market dropped nearly five hundred points in a day and the housing bubble finally threatened to burst. The Dixie Chicks topped the charts while people watched Britney Spears self-destruct. I surprised myself by changing almost nothing. I soldiered through one brittle hour after the next, making my way toward a destination I could neither see nor imagine, like a swimmer crossing the English Channel, paddling ahead on blind faith alone. Most days I tamped down thoughts of Miles until his memory became small and hard, like a fossilized ammonite buried within me. At work people remarked on how strong I was, how unbelievably well I handled things. But I was barely functioning. I moved through the motions of life, lost to everyone and everything, lost to myself.

I did make one concession: I moved out of my mother's house. I felt like I needed to be tough there, the way she had acted after my father died, and my grief seemed like evidence of some weakness I carried in me. It was too much to make it through the teeth-gritting days without weeping. I couldn't make it through the after-work hours too. I needed a place to be alone, to let my grief spool out, to unstopper myself, so I rented a house in the east part of town, a run-down neighborhood that felt reassuringly familiar. The house was yellow with purple trim, and it had laminate floors, a large backyard, and neighbors who didn't know me. There I could let myself disappear day by day until one day, if I was lucky, I would disappear into nothing.

Soon after I returned to work, the farm manager came to my office but didn't step in. He knocked gently on the open door, took off his hat, and worked the brim between his fingers. I looked up from my desk at his ruddy face and rough hands.

"I haven't seen you since—" he said.

He looked at the empty space between us for a time, and when he raised his eyes to mine, it was my turn to look down. I stared at the metal grommets on his work boots and the potting soil caked to the toes.

"I just wanted to acknowledge it," he said, looking at the top of my head because I could not meet his eyes. "I wanted to acknowledge your husband's death."

I stared at the frayed cuffs of his jeans and looked briefly into his face. I wanted to thank him but I could not speak. He nodded once, a quick jerk of the chin, and then stepped out of the doorway and was gone. I sat at my desk until I could stand to shut the office door.

People kept giving me space, all of us hoping my grief had a half-life, but I didn't need space. I needed people to say Miles's name out loud. I needed them not to flinch when I said it. I needed them to ask about him. Weren't they curious about the color of his eyes? I needed them to acknowledge not just that he had died but that he had lived.

That he had lived and loved me and for a space of time we were whole.

But I am lying. Even now I struggle to tell the truth of what I needed.

I needed Miles.

I looked at my scattered desk—the highlighters, paper clips, pens, loose change and business card holders, a mug half-filled with tea— and I swept it all aside so that I might lay my head down and weep for the things I needed and could not have.

I mostly cried like that, behind closed doors. To anyone who asked— anyone who remarked on my strength or bravery or the fact that they couldn't tell anything had happened—I liked to say I only grieved on Tuesdays. That was when the local hospice held its grief group meeting, where I made my way to sit with other mourners in perpetual shiva. We were mostly women and I was the youngest by two decades. The other widows had lost their husbands to cancer or stroke or heart attacks— old men's diseases. Some died from suicide or vehicle crashes. We were unalike in most ways and alike in the only one that mattered.

On my first night with the group I hesitated on the sidewalk for a long while before opening the door and crossing the threshold. On the back counter, coffee brewed beside a scattering of pink sugar pack- ets, and a stack of name tags sat beside a red Magic Marker. I looked around the room. Chairs shouldered against one another in a circle, and someone had placed boxes of tissue on the outskirts of the ring; I imagined they would become a commodity as the night wore on. I stuck my name to my chest and reluctantly took a seat in a spot with a good view of the door; that way I wouldn't have to cut through the center of the circle if I decided midway through that the grief group was not for me. The chairs slowly filled, and not long after I sat down the counselor, Richard, opened the meeting.

"How's everyone feeling this week?" he said.

A woman with a black dome of hair and gold-rimmed glasses twisted a bracelet on her wrist. Her lacquered nails glinted in the hard light. I read her name tag. *Bea.* Across the circle, a small woman with dark hair and a delicate frame clutched a tissue. *Linda.* They each spoke about loneliness, which stemmed from aloneness, about sitting down to dinner at a table set for one. I kept my arms crossed over my chest and my eyes fixed on a spot in the carpet just in front of my feet. I refused to look at anyone, just soaked up the sadness in the room. I let their grief draw close to mine until, near the end of the session, Richard turned to me.

"Would you like to say anything?" he asked.

I had my eyes fixed on the ground and I felt more than saw the circle's attention as everyone waited to hear what I would say. I knew—as they knew—that I did not belong there. What had claimed their husbands could not have been what had claimed mine. I opened my mouth but the words caught in my throat.

Finally I managed, "My husband was killed in Iraq."

A woman across the circle covered her mouth with her hand. Someone took in a sharp breath.

"How did it happen?" someone asked.

"A helicopter crash," I said.

I raised my eyes to the people gathered around the circle and they looked back at me with such gentleness and compassion that I lowered my head to my hands and cried with relief.

———

The literature on mourning agrees that grief can be exhausting. Here's what's exhausting: holding yourself steady. I had to steady myself the way a person steadies a broken arm, to keep from knocking into the hurt. And still, despite my best efforts, I often bumped against the pain.

In my office one afternoon I looked up from the newsletter I had been editing to see Holly, the receptionist, standing in my doorway.

"Want to go to the deli for lunch?" she said.

"I don't know." I looked at the pile of work on my desk. "I brought a sandwich."

"Come on," Holly said. "It's Friday."

I flicked my eyes to the half-finished letter on my computer, to the square of blue sky through the window beside my desk, to Holly with one hand on her hip.

She smiled. "I'll drive."

I pushed back my chair. "I didn't want to eat that sandwich anyway."

The deli was a tiny sweaty place that served homemade iced tea and fried bologna. Steam from the griddle hazed the dining room, and I had to use a pile of napkins to soak up the grease from my lunch. Holly and I talked office gossip and eyed the boys with the big pickups out front. When we were done eating, Holly waited outside while I paid the check. The wife of the couple who had bought the deli a few years back worked the register. She was young and pretty, with a big open smile. She knew most of us from the farm, by face if not by name, and she chatted with me as I handed her my credit card.

"What's this symbol here?" She tapped the front of the card with her finger. "I see a lot of different types but I've never seen this one."

The card came from my bank, a bank for military service members and their families.

"It's for the Army," I said.

The woman ran the card through the machine and handed it across the counter.

"Are you in the military?"

"No," I said, and because it needed an explanation—because she was waiting for an answer with her smiling face—I said, "My husband was."

The receipt made a clicking sound as it ticked out of the machine and the woman tore off the paper and handed it to me with a pen.

"Did he have to go overseas?" she said.

I hurriedly signed the receipt. She may not have known where the conversation was headed, but I did. I knew where we would both end up.

"He did," I said without meeting her eyes. "He went to Iraq."

She handed me a copy of the receipt and I stared at the toothpick jar on the counter and the pennies in a Styrofoam cup by the register.

"When did he get home?"

I stood stiffly, conscious of the people in line behind me. What could I say? There was only the truth.

"He didn't come home."

There was a moment, a shared few seconds, when the woman and I looked at each other and I watched my meaning shadow her face. I felt my cheeks flush and the tip of my nose go red like it does when I'm about to cry and the sadness that flowed like blood beneath my skin threatened to spill out.

"I'm sorry," the woman said.

I ducked my head and turned to the door before I could bleed all over her floor.

"Me too."

But I didn't always tell the truth.

In the front yard of a foreclosed home, I watched people crawl over the property, all of us looking for a deal. What had we learned from the market collapse? Not a damned thing. A man with a two-day beard and dirty clothes peered through the dusty windows.

"You an investor?" he asked me.

"Yes," I said, and it was hard not to laugh at the absurdity of it. Not that it mattered. He called himself an investor too.

"What's your husband do?"

Did I hesitate? Would it sound better if I said I did, that the lie didn't slip from my mouth like a fish through water?

"He's a teacher," I said, "and he coaches football."

The man nodded and wiped his dusty hands on his jeans. He jumped down from the porch and moved off through the ferns and left me standing there with the lie hot on my tongue, feeling so right I wanted it to stay there forever.

I went back to the hospice group every week. The conversation would pass around the circle, each woman offering up some bit of truth she'd been saving all week, and I found that I started doing that: putting away a morsel to share. I would chance on some memory of Miles and I'd sculpt my story throughout the week, knowing it would be the one time I'd let myself speak about him.

"Tonight I'd like to talk about needs," Richard said one evening.

The fluorescent lights hummed overhead and I hunched inside my sweater. Elsewhere in the hospice building, down corridors I never saw, people were dying. Their relatives stood close, not fully understanding that soon they'd be like us. Some of them would make their way to the Tuesday night meetings and we'd fold them in, as I had been folded in.

"What do you need right now?" Richard continued. "Take a moment. Look inside yourself. What is it that your body or your mind or your heart needs?"

There was a pause as we considered. We were all widows that

night—the widowers rarely came for more than two or three sessions. "Looking for dates," Linda would say.

"How about you, Artis?" I looked up from the piece of carpet I had been examining. "What do you need?"

I considered my response for a moment and then I offered the tidbit I'd been keeping all week.

"There was this time Miles and I went tubing behind John's boat," I said. "You know, where they pull you?"

My voice was rough and I had to clear my throat. The other women nodded encouragement.

"Miles and I were facing each other in the tube and the boat was pulling us hard. We hit a wave and my head snapped forward and my mouth smashed into the top of Miles's head."

I twisted a tissue between my hands as I talked, working it back and forth with my fingers.

"I touched my face and there was blood all over my hand. I thought I'd lost my front teeth. I looked at Miles and I could tell from his face that I looked pretty bad. I asked him, I said, 'Am I okay?' And I think he was scared because there was a lot of blood coming out of my mouth but he said, 'Yeah, babe. You're okay.'"

They were listening, the other women, Richard. I kept working the Kleenex between my hands.

"That's what I need," I said. I looked up into their faces. "I need someone to tell me it's going to be okay. Even if it looks like it won't."

The sun had set by the time Jimmy Hyde pulled into my driveway, and when I went to greet him, all I could see was his silhouette in the dark. It was better that way. Easier to negotiate the space between us.

"Let me grab something out of the trunk," he said.

He stepped around to the back of the Jeep and lugged a rectangular cardboard box out of the rear compartment.

"What's that?" I asked.

"You'll see."

He walked past me, through the carport and into the backyard.

"Can I get a light out here?"

I flipped the switch to the twin bulbs overhead and he smiled at me in the suddenly bright light. He looked the same as the last time I had seen him at Fort Rucker.

"I bought you a grill," he said. "Had to run by Walmart to pick it up. That's what took so long getting here."

"You bought me a grill?"

"You said you wanted me to cook kebabs."

I laughed. I had. Jimmy, who was also deployed, had been one of the few soldiers to contact me after the notification and the only one to keep messaging me after the others had stopped. I was in the habit of writing Miles, as I was in the habit of loving him, and Jimmy's e-mails slid easily into the space created by Miles's absence. But now I wondered what I implied in those messages. Did I suggest that if Jimmy came for a visit, there might be more than friendship between us? Did I hint at romantic possibilities? Did I flirt? I must have. Because a subtext beat beneath our every action, a thrumming reminder of a promise I seemed to have made. I'd like to tell you I didn't know what I was doing, that I was somehow innocent in all this. But I was not. God help me, I wanted Jimmy there—and not just for dinner. I wanted his hot breath in my ear. I wanted his rough hands on me. I wanted to close my eyes and let myself imagine this was another R & R, another long-anticipated return.

I watched Jimmy assemble the grill from the back step of the porch. We were almost the same age and nearly the same height. He was a little older, a little taller, built slim but broad through the shoulders, self-assured and cocky in a way I am not. I disappeared into the house to put on a pot of yellow rice, the kind you buy at the grocery store in gold foil packets, and I stood at the stove and stirred while the sound of tinkering floated in through the open kitchen door. After a time I covered the pot with a metal lid and stepped outside to check Jimmy's progress. The grill stood upright—finished. I handed Jimmy a box of matches and he laid one to the pyramid of charcoal briquettes he had stacked. The flame caught and crept upward, spreading from black square to black square, until the entire pile glowed. I carried out a tray of skewered beef and he arranged the kebabs on the grill. While Jimmy cooked, I went back into the house to the bathroom off my room. I looked at my face in the mirror. My nose was red from the cold and my eyes seemed smaller somehow. My face looked all wrong; I had become unrecognizable to myself.

In the kitchen I grabbed two beers from the fridge and outside I dragged a white plastic chair close to the grill.

"How are things in Iraq?" I said.

Jimmy took a sip of his beer. "Not too bad. We fly a lot."

"Is it hot?"

"It's cold this time of year."

The meat smoked over the fire and he turned the skewers with a pair of tongs.

"How's it feel to be home?"

"It feels weird," he said. "Hard to relax."

He took another mouthful of beer.

"Anyway, R & R's only for two weeks."

When the kebabs finished cooking Jimmy set them on a platter and carried it into the house. We ate at the table in the dining room and Jimmy did most of the talking. He spoke about his family, about people we both knew from flight school, about the deployment. He started to tell me about a mission, a dangerous flight during a night storm, but I stopped him.

"Could we not talk about this, please?" I stared at my plate.

Jimmy looked over at me, surprised, before catching himself.

"Of course," he said. "Sorry about that."

After dinner he washed the plates and silverware by hand and I dried and put everything away. When we had finished, he leaned against the sink.

"I guess it's time for bed," he said.

"I guess it is."

We stood facing each other but neither of us moved.

"Good night, then."

I turned as if to go into my room, but slowly.

"Wait."

I stopped.

"Come here."

Jimmy put out his arms and I stepped into them. I buried my face in the spot below his shoulder and he stroked my hair. But when he put his hand under my chin and tilted my face to his, I turned away.

"I can't kiss you," I said.

He stepped back, uncertain. Hadn't everything we'd done led to this point?

I stepped close to him again.

"I mean, not yet," I said.

He led me into the room that I would think of from then on as Jimmy's room, a place I abandoned after his visit.

"Could we light a candle?" I said.

I listened to Jimmy walk into the guest bathroom, where I had placed two votive candles in round glass holders, leftovers from the wedding. He stepped outside to the grill for the matches and then carried the lit candles back into the room, shutting off the lights in the house behind him. He set one candle on top of the dresser and one at the side window. As I stood beside the bed, he lifted my hair away from my neck then leaned down to kiss the place where my neck joined my shoulder. I let him kiss my collarbone. When he reached for the hem of my shirt, I raised my hands over my head. He slipped off my blouse, turning the cotton inside out, and the pearl buttons skimmed my nose on the way up. I pulled my hands down quickly to cover my breasts.

"I'm not wearing a bra," I said.

Jimmy smirked. "I know. I've been trying to get a look all night."

He rested his hands over mine, cupping the fingers that cupped my breasts. The fine hairs on the underside of his arm brushed my wrist. Already the room felt warmer. I sat on the bed and he sat beside me, kissing my bare shoulders. I dropped my hands, my face red and hot, and then I closed my eyes and let him look at my body. After a time I reached down to unsnap my pants, then rolled onto my back and pulled them off. I wore white underwear, laced, with a gold clasp on the left hip. I reached to him beside me and tugged his shirt over his head. I could feel the heat from his body on the cloth. His skin was light, like mine, and freckles covered his torso. A light patch of hair stretched from his chest to under the waistband of his jeans. He stood up to unbutton them and then let the pants drop to the floor. We were both in our underwear. He climbed back onto the bed and we sat together on the comforter patterned with chrysanthemums in red dye. I hugged myself against the chill and Jimmy pulled back the covers and together we slid into the sheets. From that vantage point the bedspread looked darker, like lips reddened from too much kissing, like the normally pale parts of the body that go flushed and livid from lovemaking. It blushed as if ashamed.

In tennis they talk about muscle memory, about the body learning the moves of the game so that during a match a player can react without thinking because the body already knows what to do. My body remembered the steps but not the partner. He was smoother in places, rougher in others. His frame was all wrong. When I finally leaned down to kiss him, the shape of his lips felt strange against mine and I realized this is what it feels like to betray someone you love.

The candle on top of the dresser burned down to a nub, and the low flame cast shadows against the wall. I thought of Van Gogh's night café at the long end of the evening, the darkness drawing in on itself, the absinthe already drunk, the madness gathered and dissipated, leaving only the taste of burnt sugar on the tongue. The room had been cool when we first stepped in but the air had warmed from our bodies, from hot breath on breath, from fingers on thighs, stomachs, hips. In the heated space, Jimmy's palms smelled like ash. The room filled with the scent of him and soon I smelled like him too. He smudged over me like a handprint on the wall.

The loneliness that followed Jimmy's visit felt like a physical blow. It left me panting. But over the next several weeks I abruptly ended what had been between us. I stopped writing and I became distant when we spoke on the phone.

"I need—" I searched for the right word. "Time."

Later I combed through my e-mail archives and deleted every message Jimmy and I had exchanged. I threw away his letters. I told almost no one about his visit and I erased all evidence of him from my life. I was terrified someone might discover what I had done.

In the military certain myths circulate. When men are deployed they rag on each other about "Jody," the imaginary man back home who's fucking their wives.

"Better watch out," they say. "Jody's going to get her good."

Another myth: the widow who sleeps with half her husband's unit. The men talk about it and so do the wives. Mostly the wives. They talk about that poor woman in Charlie Company who slept with her dead husband's commander, and when he left her she slept with one of his stick buddies. He left her too. She moved on to the enlisted guys and slowly worked her way down the ranks. The wives shake their heads at this part of the story and roll their eyes because everybody knows that's what widows do.

"What, I'm going to date somebody a year and a half, two years after John died?" Teresa said to me much later. "Everybody would call me a whore."

14

The knocking came in the night. The sound pulled me sharply, angrily out of sleep but in the bedroom all was dark. No headlights poured in from outside, no porch light shone from across the way. I pushed back the covers, waited for the blood in my head to settle, and crept first to the kitchen and then to the living room. A nimbus from the orange street lamp glowed behind the curtain as I lifted the edge and peered into the yard. Nothing. I moved through the house and onto the rear porch, irritated, my eyes straining against the night as I peered out every window, searching for some clue in the dark.

A few days later, the microwave started coming on in the night. A sharp *beep!* followed by a volley. *Beep! Beep! Beep!* The interior light glowed and the rotating plate whirled while I stood barefoot in the kitchen, fumbling for the power cord in the dark.

When the landlord phoned to check in, I mentioned the problem.

"Everything okay in the house?"

"Sure," I said. "Everything except the microwave."

"The microwave?"

"You know, how it comes on at weird times? By itself?"

"I never had that problem," he said. "The microwave worked fine when I lived there."

At the library I checked out books on ghostly visitations that said hauntings often occur in the early hours of the morning, the time when the veil between the living world and the afterlife is thinnest. I shook my head, disbelieving. But also believing a little.

After the Tuesday night hospice meetings, I started having dinner with some of the widows from the group. One night I brought up the knocking.

"Oh, that's happened to me," Bea said. She waved her manicured nails dismissively, like this was nothing. Like she wasn't surprised.

"I'll hear pans clattering in the night," Linda said. "Loud banging from my kitchen."

I toyed with my fork. My pots banged in the night too.

"Or the lights will go dim," Connie said. "I've heard—I know this sounds crazy, but I read it somewhere—that spirits can tap into electric currents."

I nodded. My lights also dimmed. I looked around the table at those women, all of them educated, none of them unsophisticated, and yet each of us desperate to believe.

Teresa called on a weekend afternoon as I stirred a pot of beans in my kitchen.

"How are you doing?" she said.

I turned off the stove and moved the pot to the back burner. "I'm all right."

"I'm going through the files from the crash investigation," Teresa said. "None of it is matching up."

Late afternoon light filtered in through the window over the sink as I held the phone with one shoulder and folded the dish towel on the counter.

"You know how I requested John's audio? From the cockpit? Well, they edited the tape," Teresa said. "They cut parts of it. What I listened to wasn't the whole thing."

I picked at the frayed corner of the towel and pulled out threads that I dropped onto the floor.

"If I had Miles's voice recording," Teresa said, "I could figure out what's going on."

I stopped with the towel and stared out the window. Leaves had scattered on the roof of the house next door like buckshot. If I requested Miles's voice recording, then I would have to listen to the tape. If I listened, I would hear his voice in the last seconds of the flight. I would know if he had been afraid. Teresa stopped talking and I realized she was waiting for my answer.

"I can't, Teresa," I said. "You're going to have to do your investigation without it."

She was quiet as I leaned against the counter and closed my eyes.

"Okay," she said finally. "Okay."

Eastern mystics say dreams are a way of stepping into another realm. They call the space between the material and immaterial worlds the *barzakh,* or isthmus. In the *barzakh* the dead can mingle with the sleeping living. Often they share secrets of the afterlife. Buddhism, too, has an intermediary space between the visible and invisible worlds—the *bardo.* There are six *bardo*s in fact and one, the *milam bardo,* is the dream state. Buddhists say the dream state is like the death state only shorter.

One night Miles flew into my dream in a helicopter. I waited for him on the tarmac, the thin strip of asphalt that joined this life and the next. After he landed, Miles raised the cockpit door and lifted his visor.

"Hey, babe," he said.

I shielded my eyes with one hand and stared up into his face.

"Were you scared?" I said, meaning the crash.

"I was so scared," he said. "But it was over fast."

"What's it like?" I said, meaning death.

"It's like a dream."

Already I could feel the moment fading, the threads of the vision slipping through my fingers.

"What's like a dream?" I said. "Where you are now or the life you lived?"

Before he could answer, I woke in the dark.

I started obsessing about Psychic Suzanna. I convinced myself that she had foreseen Miles's death and deliberately withheld the information. I worried incessantly if it would have made a difference. If Suzanna had looked across the table in the low-lit hotel bar and told me that I would meet a man of loyalty and integrity, handsome and brave and kind, a man like my father—if she had told me then that I would lose this man, that he would die a violent and terrible death, so terrible I would not be allowed to look on his face after his body came home—if she had warned me of the immensity of the suffering to come, would I still have chosen this life? Would I still have chosen Miles?

There was only one way to know: I arranged a phone consultation.

On the night of our appointment, I stayed at my mother's house. I sat on the edge of my old bed as I dialed and looked at the cowboy boots in my closet. Suzanna answered on the second ring.

"How are you doing, honey?" she said.

There was that voice again, all smoke and ash.

"Fine. I—"

"How old are you, honey?"

"I'm twenty-six. But that's not why I'm calling." I imagined her gearing up her pen, ready to trace out my fortune on scrap paper. "I'm calling about my husband."

"What do you need to know?"

"He was killed," I said. "In Iraq."

There was a long silence on the phone.

"I can tell you what he saw when he crossed over," Suzanna said. "A white dog. There was a white dog. In a field. And—" She paused, then moved slowly through each detail. "A man on a tractor. In overalls. An old man. That your husband knew. Someone who has already passed over."

I wrote all of this down as if it offered some clue. But I was irritated that she wasn't giving me what I wanted to hear. Suzanna took in a long breath like an athlete after a hard run.

"Does that mean anything to you?" she said.

"Not really."

I waited and she steered the conversation to familiar terrain.

"I can tell you that you'll get married again. To a man who also wore a uniform."

I tucked my legs beneath me and pressed the phone to my ear. This was not why I was calling.

"You'll still have a daughter," she said. "And a son."

I listened without speaking, one arm wrapped tight across my chest.

"Something you write will be published."

"A book?" I said. "Or, like, an article?"

"Honey, I can't tell. I just see your name in print."

"Oh."

"Do you have any other questions for me?"

I started to voice the reason I had called—*Did you know?*—but I must have bungled it somehow, must have tripped over my words or stumbled over my meaning, or she didn't want to answer, because what she said was "Oh, honey. You are in hell right now."

I looked at the clock on my nightstand. We had ten minutes left but it was clear there was nothing to say. Just as I began to get off the phone, Suzanna stopped me.

"One more thing," she said.

I gripped the receiver. *Tell me something I need to hear.*

"I see that you've been angry with your mother. Is that right?"

I nodded dumbly into the phone.

"Well, when we hang up, I want you to go give your mom a hug."

I almost laughed. My mother and I hadn't hugged in a long time.

"You give her a hug, and you say you're sorry. You tell her you're sorry for being so nasty."

"Okay," I said.

"Will you do that for me?"

"I will."

After I hung up the phone, I sat on the bed for a few minutes, debating. I could hear my mother downstairs in the kitchen, putting away the pots from dinner. I thought about letting the moment pass. But then I remembered something Annabelle had said about the first week after the notification when we were all crowded into the house. In a moment when she and my mother were alone together, my mother had said to her, "It's just me and A.J. now. We're all we've got."

With all my courage, I climbed off the bed and walked downstairs.

"Hey, honey," my mother said when I stepped into the kitchen. She poured detergent into the dishwasher. "I thought you had gone to bed."

I stood there unable to speak until she turned to look at me.

"What's up?" she said. "Everything Okay?"

My face collapsed on itself the way it does when I cry: my chin drew in, my lips arced down, my eyes squeezed shut.

"I'm sorry, Mommy," I said. "I'm sorry I've been so awful."

I stared at the brown tile of the kitchen floor and held myself stiff.

My mother came to me then and put her arms around my shoulders and I let myself be held. I could smell the VO5 conditioner she uses, the Arrid deodorant she wears, the Tide on her clothes. She held me for a long time and I think she cried, too, and when it was done some of my anger had leached away.

15

I once sat in a crowded room of military survivors and watched a clip from a documentary film about military widows. It was immediately clear why the producers had selected the women they chose to profile. They were pretty and articulate and their husbands had a handsome fresh-scrubbed look. When one of the widows in the film spoke about her husband, his photo appeared on the screen and the room full of people literally gasped—he was that good-looking. But then his pretty wife explained how he had died. He was napping in his bunk in Iraq when a worker mistakenly dumped a truckload of sand on his shelter. A foolish accident. I felt more than heard the second reaction from the crowd. Disappointment. We wanted a hero's death for the young husband with the movie star's face. We wanted, if not a happy ending to his story, then at least a heroic one. His death made all that we were trying to make sense of hopelessly senseless.

Teresa was the one who told me Miles and John would not receive the Purple Heart. It never occurred to me that they wouldn't. I had assumed a soldier killed in combat automatically earned the medal. As it turns out the Purple Heart is reserved for those pilots who are shot down, not downed by their own mistakes.

During one of my visits to North Carolina, Teresa showed me her investigation file, a thick manila folder stuffed with pictures, transcripts, and government documents.

"This thing we got right here," she said as she handed me a photo, "this crap. This is the worst to me."

I looked over the image of the crash site.

"You remember they said 'massive ground fire'? That wouldn't be green if there was a massive ground fire."

She pointed to a section of the photo where broken tree branches knocked together like knees.

"Remember they told us they went flip-flopping in there? It wouldn't happen like that. You know what I'm saying? There is no ground damage. If you look at these pictures, the irrigation ditches are perfect. The ground's not even burned. This would have been burned if there was a massive ground fire."

She looked over my shoulder at the photo in my hand.

"And notice they didn't take any trees out on the right or left? They took out a row of seven trees. That's it."

"So, what does that mean?" I asked.

"That means they fell out of the sky."

She shuffled through the papers on the table and pulled out another photo.

"Here's the black box. The infamous black box. Massive ground fire and it's not even burned."

She handed me the picture and turned back to the pile.

"All this information, I'm trying to find this picture that I showed you. There's another one in here and it's not the same. Nothing's the same. I have three reports and nothing matches. This is the official report, this one that I have in my hot little hands. Like all the stuff I high-lighted? Something's not right."

She handed me another photo of the crash site.

"They landed in the lemon trees," she said. "Are they big?"

"The lemon trees? No, I don't think—"

"I don't think so, either. They don't look big in that picture. But all this stuff—nothing matches. None of it. Remember, you saw this? There's no ground damage. They took out seven trees and that's it. No ground damage."

I took the photo she handed me.

"And then here again the same picture. It's green. It's not burned, you know, and the irrigation ditches aren't tore up. Look—more green. Massive ground fire, my butt. Look—no fire there, either. That's the tail rotor, by the way."

I looked at the warped piece of metal that had once been part of the aircraft.

"Why would—"

"That's what I'm saying," Teresa said. "Nothing's damaged. They did not go flip-flopping in there like they said they did. I don't care what they tell you."

The clock on the living room wall chimed.

"Come on, come on," Teresa said, searching through the pile. "You won't believe all the stuff I have."

She pulled out a sheet and scanned the writing.

"You know, also, there's a box in the helicopter that if they go down it lets off a signal so the satellite picks it up to find them. That didn't work."

She paused, reading.

"See, I don't know how much you want to know."

"I don't really want—"

"Here it is. Here we go." Her voice dropped to a whisper. "They don't show us where the guys are in this one. The way the gun's angled.

The impact point's different. The engine's lower. See, they're kind of making up their own story."

She handed me a printed invoice.

"You know what they did?" she said. "There's two reports. There's a safety report and then there's the cost report. They actually gave you and me a bill. How much it cost them to lose John and Miles."

"How much did they cost?"

"John and Miles were a million dollars each. The aircraft cost twenty-five."

I shook my head. "Jesus."

"Remember we got told originally—I don't know what you got told, but I got told originally—that there were two flashes in the sky. One they thought was the flares because the flares go off—I don't know if you're too familiar with the aircraft—the flares go off to make a rocket hit the flare instead of the helicopter because it has heat. So I think the flares went off but I think they still got hit."

Teresa sat down in the chair opposite me.

"How much do you want to know about Miles? Like, he wasn't in the aircraft, do you know that?"

"I knew that."

"He wasn't burned at all. Did you know that?"

I nodded.

"John was burned," Teresa said. "Bad. They told me thirty-three percent when I buried him. Well, when I got all the stuff I got, it was worse. It was ninety-nine percent. You know their protective gear? Melted to him. It takes eight hundred fifty degrees to do that. You need air and you need heat. He had to be in the sky, on fire, falling, for that to happen. See, they don't understand that I did my research."

She shook her head as she riffled through the pages.

"But let me see if I can find this. . . . Remember we saw this where they tried to tell us what the last words out of theirs mouths were?"

She waved the audio transcript, then stopped to scan the typed words.

"Like this part. Like, it's not the same, either."

She read to herself, then stopped and looked up at me.

"All Miles's stuff is blacked out. Do you think you'll ever be ready to look at that stuff?"

"No," I said.

"No?"

I shook my head.

"I'm going to do the best I can to get this fixed," Teresa said. "I'm not stopping. They pissed off the wrong wife."

She put down the page in her hand and looked across the table at me.

"If anything," Teresa said, "I want to change 'pilot error.' You know what I mean? They're the most trained soldiers we have and they fly a multimillion-dollar aircraft, and you can blame them when you don't know what's going on? That shit's wrong to me. You know, John can make mistakes. He's human. You know? I'm not saying he didn't. And that was the night Saddam Hussein was sentenced to death. So you're telling me they're flying in the home territory of Saddam Hussein and you're going to tell me nobody tried to take a potshot at our husbands? Bull. I say bull. They always miss the first aircraft and hit the second. That's the way it is. You know?"

Much later, when we were five, nearly six years out, I asked Teresa why it mattered so much that our husbands receive the Purple Heart.

"You can feel it," she said. "Some of my friends, even acquaintances, they go, 'Your husband never received a Purple Heart?' They don't say it, but you can see it. *You're not part of this.* Well, I *am* part of this.

"I watched my husband go to Desert Storm and I watched him go to Afghanistan. I watched him go to Iraq, and when he came home he didn't come home the way he's supposed to. My husband was a soldier.

He gave his life. And he—and I, and his girls—shouldn't be thought less of because of the way he died.

"I don't care what anybody says, but people make you feel less proud. He was doing his job. He didn't come home from doing his damn job.

"You sit there and you look around at the graves at Arlington and you see PURPLE HEART, PURPLE HEART, PURPLE HEART. And then you don't see it on your husband's grave. You're like, is he less of a hero because of it?"

At the Tuesday night group, Richard asked us what might bring some comfort.

"I would eat a big, heavy meal," I said. "Meat loaf and mashed potatoes. Chicken and dumplings. That sort of thing. I would eat and I would sleep and I would wake up and do it all over again. I would eat and sleep until I felt better."

"So, why don't you give it a try?" he said.

"Oh, no." I raised a hand as if to stop the idea before it could take hold. "I would never do that."

"Why not?"

"Because it would never end. The eating and sleeping. I would fall into that hole and never climb out."

But on my way home from work the next day, a box of barbecue sat reassuringly on the passenger seat. I stopped in front of my driveway, opened the gate, and nosed in. I parked the car, shut off the engine, and for a full minute I breathed in the sweet smell of barbecue sauce. On the way to the door I ignored the one-armed cactus in the front yard, the hole in the porch screen, the mud caked on my tires and flung up behind the wheel wells. I ignored the too-high grass, the chain-link fence, the BEWARE OF DOG sign left over from the previous tenants. The front door stuck and I had to push with my hip until it gave. I half stepped, half fell into the living room and the screen door clapped my heels. I didn't flinch. I carried the plastic bag of food into the kitchen and set the Styrofoam cup of tea on the counter. It sweated in the heat. I stripped off my work clothes on the way to the bedroom, kicked my sandals toward the closet, and stood in my cotton underwear. I pulled out the drawers to my dresser, first one, then the other, until I found my at-home shorts, frayed at the waistband, then a thin-strapped tank top. The light through the window gave the room an underwater quality and I could smell the barbecue from its depths.

In the kitchen a line of ants crawled over the counter. They started in the windowsill where the wall met the frame and marched to the drain and back, ant after ant after ant, past the breakfast dishes gathered in the sink, the bowl with a rim of milk at the bottom, the spoon set beside it. I didn't care. I opened the plastic take-out bag and a puff of steam rose up. I was slow, slow with it, careful. I reached in, pulled out the Styrofoam container, and slid the tab back on the box. There it was: pulled pork, macaroni and cheese, coleslaw. Red sauce smeared on the underside of the lid and condensation beaded on the top. The bottom of the box was still warm. I didn't bother to put it on a plate. I carried the box through the dining room, past the secondhand table and the mismatched chairs painted pink and green. Watermelon colors. Someone else's art project. I set the take-out box on the couch and sat beside it, my back to the armrest, facing the television. I was starving, a hole of hunger blown through me. Some people say children mistake hunger for other discomforts. They say *I'm hungry* when what they mean is *I'm sleepy*. They say *I'm hungry* when what they mean is *I'm sad*. I wanted to eat the pork in two greasy bites. I wanted to shove macaroni into my mouth, to pick up the coleslaw with my fingers and cram it down my gullet. I wanted to run my fingers around the edge of the container and collect the sauce stuck to the sides. I would raise my fingers to my mouth and suck off the sauce, even the bits caked under my nails. I wanted to eat and eat and eat until I was sick with it. Until I was full. But instead I flipped through the channels. I found a *Baywatch* rerun. I took my time. I ate the pork one slow bite after another. I took careful forkfuls of macaroni. I chewed until the food was paste in my mouth. I swallowed. I took another bite. Sunlight dripped from the picture window behind the couch and spilled across the laminate floor.

When I had finished eating, I stretched out on the couch, my toes pointed toward the television set. The armrest felt nubby beneath my head. On the street outside laborers called out to each other as they headed home, and the lozenge of light on my living room floor faded to pewter. I rolled onto my side. From that vantage point I could see the dust beside the couch, the dry carcass of a cockroach, domestic tumbleweeds of lint and hair. I batted one with my hand. When I rolled over I tried to watch TV through my toes. The actors stood on a beach far away and a woman who surely smelled of coconut oil tossed her golden hair over one shoulder. I rested my hand on my swollen stomach, ran my tongue over my back molars, and poked at a piece of cabbage caught there. My cheeks tasted like mayonnaise as I drifted into sleep.

I swam in darkness, five fathoms deep, where the black water is still, when a noise reached me. My phone ringing from the surface. I rose from that pelagic sleep and kicked toward the dark living room, to *Hercules* reruns, to my phone warbling. I sat up and reached for the receiver.

"Hello?" I said.

"Hey, honey. How are you doing?"

Teresa Priestner.

"I'm fine," I said. "Fine."

I tried to work saliva into my mouth.

"I ordered John's autopsy photos," she said.

I squinted and rubbed my eyes.

"Are you sure you want to do that?"

"I need to see him," she said. "To figure out what happened that night."

I folded my feet under my legs and the leather made a dry shifting sound. Cracks ran across the couch like tributaries, branching over the cushions.

"I know our boys were shot down," Teresa said. "I know John didn't make a mistake. That man had fifteen hundred flight hours. Two deployments. No way he did this."

I picked at the places on the couch where the leather had flaked away.

"It's hard to believe," I agreed.

"Are you going to order Miles's autopsy report?"

"No."

"Because if we had both of them, we'd have a better idea of what happened."

"No," I said again. "I never want to see that."

I could make out the sounds of traffic on the boulevard and the bark of dogs two houses down. Streetlights had come on outside and their yellow glow soaked through the curtains. I needed a drink of water.

"I understand," Teresa said finally in a way I knew meant she didn't.

———

Soon afterward, Captain Delancey called from Iraq. I was surprised to hear his voice on the other end of the phone.

"This is Scott," he said.

Scott? Of course. His real name. I'd never heard Miles call him anything but Captain.

"How are you doing?" he asked.

"Okay, I guess." I looked around at the spare interior. "How are things over there?"

"Fine," he said. "Hot. And sandy."

I held the phone close to my ear to hear him over the static. There was a long pause. From him or the phone line, I couldn't be sure.

"Do you need anything?" he said after a while.

I needed everything. I needed someone to fix the hole in my screen and to move the heavy boxes on my patio. I needed someone to plant the mango tree I was always talking about buying and to paint the dining room chairs. I needed someone to come home to, to speak to, to listen to. I needed someone to hold my hand at night. But instead of telling him any of that, I talked about the thousand mundane things that filled my life. I talked about work, friends, and the man next door who beat his wife. Scott talked about flight schedules, long hours, and when they might be coming home. We spoke like that, circling, until there was nothing left to talk about but the crash.

"Were you there?" I said. I sat with my feet tucked under my legs and in the light of the living room I traced the hollows of my knees. "On the ground. When they recovered the bodies."

Scott's voice sounded far away. "No. I wasn't."

"Did you see him afterward?"

"No."

The skin beneath my fingers felt thin, as if I might split it with a nail.

"So you don't know how he looked? The condition of his body?"

"No," Scott said, and the house shuddered in the silence that followed.

Of course, I could have ordered the autopsy report. I could have read for myself what made the Army decide that Miles's casket should stay closed. I could have examined the autopsy photos and inspected exactly what had made him unviewable. I could have been as brave as my mother and looked and looked and looked.

People told me—or perhaps I told myself—that I imagined it worse than it was. But much later I spoke to a military doctor who worked in Iraq, a man who talked gravely of what he had seen in-country, and he told me that mortuary affairs does an admirable job with the bodies. They have tools at their disposal like Dermabond, a skin adhesive.

"It's like superglue," he said. "If there was any way they could have made him viewable, they would have."

He told me this across a wooden conference table with a top smooth as glass, and I knew it wasn't true what people told me, what I told myself. I had not imagined it worse than it was. I cried quietly then because I finally understood how Miles had come home.

16

In Saint Peter's Basilica in Rome there is a statue of the saint whose feet pilgrims have touched for centuries. The stone has slowly been rubbed away so that the toes are worn to nubs. In my rented house, I stubbornly kept Miles's pencils in my desk drawer. I shelved his books in my bookcase. I mixed his socks in with mine. That way I would come across his things by accident and I would have such a feeling for him, such a sense of knowing, that for the space of a second I could believe he was alive. But over time the socks and books and pencils began to lose their effect. It was no longer like at the beginning, when I would have to step back and press a hand to my chest, the feel of Miles sharp there, as if just then remembering he was gone.

This is how I came to understand why my mother had stored away my father. The lines of his memory must have begun to soften and fade. His image grew muddied. She must have known she was losing him with each pass. I would not lose Miles. I would not wear him to nothing. So, like my mother before me, I made my husband disappear.

I began by asking Miles's mother, Terry, to come to Florida to collect what had once belonged to her son. Together we dragged the tough bins close to the open garage door while sheets of rain poured over the door's metal frame and drove divots in the sand on the other side. I brought over two wooden chairs, one missing half its back and the other shedding paint in green strips. I released the clasp on the largest tough bin, steeling myself for what lay inside. Sunlight filtered through the curtain of water and swam down to us to reveal the contents, the rolled socks and stacked magazines I'd left when I first sorted through the bins and had not touched since. They still held so much life in them, as if Miles had just folded the shirts, just turned back the pages of the books.

"Look at all this," Terry said.

She reached into the pile and lifted out a pack of unopened boxer shorts.

"I sent these to him," she said.

She glanced over the clear plastic wrapping and the folded underwear inside and then set the package beside the bin. She pulled out a cotton T-shirt printed with the Army logo across the chest and held the shirt in front of her before draping the material against her own chest.

"Do you think it will fit?" she said.

"I think so."

"I might take it to run in."

"Take anything you want," I said. "This is all yours."

I wanted none of it. No reminders of Miles. Nothing to speak of his life or death. Rain splashed off the concrete driveway and into the garage, fine as mist, covering my arms while Terry bent over the box again and lifted out two books she had sent to Miles in Iraq.

"I might take these."

I nodded. "Okay."

She leaned over the black tough bin again and sorted through the items in a way that I recognized, slowly and deliberately, as if she were looking for something that might ease her heart. I did not tell her she would not find it. When it was all too much—too much to remember, too much life packed into those plastic boxes—Terry pulled another T-shirt from the pile and pressed it to her face. She breathed deeply, as I had, searching for some trace of Miles, not knowing as I already knew that they had washed his clothes before sending them home. Losing a spouse is in no way like losing a child but all loss is in some way like losing ourselves. I stood from the chair with the paint peeling off in strips and reached for Terry, and though I am taller and broader through the shoulders she is built wiry and strong, like Miles. It was impossible to say which of us held the other up.

Into the now-empty tough bins I relegated the last traces of Miles. On a weekend afternoon when I knew my mother would be out, I drove to her house and headed to the back bedroom where I had set aside the clothes for Miles's R & R, a respite from the war he never made. The clothes were left waiting—as I was left waiting, as we were all left waiting—for Miles to come home. In their waiting they gave off a signal, a homing beacon, a message broadcast daily as if from an abandoned radio tower.

Welcome home, they said. *Welcome home.*

I could not stand to listen anymore.

On my way to the guest room I set the muscles in my face so that if I glanced at myself in the mirror above the dresser, I would look stern. I squared my shoulders and walked with purpose, all composure and good sense. I was sure I could handle the task the way my mother might, without tears, without making a scene. I was proud of

my resolve as I pulled open the top drawer and saw his clothes the
way I had left them. The smell of the detergent I used in North Carolina rose from the open drawer, and without thinking I smoothed the
top of the pile the way I had once smoothed our clean laundry. I lifted
a brown polo shirt with white plastic buttons from the pile and set it
on top of the dresser. I pulled out a pair of jeans with a faded stain at
the place where a man might wipe his hands after changing his oil.
There was a set of thermal underwear in case R & R came during the
winter and Miles and I decided to go skiing, and a pair of flip-flops
if we spent time in Florida. Beneath all this, there was the blue glass
bottle of his cologne. I raised my gaze to the mirror and I was glad
for my steady face, my dry eyes, the way I pulled each item from the
drawer and laid it on top of the dresser. I made the mistake of thinking myself brave. Convinced of my own courage, I raised the cologne
bottle to my nose. Often we become aware of our lover's smell only
through absence and distance, and here was the indelible scent of
Miles. I felt him in a way I had not since he deployed. My knees went
loose and I had to sit on the edge of the bed as the composure I had
worked so hard to construct evaporated. I cried quietly with my head
bent to my chest as I realized for the first time that the hurt was never
going to go away.

After a time, my face red and my eyes swollen, I stood, steadied
myself on the dresser, and gathered the last of my resolve. I picked up
the clothes and the cologne and made my way to the garage, where
I lifted the lid to one of the tough bins. I placed the items inside and
sealed them away.

All that remained was my wedding ring, and in July, on the one-year
anniversary of our wedding, I decided to take off the band. I sat for a
time in my backyard as the light drained from the day, holding myself

with both arms. A friend once told me the story of a party he attended in London with a middle-aged man who had recently lost his wife. Over the course of the evening the widower cornered one guest after another.

"How long will I feel this way?" he demanded as his drink sloshed on the carpet. "How long?"

I had decided—as we often decide these things: arbitrarily—that I would feel this way until July. If I just stuck to it, to the hospice group and the long nights of crying and the sick feeling of loss each morning, I was convinced I would be healed. But I had made it to July and I was not better.

"I am not better," I said to the empty backyard.

I sat in silence until a cloud of mosquitoes had gathered at my feet and the yard was lost in shadow. Then I stood, walked back in through the porch, and locked the door behind me. In my room I picked up the wooden box Miles had once kept beside the bed that now held his wedding ring. I walked into the living room and lit a few candles. The books I read on grieving talked about ritual and I wanted this to be a ceremony. There was no script and, besides, there was no audience to hear what I might say. So I said nothing. I closed my eyes and let myself think about Miles. I thought about the way he had slipped the ring on my finger. I thought about the jewelry shop in Texas where we'd found the rings.

"How about these?" Miles had said as he bent over the glass display case.

I moved close to him in the wood-paneled store, my hands stuck in the pockets of my coat.

"Those could work."

I let my sadness well in me until it coursed through my body. I sat in the white-hot space of my hurt. It worked its way through me and poured out my eyes in stinging tears. It seized my heart and shook the muscles in my chest. I shook with it. I rocked back and forth, the ring still on my finger, my hand pressed flat against my breastbone, and cried until my eyes ached, until my veins burned, until my throat stiffened with the force of it. When I stopped, I lowered my hand.

"I'm sorry," I said.

I scrubbed my eyes with the hem of my shirt. I took a steadying breath, slipped the ring off my finger, and held it in both hands. I shut my eyes so that I was blind to the room, blind to the flickering candles, blind to my blank walls and secondhand furniture. I closed my eyes so that all I could see were the blank insides of my eyelids.

"Please," I said. "Please help me."

I spoke the words as I squeezed the ring in my fist.

"Please."

I shook my head as I said it, slowly, from side to side.

"Please help. Please."

My sense of things faded and the words lost all meaning. Soon I was chanting a wordless prayer, an om of sadness, a sound that was pure grief. I continued until my lips numbed and my fingers locked in their grip. I sat with my eyes closed and my breath low in the back of my throat, feeling the candle flames and the empty space of the living room. I felt the emptiness in me. I lowered my hand from my chest and opened my fingers, raised the lid to the wooden box, and set my wedding band inside. The two rings glinted in the light from the candles and I sat with my bare hands in my lap, trembling.

———

Time pressed relentlessly forward and the one-year anniversary of Miles's death loomed. I had spent the days and weeks and months after the notification inside an iron lung, taking one joyless breath after another, not living really, just sustaining. There had been nothing beyond the next breath and still people told me the second year would be worse.

"Once you make it through the first round of important dates," an older widow told me, "you'll be disappointed to discover what follows."

"What follows?" I asked.

"Another year."

Widows who were further along told me that the challenge becomes not just surviving but living, less a question of *How do I make it through the day?* and more of the dilemma, *What now?*

I planned to take a personal day from work on the anniversary itself. I thought I would drive to a park on an undeveloped stretch of estuary, pack a sandwich and a book, sit under a cabbage palm and listen to the raccoons in the buttonwoods. I thought I would walk the sand paths until they gave out on the shore. I would collect lightning whelks and lilac augers and drag my toes in the surf. But when the day came I did none of these things. I drove to my mother's house and sat on a chair facing the beach as I had done in the first days after the notification. I watched the waves for hours, let them come into me, into my eyes, past the corneas and through the lenses and against the retinas, let the images penetrate my brain until they had wiped away all trace of what lay inside.

I had recently read an article about a woman whose son had been killed in Iraq. She quit her corporate job to start an organic farm, and when people asked how she could be so foolhardy she simply shrugged them off.

"I've already lost everything," she said. "Why wouldn't I try this?"

A late-autumn cold front had blown in earlier in the week, bringing days of wind and rain, and I was cold as I sat in the wicker chair. I folded my legs to my chest and watched the waters of the Gulf churn the color of strong tea. I wondered what it would feel like to step outside my life, and I thought of the last line from Miles's good-bye letter. *Follow your dreams with all your heart, and with honor and decency.* I realized then that the way through the days and months and years to come depended solely on me, and I saw for the first time that I could stay in the same house, in the same job, in the same city, drowning slowly, or I could step out and away. There on the eve of my second year without Miles I asked myself, *What now?*

Part III

17

A contest. That's how this all begins. The local daily paper, the *News-Press*, ran a contest looking for someone to write for their new community website. Annabelle, who worked as a sportswriter for the *News-Press*, encouraged me to enter. I did. The editors selected three finalists, me among them. For two weeks we submitted sample stories while the public voted, and at the end of that stretch an editor from the *News-Press* called to tell me I'd won. I hung up the phone and pumped my fist in the air and did a frantic jerking dance around my living room.

"I won!" I shouted. "Holy shit."

I wrote for the *News-Press* every week—personal essays and slice-of-life pieces about southwest Florida. The stories were unpaid and unedited, but at least I was writing. One afternoon my boss on the farm called me into his office.

"I've got somebody you should meet," he said.

He wrote an e-mail address on a slip of paper and handed it across his desk.

"She's a friend of mine. A writer. She does PR work now but she might be able to point you in the right direction. If you're serious about this writing thing."

I looked at the address in my hand, uncertain.

"Go ahead," he said. "Contact her. What do you have to lose?"

Back in my office I sat with the piece of paper propped against my keyboard. I could not imagine what I would say to this woman, but I invited her for coffee anyway.

It rained the night of our meeting. Water slid off the waxy leaves of ixora hedges in the parking lot, seeped through the mulch, and puddled on the pavement. I hurried beneath the roof of the shopping center to the soft light from the coffee shop spilling onto the wet sidewalk. Under the awning I shook out my umbrella and peeked to see if she waited inside. Not yet. I nervously ordered a cup of tea at the counter and found a table near the door. An anxious refrain beat against my skull, a version of *What are you thinking?* set on repeat. No one ever told me that the act of courage actually feels like fear. By the time the woman arrived, I had sweated through my nice blouse. We shook hands and she took the seat across from me.

"So I hear you want to be a writer," she said.

I looked at the mug between my fingers. *Say it,* I dared myself. *Claim what you want.* I raised my eyes to hers.

"I do."

The rain fell outside in a windless downpour and the woman nodded.

"I have some ideas. Places where you might start." She reached into her purse and pulled out a newspaper. "This is *Florida Weekly*. A new publication, started by guys who left the *News-Press*. It's a good paper with quality writing, but you can tell they don't have enough reporters."

She peeled off the front section and pointed to a byline.

"See this? 'Special to *Florida Weekly.*' That means it came from out-side the paper, probably from a PR person."

The cappuccino machine whirred, briefly drowning out the guitar chords that pumped through the stereo, and I looked at her without comprehending.

"That means they need writers," she said. "This could be a good place for you to pitch."

She handed me the paper and I scanned the front page. It had a good look—clean, professional, with quality photos and a clear layout.

"So, how do I pitch them?" I said.

"Write the editor. His name is Jeff Cull. Tell him what you'd like to do—that you want to be one of his freelance writers. Maybe for the Arts and Entertainment section? I think that would be a good fit for you. Then send him clips of the stories you've written for the *News-Press*. That will give him an idea of what you can do."

"And then what happens?"

"Then you wait to hear back."

The smell of guavas hung heavy and sweet as I lapped the farm's main office. I followed the porch that skirted the building, past the jackfruit trees that stood beside the south wall, the spiked fruit big enough to kill a man if they fell. I moved clockwise around the porch, past the door that led into the kitchen, the windows of the front office, the main entrance where papayas turned soft and brown in the heat. I hardly noticed, I was so intent on composing a message in my head.

I had paged through a copy of *Florida Weekly* over lunch, reading the articles in every section, looking for gaps and figuring out where I might fit in, when a thought occurred to me. I remembered the friend of a friend from college, the one in the running for the editorial job, and his idea for a relationship column. I was still fascinated by the big questions that love asks, specifically how to negotiate the terrain between what we want from our lives and what we want from a partner. I still had strong opinions about a woman's responsibility to herself. And I still thought about sex. My God, did I think about sex.

The back door gave a metallic yawn as I moved into the air-conditioned building. I took a seat in front of my computer and typed out the message I had composed in the afternoon heat. I attached three of my recent articles, scanned the e-mail carefully for errors, and before I could lose my nerve I hit Send. It was exhilarating and terrifying and perhaps the most foolhardy thing I had ever done.

And then what happened?

Then I waited to hear back.

But not for long.

"I really liked the dating piece," Jeff replied that afternoon. "Let's talk about this when you have some time. If you get a chance, stop by and we'll chat."

I gulped great lungfuls of air and then covered my mouth to stop the cheer that was building in the back of my throat. I snuck out the side door to a picnic table beneath the oaks and tented my hands over my mouth.

"Oh, my God," I whispered into my cupped palms.

Shaking my head, I lowered my eyes so that I stared into my lap. I felt a bittersweet pang as I sat on the picnic table processing the best news I'd had in a long time. Because I didn't know what else to do and also because it felt right, I bowed my head and folded my hands.

"Thank you," I said.

———————

The sign in the parking lot said FLORIDA WEEKLY. Blue letters on a white background with a palm frond motif. I parked with a knot in my belly where my nervousness had drawn down to a hard pit. The pit stayed there as I crossed the hot expanse of asphalt, stayed as I reached the shade under the awning, stayed as I opened the door and stepped into the cool interior. The office was empty.

"Hello?" I said.

There were half-unpacked boxes stacked against the side wall, a mess of books and office supplies spilling onto the floor. The lights in most of the rooms were turned off. I stepped down a side hallway.

"Anyone here?"

A man in a button-down shirt and tie stepped out of a back room.

"Hey, there," he said as he walked down the hall. "I'm Jeff."

He was in his early forties and had an air about him—genuine, curious, intelligent—that I have since learned to associate with editors in general and newspaper editors in particular. I liked him instantly.

"Come on back," he said after we shook hands. "We're just now getting the office set up."

I followed him into another room and he offered me a chair. There was no stiffness to him, no formality, just a direct earnestness.

"I looked you up after I got your e-mail," he said. "I'm sorry to hear about your husband."

There it was where I least expected it—the hurt I was always bumping into. A moment of worry crossed my mind as I imagined choking up in front of this man I so desperately needed to give me a shot. But he deftly diverted the conversation and I let out the breath I had been holding. I'd like to tell you there was more of a preamble, but newspapermen—and Jeff in particular—have a penchant for getting straight to the point.

"We'd like you to do a column for us," Jeff said. "Like you pitched. A dating column."

I kept my gaze steady, afraid if I moved I'd betray my excitement.

Nonchalance, I whispered to myself, mentally gritting my teeth. *The goal is nonchalance.* I pressed my lips together. It was all I could do not to leap across the desk and wrap my arms around him.

"We'd like you to start next week."

Sweet Jesus, I thought. *Just like that?*

He told me how much they'd pay me. On the drive over I'd mentally reviewed what I thought would be an acceptable amount. He quoted me twice that figure.

"What should I write about?" I said. "Anything in particular?"

"We liked those samples you sent in. Just keep doing what you're doing."

I nodded as if I understood. What *was* I doing? I didn't know, but I wasn't about to admit it. I stood to leave and we shook hands.

"And, Artis?" Jeff said as I moved toward the door.

I turned back to him, one eyebrow raised.

"Don't be shy."

I laughed.

"I'm not shy," I said.

2008

18

There are more than a thousand widows of the wars in Iraq and Afghanistan, but during my first time at the National Military Survivors Seminar held each year over Memorial Day weekend by an organization called Tragedy Assistance Program for Survivors—or TAPS—I worried that none of them would be like me. When I walked into the upstairs lobby of the hotel on the first day, I saw that all of the women seemed to know each other, as if they had come from the same unit. They hugged and cried in small circles, everyone but me in red T-shirts.

"Is this registration?" I asked a woman behind a wooden table.

"Sure is," she said in a voice that struck me as too high and too light.

"Henderson," I said as she thumbed through the registration packets.

"Here we go." She handed an envelope across the table and beamed up at me. "You can pick up your T-shirt over there."

She pointed across the lobby and I turned in that direction.

"Don't forget your button," she called after me.

"My button?"

As I looked at the table next to hers I understood. The TAPS registration form I'd filled out months before had asked me to submit a picture of my loved one. I remembered having sent in a photo of Miles, but I couldn't have told you which one. I moved to the adjoining table and gave the woman there my name. She handed over a small manila envelope and I pushed open the brass clasp. Inside was a photo button: Miles on the deck of a deep-sea fishing boat, a yellow-finned grunt in his hand. My breath caught in my throat.

"What do I do with this?" I said to the woman behind the table.

"You wear it," she said. "Like this."

She took the large envelope out of my hand and dug through the contents until she found a small black pouch with a nylon cord.

"The string goes around your neck," she said, "and your button goes right here."

She lifted the pouch out of my hands and pinned the button to the side.

"Don't forget your ribbons," she said.

She pointed to the next table over, where colored ribbons lay in neat rows, each with a printed label: LOVED ONE, SIBLING, PARENT; MARINE, NAVY, AIR FORCE. I took a green ARMY ribbon and a purple SPOUSE ribbon. As I pulled the strips of paper off their adhesive backs, I noticed a woman in line behind me. She dropped the black cord of her pouch around her neck.

"Who did you lose?" she asked as she reached around me for a SPOUSE ribbon.

I was shocked for a moment at the casualness of it, the way this woman I didn't know could ask me about something I rarely discussed. But I reminded myself that I was at the conference to talk about Miles and to meet other grieving survivors. Otherwise, why bother?

"I lost my husband," I said. "Miles."

"Can I see?"

The woman pointed to the button hanging on my badge. As I

passed the photo to her I realized how young the man in the image was. It occurred to me that someday I will be an old woman carrying a photo of the boy I love.

"He's cute," the woman said.

She handed back the button and I smiled despite myself.

"We regret, those of us who have lost a loved one suddenly, that we didn't have the chance to say good-bye."

A speaker with soft arms and an expansive bosom, the kind of frame made for hugging, stood at the front of the conference room while I sat at a crowded table in the audience. A woman across from me reached for a box of tissues at the center; it looked like she'd been crying all day.

"We think if we just had one more minute with them, we'd say all the things that didn't get said." The presenter moved across the floor as she spoke. "Now, this may make some of you sad. And it may make some of you angry. But listen to what I'm going to say. You think if you had another minute, you think if you had more time, you would tell them good-bye. But that's not what you would say. Here's what you would say. *I love you.* And *I'll miss you.* And *Remember that time we—* You'd say all that. But *Good-bye?* Never."

I scanned the room: everyone had the same look, a mix of devastation and hope.

"Now, this is blank paper," the speaker said as she handed out white strips. "Don't write anything on it."

She stopped beside my table and laid a stack in the middle.

"I mean, I want you to write on it. But let me tell you what it's got to say first."

People laughed the way they will when they're steeling themselves, when they know the hard part's coming.

"We all have unresolved issues with our loved one," the speaker said. "It's the nature of love. We all have issues that we didn't work out, problems that never got fixed. I want you to think about what that is for you. Go ahead. Take a minute. Close your eyes if you want to."

I closed mine, weary from looking at all those wrecked faces, and shuffled through what Miles and I had left undone, unsaid.

"Now think of the issue that weighs on you the most," the speaker said. "What is it you wish you could say to them if you had one last time together? What do you need to apologize for? What do you need to get off your chest?"

I scrolled down the list of things I wished I had done differently. If only I had kept my mouth shut—about the house, about the military, about my worries for the future. If only I had been kinder, gentler. If only I could have brought Miles home.

"Go ahead and open your eyes now," the speaker said.

The conference room was the same, all brokenhearted parents and sisters and wives. All of us sick with our grief.

"Now, what I want you to do with this scrap of paper"—the speaker held up one of the blank sheets in front of her—"I want you to write down what you would say to your loved one."

I met the eyes of the young woman next to me and we both raised questioning brows.

"I'm going to take the papers—now, fold them up good when you get done writing—and I'm going to take them home. I'm not going to look at them. I'm going to burn them and they'll go up in smoke, and that way—now, you may believe this and you may not—but I like to think your loved one will get the message."

The young woman to my side passed me a pen.

"Take a minute now," the speaker said. "Don't rush yourself. Write what you need to write."

I thought of the fear that I nursed daily, the fear that I slept with at night and woke to in the morning, the fear I carried like my mother carried her silence, like Teresa carried her blame. I held the slip of paper and picked up the pen.

I'm afraid I didn't love you enough to save you, I wrote.

The pain that came with it wrung my lungs and seared my eyes. Around the other tables, men and women were also weeping. I reread what I had written and it occurred to me that perhaps my fear was groundless. In a way that I had previously been unable to see, I realized my love had not factored in his death. There was action and fate and pure dumb luck. There was the absurdity of circumstance, that two good pilots could be brought down by bad weather they had seen coming. There was the reality that sometimes one helicopter goes down and the second does not. There was the unfairness that sometimes your husband is on the one that goes down. Bur my love for Miles? There had been more than enough.

"Just leave your paper on the side table on your way out," the speaker said from the front of the room.

I folded mine quickly before anyone could see what I had written, and as I filed out of the room I added my small slip to the others stacked on a table against the wall. Much later I tried to describe the experience of the conference to someone—the photo buttons and the seminars and the crying with strangers—and he said, "That sounds awful." But it wasn't awful. It was difficult and painful and terribly, terribly hard. But it was also redemptive, like a brush fire to clear the land.

For the TAPS Saturday night banquet, I dressed in a black cotton dress cut low in the front. Too racy for that crowd, I figured, but I wore it anyway. I wondered if there would be dancing. The experience had been so surreal—all that laughter, all that festivity in the midst of overwhelming sadness—that I had ceased being surprised. People milled outside the reception hall in their nice clothes, suddenly strange without their red T-shirts. A few men circulated, fathers and brothers and friends, but the crowd was mostly women. A pretty blonde stood to my left and smiled when I glanced over. I smiled back.

"Are you here by yourself?" she said. The woman, who looked my age, stuck out a hand. "I'm Laura." She turned to the small group beside her. "We're all wives. I mean, widows."

I shook each of their hands—Mindi, Jocelyn, Jaime, Sarah—and we fell into a conversation that surprised me with its instant intimacy.

"How long were you married?" Jaime asked.

"Just four months," I said. "You?"

"Eight years. I met Dave in high school."

"What branch was your husband in?" Mindi said.

"Army."

"I'm Army too. Which unit?"

"The Eighty-Second. Out of Bragg. Yours?"

"The Two-Six Cav out of Hawaii."

"How did your husbands die?" I asked and was shocked for a moment at my boldness. But they answered without hesitation.

"A Kiowa crash," Mindi said.

"An IED blast."

"IED."

"And yours?" Mindi asked.

"Helicopter crash," I said.

They nodded, knowing.

"Did you meet before TAPS?" I asked the group.

Laura laughed.

"No, we just met," she said. "This is our first time here."

The crowd shuffled slowly into the ballroom and our group of widows claimed a table in the back. Sarah bought a bottle of wine. I bought a second. A keynote speaker talked about honor and sacrifice and a woman sang "Amazing Grace." Jocelyn, who was only a few weeks in, covered her face with her hands and Sarah wrapped her in her arms. I looked around the table and saw that we were all crying. For the first time in a long time, it felt all right. We ate the baked chicken and asparagus that the waiters served. We drank our cheap hotel wine. At one point Mindi pulled a rose from the arrangement in the middle of the table and soon we each had a flower stuck in the neckline of our dresses.

"Our 'bereavage,'" she called it.

There was no dancing, as it turned out, just a slow end to the evening. I laughed in a way I had not laughed since Miles died. As we headed out of the ballroom and to our separate hotel suites, I wondered why I hadn't known women like them before. Where had they been when I was trying to make a life alongside the military?

The answer, of course, is that they had been there all along.

On the morning of Memorial Day, TAPS arranged a shuttle from the hotel to Arlington National Cemetery and our small group of widows joined up at Section 60. We followed Mindi to her husband Tuc's grave, in the row in front of John's, and we fanned out around her on the grass. We sat for a time without talking and then, in the way of military widows, we talked about the grim details of our husbands' deaths. This was the new language I had learned to speak, a lexicon of *briefings* and *autopsy reports* and *partial remains*.

"You said Tuc died in a helicopter crash?" Sarah asked.

"Yeah," Mindi said. "They got shot and went down hard."

"Did you get to see him after he came back?"

"In the funeral home."

I sat back on the grass. "You saw him?"

"Just from the waist up. In the coffin."

"How was he?"

"He looked all right."

"I saw Sean," Laura said. "As soon as they got him to the funeral home."

"What was it like?" I said. "To see him, I mean."

"Not too bad. I got to hold his hand."

"How was it?"

"He was cold," Laura said. "They pack them in ice."

I imagined Miles's body gone stiff and cool, and I shivered. Other families had started to fill the cemetery, and a group of young men smoked cigars a few graves down. They had brought folding chairs and a cooler of beer, as if they planned to be there all day.

"I didn't see Dave," Jaime said. "The IED blew apart his Humvee. I don't want—"

She looked at her feet and back at us, and we returned her look without flinching.

"I don't want to think about how he came home."

I ran my hand over the grass and felt the day's heat gathered there. To the east the brown waters of the Potomac churned toward the sea, and I thought of rivers running red with blood. At Arlington the grave markers are white like ivory or teeth or bone. I looked at the young women beside me and considered the terrible knowledge they carry inside them—knowledge I carried too—and I felt a sudden responsibility to tell their stories, our stories. I wanted everyone to know the things we knew.

19

The 1st Attack Reconnaissance Battalion of the 82nd Airborne Division came home from Iraq in October 2007, fifteen months after the unit deployed. I refused to let anyone tell me the exact date the soldiers would fly to Fort Bragg. If I had known that the families were reuniting while I sat alone in my rented house with its ragged backyard and half my things in boxes, it would have felt like a betrayal of the gravest kind. I preferred to think that one day the unit would be in Iraq and one day it would be home, with nothing in between. No dramatic welcome reception with flags and balloons and signs, the reunion sweetness I will never know. There are widows who go to the homecoming. They say being there and not seeing their husbands walk off the plane confirms the truth of what happened. They say it brings them closure. I do not believe in closure. But knowing the unit was home felt like an ending of sorts to one story, and I liked to think it created room for the opening of another.

———————

When I first thought about quitting my job on the farm to write full-time, I e-mailed an editor friend to ask her opinion.

"Are you nuts?" she wrote back.

I laughed. I was.

I took time off and visited Vietnam and Cambodia. The *News-Press* commissioned a travel piece and the editors published my article on the front page of the Sunday travel section, my favorite section, the section I read every morning growing up, where the stories that first inspired my dreams of writing had appeared. I took more time off and visited India; I sold an article on the desert cities of Rajasthan. I pitched a local lifestyles magazine and the editor there gave me an assignment. One of my essays appeared in a literary magazine. On a cool afternoon on the farm, I gathered my nerve, walked into my boss's office, and told him I was quitting. He looked completely unsurprised.

The Sunshine Café had two recommending qualities: it served breakfast and cocktails all day. The early-bird special was invented for places like that, and by the time our group of hospice widows rolled in after the Tuesday night meeting, most of the diners were finishing their banana pudding. We took our usual table by the window and ordered drinks.

"I got to tell you," Bea said as she took a sip of her Bloody Mary, "I am tired of being alone."

"I hear you," more than one of us said.

She set her glass on the table. "What I wouldn't give for a man to hold my hand."

"Or to take me out to dinner," Linda said. "I wouldn't mind that."

"Or just to have someone to talk to," Lan-fah said.

The table was quiet as each of us mulled this over, and when Jeanie spoke we all turned to listen.

"Well, I have some news," she said in a low voice. "I'm not sure what you girls are going to think."

The other tables sent up the combined noise of silverware against plates, glasses clinking, napkins shuffling. We waited for Jeanie to finish.

"I'm seeing someone," she said.

There was a beat of silence at the table as we took in the news, and then we were cheering and our questions spilled over one another.

"Who is it?"

"Where'd you meet him?"

"What's he like?"

Jeanie laughed. "If I had known you were going to have this reaction—"

"This is great news," I said.

"Do you like him?" Lan-fah asked.

"I do," Jeanie said. "I really like him. He's a good guy."

Linda lifted her wine glass in a toast.

"I'm so happy for you," she said.

Lan-fah raised her glass and I touched mine to both of theirs. Bea added hers last.

"Me?" she said. "I'm jealous as hell."

We laughed then, all of us, because we were jealous too.

Thirteen months after the unit returned home and two years after Miles's death, Captain Scott Delancey came to see me in Florida. Some of the soldiers did that—stopped by or called to pay their respects. In my driveway Scott looked taller than I remembered him, broader through the chest and back, and he had grown older in the time since we had last seen each other. I suppose I had grown older too. When he bent down to hug me, the feeling of being so close to someone I associated with Miles was nearly overwhelming. I pressed my face to the crook of his neck and breathed him in.

"How've you been?" he asked when we pulled apart.

"Good," I said. "Happy to see you."

On a dare we drove to an arcade north of town where there were batting cages and go-cart tracks and we were the oldest people by a decade. We played rounds of air hockey and Scott beat me every time, but he had the courtesy to let me win on the go-cart track. It felt good to be with someone who had known Miles, and I liked that Scott was generous—he gave me tokens by the handful—and funny. I liked, too, the way other women watched him.

On the drive home from the arcade, Scott reached across the car and took my hand.

"Do you know how to drive a stick shift?" he asked.

"No," I said.

He placed my hand on the gearshift and kept his fingers over mine. "Now's a good time to learn."

We drove like that for a while, my hand cupped in his as he shifted gears, my face flushing each time his skin pressed against mine. When we were nearly home, Scott pulled off the road and into an empty parking lot.

"Your turn now," he said.

"No way. I'll destroy your transmission."

"You'll be fine. I'll be right here to help."

We switched seats and I took the car on a halting tour around the parking lot. The gears ground and the engine stalled but Scott just laughed.

"Keep going," he said. "You'll get it."

I was nervous—from the driving, from him—and my body temperature climbed. I sweated and the windows fogged over, and after a time I called the lesson done. Scott drove the rest of the way while I sat in the passenger seat and wondered what was building between us—if anything. At home, Scott walked me to my front door and said good night. Before he turned to leave he placed a kiss at the corner of my mouth, that small stretch of skin that is for neither friendship nor love but some nameless place in between.

———

The *Florida Weekly* office had grown in the time I'd been writing for the paper. Framed copies of prizewinning editions decorated the walls, and the space buzzed with a low hum of activity. Phones rang in the sales office and I could hear a reporter speaking to an editor in the back room. Somewhere a coffeepot percolated and the smell gave the space an industrious feel. Jeff came to fetch me in the reception area wearing new square-framed glasses that made him look hip.

"You guys are busy," I said on our way to his office.

"We're putting out the paper in four counties now," he said. "Our circulation's up to a hundred thousand."

"Not bad."

Jeff laughed. "Not bad at all."

In the office, I sat across from Jeff's desk and admired the framed newsprint that hung on every available space. The paper had reported a story on local casualties of war, and Miles's photo—the cropped picture from our courthouse wedding—looked down from a copy of the article. Life is funny that way.

Jeff leaned back in his chair, cocked his elbows, and put his hands behind his head.

"So I hear you need a recommendation letter."

"For journalism school," I said. "At Columbia."

Jeff whistled. "That's serious. You ever lived in New York?"

I shook my head. "I heard it's a crazy city."

Jeff lowered his arms and leaned forward. "So, why journalism school? You've already got a gig here."

"I need to figure out how to do it right," I said. "How to tell the big stories."

I promised to send him information on the recommendation letter, and when I stood to leave he walked me to the front office.

"Thanks again," I said, my hand on the door.

"Keep me posted," Jeff said. "And good luck."

My time with the Tuesday night grief group was nearing its end. I'd watched the women who were there before me graduate themselves out of the group. Some remarried, some moved away, most simply learned to balance the realities of this new life. On one of my last nights, the usuals gathered, plus the newcomers just testing the place, deciding if the group would work for them. There were the usual flimsy tissue boxes, and we told the usual stories in familiar rhythms. When there was a lull, we sat in companionable silence for nearly a minute before Richard, whom we gossiped about at dinner, who had a beautiful wife—Linda saw them at the grocery store—and whose young son had died many years before, told us this story.

"My grandmother used to say—"

We clutched our rough tissues and looked at him with our swollen eyes.

"She used to say that if you took all the sorrows of all the people in the world and hung them from a tree like fruit and then you let people choose which one they wanted, we would still pick our own."

I thought back to the phone call with Psychic Suzanna months before and to the first time I met her in the hotel bar. What if she had told me then what was to come? Not just meeting Miles, not just his death, but afterward. That Miles would be the catalyst for this blossoming life, that my time with him would lay the foundation for some braver, more fearless me. That through knowing him and loving him I would become someone with the wherewithal to seize my dreams. I searched across the circle and saw that the other women had turned inward, as I had turned inward, and I imagined us meeting in that orchard of sorrow. Perhaps my mother would be there. Would she still choose this life with its sadness and memories and hopes?

I looked up to see the other women nodding and I found myself nodding too. *Of course,* we seemed to say, all of us. *Of course we would pick our own.*

2009

20

At Fort Bragg the memorials to fallen soldiers are scattered through-out the base, often tucked behind unit headquarters and forgotten by nearly everyone except the families of those who have served and died. MILES HENDERSON is carved into the memorial for the 82nd, and I like to imagine the strangers who might someday run their hands over the stone. Will they trace the letters with careful fingers? Will they say his name out loud? Perhaps they will ask themselves if the war was worth even this one life.

On the third Memorial Day after Miles's death, Teresa parked her Buick on the paved road that runs alongside Section 60 at Arlington. An old oak stood at the edge of the cemetery, its branches reaching in-ward toward the graves, as blistering heat blanketed the city. I imagined scorched earth as we walked across the grass, the bones beneath our feet blackened and burned, the world set on end. In grief parlance they call this upended life the "new reality." They don't tell you it doesn't feel like any sort of reality at all.

Teresa stopped in front of John's plot and I stopped beside her. She first sat back on her heels and then stretched her legs in front of her while I stepped out of my sandals and lowered myself to the ground. I kept to the space between John and his neighbor but Teresa sat directly over his grave.

"I wish I could sleep here," she said. She smoothed the ground the way a person might smooth a bedsheet. "I miss him so much. Both of our boys. Miles too. You know, I never think about John without thinking about Miles."

I nodded. I missed them too. I missed the days on the lake in John's boat, crystal-clear afternoons of heat and cool water. I missed Miles beside me. I missed the way Teresa had been when John was alive, sure of this world and her place in it.

"You and me," Teresa said. "Who would have thought?"

I would have been the last to think it. But there we were. She scooted forward so she sat next to the headstone, and I watched her from the corners of my eyes. She traced John's name with one finger and ran her thumb over the line that said BRONZE STAR. She touched the places where John's birth date and the letters of his rank had been carved into the stone. She did not turn her eyes to the left and right, to the graves beside John, the ones that said PURPLE HEART beneath the names. She had trained herself to stop looking.

But I had not stopped. I looked at all of them, the markers stretching out in a sea of white. When we buried John his grave had been the last in the line. Now the plots snaked in front of his, grave upon grave, reaching to the edges of the field. I tipped my head back to the hot sun and took the brunt of the glare full in the face. I did not turn away from any of it—the sky, the sun, the graves, Teresa and her worries. If I were another kind of woman, I would have put my arms around her and told her how thankful I was that we were in this together. I would have said how proud John would be of her and how much I admire her. But I am not that kind of woman. Instead I offered the only things I know how: my silence and my presence.

"This is so hard," Teresa said. "You know?"

I watched her sit back in the grass and run a hand over her damp brow.

"I know," I said.

She leaned forward to crawl onto her knees and stand slowly, one leg at a time. I followed, fanning my shirt like a bellows. Teresa touched John's gravestone and turned toward the road while I let my own hand linger on the marble. I followed her to the car, and in the shade of the old oak I sensed the roots pressing into the earth. I imagined a time when the heat might subside.

———

I have read that the human heart is roughly the size of a fist. This is how I saw my own heart: as a fist curled in the space behind my breastbone. The fingers of that fist ached, they'd been cramped together so long. Sometimes I tried to imagine what it would feel like to unfurl them and extend an open palm.

In the late summer, I told Scott Delancey the good news about journalism school.

"New York City," I said. "Can you believe it?"

"Amazing. When are you moving up?"

"Before school starts. In a month or so."

"Need any help?"

I laughed. Was he joking? Of course I needed help.

But instead I said, "I've got it."

"Seriously?" Scott insisted. "It's no problem."

"I'm staying with a friend until I find my own place. There'd be nowhere for you to stay."

"I'll get a hotel room."

"You're serious?"

"It's too easy," he said.

New York was steeped in heat the day Scott flew in and a dense jungle humidity lay over the city. Sweating bodies crammed the streets and the asphalt boiled beneath our feet, but Scott laughed off the hot weather.

"This is nothing compared to Iraq," he said.

That night we made our way to a bar in Hell's Kitchen where candles flickered on the tables and reflected off the red walls. I was on edge in my nice clothes, trying to figure out if Scott was there because of me or Miles. He ordered a whiskey and Coke for himself and a club soda with lime for me. He finished his second drink before I broached the subject of where I would spend the night.

"So," I said, "it's too late for me to go back to Queens."

Technically untrue. I could have caught the subway, which ran all night, and walked back to my friend's apartment, twenty minutes from the train station. Not the safest trek but doable. Scott waved a dismissive hand.

"Stay at the hotel with me."

I gave him a sidelong look. I didn't want him to think he had me so easily, that I was like any other girl he could pick up.

"But we can't sleep together," I said. "You have to promise."

Scott tilted his head back and laughed, then he leaned over and kissed me on the cheek.

"You're my friend's wife," he said. "Nothing will change that. I'll always be here to look after you and protect you. But we're not sleeping together. You're not even in my orbit."

Suddenly I felt like a fool in my dress and high heels. I had hoped—

what? That Scott would come to New York and save me? That we might share the hurt between us? That I might start a new life with this man while still holding on to Miles?

"Let's play a game," Scott said to change the subject. "Let's look around the bar and say who we'd sleep with."

I hoped the hurt didn't show on my face.

"Okay," I said. I wanted him to think it was no big deal.

"I'll go first," Scott said.

He pointed to a table of women across the room. They were New York sleek, with shiny hair and expensive clothes, pretty and sophisticated in a way I will never be. All at once the bar felt too warm, too close. I sipped the last of my drink and rattled the ice in the glass.

"You know what?" I said as I set the tumbler on the bar. "I don't want to play."

Scott looked at me from where he sat on his bar stool.

"I'm ready to go," I said.

He didn't fight me. He paid the check and hailed a cab. On the way back to the hotel, people streamed by on the sidewalk as we passed. It had rained earlier and puddles on the concrete caught the glow from neon signs. Neither of us spoke.

At the hotel we took the elevator to Scott's room, and I walked in front of him down the carpeted hallway.

"Your ass looks good in that dress," he said.

I rolled my eyes. This was the Scott I remembered.

He lent me a shirt to sleep in and I showered in the marble bathroom. He was already in bed when I came out, and when I lifted the comforter to slide in beside him it was as if we had shared this routine our entire lives. Scott turned out the light and I lay on my back in the dark room. The curtains were pulled tight against the city lights but I could hear the noise of New York below. A horn honked and someone called out on the street. I felt Scott beside me, awake and listening.

Finally, he spoke in the dark.

"Tell me again why we're not sleeping together?" he said.

"Because I don't sleep with men I'm not in a relationship with," I said.

Not strictly true, but I refused to be one of the women who came and went in Scott's life.

"But I thought you said you didn't want to be with me," he said. "In the bar."

I shook my head and the pillowcase rustled beneath my hair.

"That's not what I meant," I said. "I didn't want to sleep with you if you weren't serious about me."

Scott turned to face me and I could feel his breath against my cheeks.

"Does that mean you would consider dating me?" he said.

"I thought I wasn't even in your orbit."

Scott lay without moving and I listened to him take in a careful breath.

"You're the only one I want," he whispered. "The only one I've wanted for a long time."

His words split me open and all that I carried inside rose from that parted place. Here was a man who was nothing like Miles. Yet he remembered the way Miles looked, the way he laughed, the way he carried himself. He remembered the sound of Miles's voice. When Scott reached his arm across the bed to pull me to him, I let the curves of my body fit close to his. Outside, the city had stilled. We stayed silent for a long time, and then I asked Scott if I could see the tattoo he had mentioned once on the phone, a memorial he had inked on his skin after the deployment.

"Yes," he said.

He rolled onto his stomach and in the glow through the curtains I could see the design that covered half his back. John and Miles were there, rendered as skeletons, and I recognized Miles instantly. His face, his smile, his posture—all delivered as bones.

"It took twelve hours," Scott said. "Two sittings. The pain felt like penance."

I traced the ink with my finger.

"I should have grounded the aircraft that night," Scott said. "I was the battle captain. I was in charge. I knew the weather was bad. I knew visibility was limited. I should have told them to stay at War-horse."

What could I say? *I know.* Or: *Yes.* Or: *There was nothing you could have done.*

I ran my hand softly over his back.

"You did all you could do," I said. "It was no one's fault."

The traffic in the street hummed quietly and I listened to the steady rhythm of Scott's breathing. When he spoke next, I had to lean close to hear.

"I would trade my life for Miles," he said.

Without speaking, I laid my face against his skin so that the ink of the tattoo touched my cheek. I would let him.

Early after Miles's death, I asked myself how I would know when I was healed. This is what I decided: when I would not trade everything in my current life to have Miles back. Every new moment, every new experience, every new love. But now I see this for the impossible bargain it was. In the dim hotel room, I could feel the life I had known slipping through my fingers. Even as I held tight, I let go.

———

When the sharpness of Miles's loss had faded but the sting was still there, as I am learning it always will be, my mother and I spoke for the first time about my father's death. I called her from my apartment in New York and she carried the phone out onto the deck.

"I still remember that nurse in the hospital," my mother said. "The one who walked me down to the morgue. I remember her saying, 'You're not even crying. How can that be?' And I thought, *Lady, I ain't got time for that right now*."

Here was the mother I had always known, rough, a fighter. But what she said next surprised me.

"I made up for it later," she said. "I wept for months."

This woman I did not recognize.

"I always made sure I didn't cry around you," my mother said. "I had to be the strong one. You were counting on me totally. It was me. Just me. You needed all of your strength and all of mine and me sitting around crying? We couldn't do that."

Here was my mother with all the fight gone out of her, and it occurred to me how exhausting it must be to seem so hard all the time.

"What was it like to be with Dad?" I asked.

"It was magical, right from day one. I didn't realize that you could feel that way about a guy, that you could be that happy. It was really, really good what we had. You can't replace that."

Yes, I thought. *I know. Or I'm beginning to know.*

"Was there ever a time when it started to hurt less?"

"It still hurts," my mother said. "It's never going to go away."

I leaned my head against the frame of my bed, understanding in a way I had never understood the weight of the grief my mother had carried for so long. She was quiet for a time and I could hear the sound of the waves beneath the deck.

"You and I have never really sat down and talked about this, have we?" she said.

I gripped the phone in my hand and took a slow breath.

"No, we haven't. Why do you think that is?"

My mother spoke so softly, I had to press the phone to my ear, and even then I had trouble hearing her over the wind and water.

"Too painful," she said. "Too painful for me."

I closed my eyes and listened to the sound of the Gulf as the waves drew in on themselves and spilled back to shore. The weight of my mother's courage seemed to press through the phone and across the receiver, so that it flowed into me and joined us like a cord.

"Would you still have chosen to be with Dad?" I said. "Even if you had known how everything would turn out?"

My mother did not hesitate.

"In a heartbeat," she said, and I smiled.

Of course.

2011

Five years after Miles's death, I spent time at a residency in Florida working on this book. I had graduated from Columbia University's School of Journalism in 2010, spent a year in West Africa, and recently returned from a stay in the South of France. On a warm fall afternoon, I took the day off writing and drove to the middle of the state to the town of Cassadaga, where a community of psychics and mediums live. It was mid-October and the city had been outfitted for Halloween: plastic bones leaned on stone benches and Styrofoam tombstones poked from the ground. An eerie scene for a town that specializes in communicating with the dead.

I parked at the welcome center and walked through the gift shop, sliding past the incense and crystals to the bulletin board at the back of the store. I found a business card tacked to the board for a woman named Maeve who called herself a "psychic/medium."

"I'm just down the street," she said on the phone when I called. "You can walk here."

I set out on foot. Spanish moss hung from the trees beside the side-walk and a one-eyed cat glared at me from a front lawn, daring me to walk on the grass. I reached a row of apartments behind a screened-in porch and Maeve opened the door when I knocked, looking less like a spiritual medium and more like a schoolteacher. She wore a coral sweater and pressed khakis, silver earrings and subtle makeup, the kind of outfit worn by women who don't have to work. The room inside—her office—had just enough space for the two of us to sit at a round table draped in purple cloth.

"Would you like a psychic reading?" Maeve asked. "Or more of a medium experience?"

"I don't know," I said. "Maybe a little of both?"

What I wanted was reassurance. I was prepared—eager, willing—to suspend my disbelief in exchange for a heavy dose of optimism. What that would look like, I couldn't say.

"Well, have you lost anyone important to you?" she asked.

"I lost my husband."

"Then we should do a medium experience," she said.

I nodded and tried to imagine this slight woman channeling Miles. Maeve closed her eyes and I envisioned her placing a long-distance call.

Dear God, I thought despite myself, *let her get through to him.*

She opened her eyes and smiled.

"He had a great energy," she said. "Charming, like a boy."

A pad of paper and a pen sat on the table in front of me and I real-ized they were for taking notes. I wrote down what she said.

"He liked to have fun, to go on adventures, to try new things."

I scribbled this on the lavender notepaper.

"He didn't like to be dressed up. He liked to dress casually."

I nodded, wrote *dressed casually.*

"I sense that he died suddenly," she said. "That this was an unex-pected death and there was a vehicle involved."

I bit my bottom lip and ground the nib of the pen into the page.

"I see that he was thrown and he died from those injuries."

I thought of Miles's death certificate. MULTIPLE BLUNT FORCE TRAUMA. I looked at the clock on the table and saw that half my time had passed.

"I see the two of you walking in the woods," Maeve said. "Did you ever do that?"

I thought of the first time Miles had driven to Tallahassee to visit me, of our feet pushing through the dry leaves, Miles holding a branch so I could pass.

"And when you walked in the woods together, did you sometimes feel like you could read his thoughts? Like the two of you were having a conversation without talking?"

Miles behind me on the trail, his boots crunching on the gravel. I could feel him.

"What he wants me to tell you—"

She opened her eyes and looked at the timer set on the table. We were almost done, my session headed to a close. She shut her eyes again and drew her brows together, the way a person will when they are listening intently.

"He wants you to know that it's like those walks in the woods. He's always beside you, even if you can't see him. You can talk together the way you once did. He'll hear you. He's right there."

That night I lay on an abandoned dock that stretched into the back bay while the dome of the sky reflected in the water at my feet. It was all one: sky, sea, stars. No end and no beginning. No horizon, no dividing line. No before or after. Only the spiraling heavens and the black tides and the narrow dock like a smudging finger in the dark. Thin clouds traveled across the night sky and the brightest stars peeked through the covering veil. Mullet jumped, and the slapping of their reentry sounded

over the still water. The earth spun slowly, slowly, and I moved with it.
I was not afraid.

In the fall of 2005, when Miles was stationed at Fort Hood, we took a
trip in the rolling hill country west of the base. On an overcast morning
we drove to a lake where the wind formed whitecaps on the gray water,
and I shivered as we looked out from the banks. We shelved our plans
to go kayaking and drove instead to nearby caverns. Texas, like Florida,
was once covered with a warm shallow sea. We were the only visitors
on the tour and the air was damp and cool in that underworld. Sound
vibrated back and away, washing over us like a memory of the tides.
The guide lit each room in front of us and extinguished the bulbs over
the path we had just walked. At the end of the tour she said she would
shut down all the lights, to let us see the cave in its natural state. Miles
and I looked at each other uneasily. I raised an eyebrow. He nodded his
head. The guide flipped a switch and the metallic clicking ricocheted
off the walls. The cavern disappeared in a blackness without end. I lost
Miles then, but I breathed in the dampness of the cave and found him
there in each particle of subterranean air.

"Miles?" I said.

His voice in the dark was a whisper, an echo.

"I'm here," he said.

Acknowledgments

To my brilliant editor, Sarah Knight, who brought this book into being. When I describe you to other writers they always say, "She sounds like the perfect editor." To which I respond: "She is";

To my beautiful agent, Anna Stein, who held my hand when I needed it most. Thank you for your unwavering support and encouragement;

To Sam Freedman, who believed in this book—and me—before I knew how; and to Kelly McMasters, whose kind hands shaped this story in its early stages;

To the team at S&S—Molly Lindley, Jessica Zimmerman, Andrea DeWerd, and everyone who supported the book;

To the residencies where this book was written—the Atlantic Center for the Arts and the Virginia Center for the Creative Arts—and to La Muse, where this book was begun and where it was finished. A magical place;

To my first readers and the women of the Writing Corps;

To Dr. Richard Paritzky, who led me from the dark. "If you want to try grieving on days other than Tuesday," he said, "give me a call";

To the widows who bravely shared their stories with me—Jennie Allgaier, Debi Coffelt, Casey Rodgers, and Shellie Smith. You were with me on every page;

To Teresa Priestner, who tirelessly answered questions about the military, sat for multiple interviews, and proofread sections of this book. My sister widow and friend, thank you;

To the Hendersons for their kindness and generosity, always;

And to G., who when I said, "You saved me," answered, "You saved yourself."

About the Author

Artis Henderson is an award-winning journalist and essayist whose work has appeared in the *New York Times, Reader's Digest, Florida Weekly,* and the online literary journal *Common Ties.* She has an undergraduate degree from the University of Pennsylvania and a graduate degree from Columbia University's School of Journalism. She lives in New York.

SOLDIER

AIR RAID SEARCH AND RESCUE

DOGS

READ ALL THE

SOLDIER DOGS

BOOKS!

SOLDIER
AIR RAID SEARCH AND RESCUE
DOGS

MARCUS SUTTER

ILLUSTRATIONS BY PAT KINSELLA

HARPER FESTIVAL

An Imprint of HarperCollinsPublishers

HarperFestival is an imprint of HarperCollins Publishers.

Soldier Dogs #1: Air Raid Search and Rescue
Copyright © 2018 by HarperCollins Publishers

www.harpercollinschildrens.com
Library of Congress Control Number: 2018934065
ISBN 978-0-06-286866-4 (trade bdg.) — ISBN 978-0-06-284403-3 (pbk.)
Typography by Celeste Knudsen
18 19 20 21 22 PC/LSCH 10 9 8 7 6 5 4 3 2 1
❖
First Edition

To Joel Ross
And to all the brave people and dogs
who did their part during WWII

CHAPTER 1

JUNE 1, 1942
2:33 A.M.
CANTERBURY, ENGLAND

Twelve-year-old Matt Dawson hunched in the darkness as bombs fell outside the half-collapsed movie theater. He hugged his knees in the cramped space beneath a fallen balcony. His breath came loud and panicked. He was trapped.

He could hear his ten-year-old foster sister, Rachel, trying to stifle her crying nearby, but he couldn't see her. Rubble surrounded them both. There was no way out. Sweat pricked Matt's skin, and the air was clogged with smoke and dust.

He heard the shriek of air-raid sirens and the

groan of a wall collapsing. How long before the rubble fell on him and his sister?

He wanted to give up, but he needed to be brave for Rachel, just like his brother, Eric, used to be brave for him. He didn't feel brave, though. All he felt was scared. Still, he stretched his arm through the rubble until his fingertips barely touched Rachel's.

"It's going to be okay," he told her, but he didn't really believe it.

Matt was American. His parents had brought him to England so his father could help with the war effort. Then the entire family had moved to Canterbury to escape the air raids in London. But the raids had changed targets, and now he and Rachel were trapped inside a ruined movie theater and the bombs were still falling.

Nobody could find them. Nobody could save them.

"Do you think the raid is over?" Rachel whispered into the darkness.

"Maybe. Or maybe there are more waves coming."

"There can't be! When will it stop? When will— Oh!"

"What?"

"I think I heard people!" Rachel took a breath. "Help! Help!"

"We're in the movie theater!" Matt yelled, even though he didn't hear anyone. "We're trapped!"

He heard a shout from the street, muffled by the rubble. A bunch of voices that sounded like firemen, desperately battling a blaze. Firemen like his brother, Eric.

"Help!" Matt yelled. "We're trapped!"

"There's nobody in the movie theater," a man's voice said.

"Are you sure?" another voice asked.

"In here!" Matt called. "Hello?"

"We're trapped!" Rachel shouted, in her accented voice. "Help!"

The men couldn't hear them through the rubble. Not with the sirens screaming and the fires roaring.

"It's all clear," the first man said. "Move out."

"No!" Matt shouted. "WE'RE IN HERE!"

The voices faded away . . . then Matt heard a distant barking.

"Chief!" Matt shouted. "Chief!"

Chief's barking grew more urgent.

"Chief!" Rachel yelled.

"What is that mutt doing?" the first man said. "We've got a situation around the corner. Get a wiggle on!"

"Drag him along," the second man said, when the barks became sharper. "There's nobody in the theater. The mangy fleabag just wants to watch a movie . . ."

Matt and Rachel screamed and shouted, but the voices grew fainter and fainter.

Until they disappeared—even Chief's.

And Matt and Rachel were alone. Again.

CHAPTER 2

"**C**lean the table," Matt's mother told him after dinner.

Matt paused in the door to the hallway. "It's Rachel's turn."

"Rachel's doing her homework," his mother said.

"I'm walking the dog!" Matt trotted toward the side door, yelling over his shoulder. "I'll do it when I get back!"

"Don't go too far," his mother called after him. She'd been on edge for a month, ever since the Germans threatened to bomb historical sites in England. They *lived* in a historical site: the ancient city of Canterbury.

Before Matt reached the door, Chief loped beside him from the other room. Matt wasn't surprised. Chief always showed up when you needed him. Matt's older brother, Eric, used to always be there too. But once the United States entered World War II, Eric had joined the Marines and shipped out. He'd left Matt to look after Chief: a strong, smart, loyal German shepherd–collie mix.

Matt grabbed the leash from the rack. "C'mon, boy!"

Running outside, he heard his mother saying something about the dishes. He felt bad for taking off, but he'd promised Eric that he'd take care of Chief. Also, he hated cleaning the table.

Especially when it was Rachel's turn.

Matt's mother had been a schoolteacher in Minneapolis before they'd come to England. After the schools closed in Canterbury, she'd started teaching Matt and Rachel herself. Which was okay, except Rachel got extra classes in English, which meant Matt got extra chores.

Also, Matt missed spending time alone.

Well, what he *really* missed was spending time with Eric. Back in the States, his brother had played football and studied engineering, just like their dad. He'd worked as a fireman in the US, and after they'd come to England, he'd volunteered as one.

But despite being busy, Eric always found time to toss a ball around with Matt, to teach him Morse code and take him to a movie or for an ice-cream cone.

Then he'd joined the Marines. He hadn't even waited to be drafted! He'd just gone to the US Embassy in London and enlisted.

He left the family—left Matt—months before anyone told him he had to. And the last thing he'd said to Matt was, "Take care of Chief."

"What about everyone else?" Matt had asked.

"If you take care of Chief," Eric had said with a wink, "*he'll* take care of everyone else."

Except, after shoving through the side door, Chief was more interested in peeing on a bush.

"C'mon, boy," Matt told him. "Before Mom finds us."

Matt and Chief trotted down the street and across the lawn of an ancient building that loomed high overhead. Matt loved the old stone structures around Canterbury—especially the still-standing sections of the city walls. With round towers and heavy stones, they reminded him of castle fortifications.

Which, according to his brother, they actually were. The Romans had built forts here in Canterbury almost two thousand years earlier. Matt liked to imagine Roman soldiers with shields and spears patrolling the wall and charging into battle.

Matt picked up a stick and threw it across the lawn. "Fetch!"

Chief charged away and returned holding the stick between his white teeth. He gave Matt a playful, teasing look, like he wasn't going to give him the stick.

"You've got to drop it if you want me to throw it again," Matt told him.

Chief shook the stick once, then dropped it at Matt's feet.

They played fetch until Chief lost interest and relieved himself again on a stone wall.

"Have some respect for history!" Matt told him.

Chief watched Matt with his dark, clever eyes. He was a big dog with a glossy coat, white teeth, and a pink tongue that lolled from his mouth when he panted. He sometimes scared people who didn't know him, but he also liked lying on his back and having his tummy rubbed.

And most mornings he'd steal Matt's pillow, drag it onto the floor, and curl up tight, trying to fit his whole body on it. He always hung over the edges, but he never stopped trying.

Matt reached down and scratched behind one of his pointy ears. "Another boring night. I wonder what Eric's doing right now."

Chief cocked his head, like he recognized the word "Eric."

"You miss him, boy? I miss him too."

Chief whined faintly.

"Don't worry," Matt said. "Eric's okay. He's probably off fighting the Japanese right now."

Chief nuzzled his hand and looked toward the house.

"Fine," Matt said. "I'll clean the table. But

don't pretend you're so helpful. I know you just want to lick the plates."

He started toward the house, and a shape drifted from the shadow of the wall. Chief gave a warning bark, and Matt's heart squeezed in fear. All of his parents' worries washed over him: about staying in England, about raising kids in Canterbury with the Nazis rampaging across Europe.

Chief lunged toward the shadowy figure, never hesitating to protect Matt—

And Rachel's giggles sounded through the night as Chief licked her face.

"Down, Chief!" she said, in her accented English. "You silly bear!"

"What're you doing here?" Matt demanded. "You're supposed be finishing your homework."

Rachel ducked her head, and her curly dark hair fell around her pale face.

"Would you stop following me around?" Matt said.

"Your mother is wanting you," Rachel said.

"I know! That's where I'm going. C'mon, Chief."

Chief gave Matt a look and stayed with

Rachel, brushing his muscular side against her skinny knees.

Rachel twined her fingers in his thick fur.

Matt grumbled. Chief was Eric's dog. Why did he spend so much time trying to cheer *Rachel* up? She needed her own dog. Or even a cat!

Anything so she'd stop tagging along with *him*.

Back inside the house, Matt cleared the table, then flopped onto the couch in the living room. His father wasn't home yet. That wasn't unusual. His father often worked late into the night, busy on some hush-hush engineering project with his colleagues in the British military.

When Matt's family first came to England, they'd lived in London, which was the biggest city Matt had ever seen. They'd left after the first wave of air raids, when the government started evacuating kids to the countryside—including to Canterbury.

So they'd moved here, into a little house between the cathedral and the city center.

Except six months after *that*, the government had evacuated the same kids out of Canterbury and shut down all the schools. They were mostly sent to the north of England. Matt's family had stayed that time. His dad couldn't move that far from work, and his mom refused to leave again.

"I'm not letting the Nazis chase me out of another house," she announced.

Matt guessed that she'd had another reason for wanting to stay. He figured she wanted to let Rachel stay in one place for a while, instead of always moving to new towns. Maybe that would help with Rachel's nightmares.

Rachel had come to England a few years earlier, through the Kindertransport program, which rescued Jewish kids from Nazi-occupied countries. The program helped thousands of children flee to England from Eastern Europe before the Germans killed them—but it was only for kids. The immigration laws kept their parents and grown-up brothers and sisters from joining them.

A few months ago, Matt's parents had brought Rachel to live with them. She was quiet and shy. Matt didn't mind her, really, except she was always *there*. Like a shadow. She never left him alone.

Mostly, though, he just missed Eric. And he

had a secret. One that he'd never told anyone except Chief.

He was mad at Eric for enlisting so early. He was mad at his parents, too, for letting him go. He never said anything, because he didn't want to seem selfish or unpatriotic, but every night he went to bed angry.

"I can't believe they let Eric enlist," he grumbled to Chief as he buttoned his pajamas that night.

Chief's ears pricked, and he sniffed toward Matt's pillow.

Matt flopped onto his bed. "He could've waited."

Chief snurfled at the sight of Matt's head on the beloved pillow. Abandoning his goal of stealing it, he turned in circles, then lay beside the bed.

Matt yawned and said, "See you in June," because it was the last day of May, and it would be June 1st in the morning.

He tossed and turned for a while before falling asleep. And he woke shortly after midnight, when the air-raid sirens shattered his dreams.

CHAPTER 3

Matt burst into the hallway in his pajamas, heart pounding. Chief was already in Rachel's room, barking to wake her.

"Shoes and coats!" Matt's mother called. "Front door!"

Matt knew exactly what she meant, because they'd prepared for an air raid. He galloped down the stairs. He flung open the closet and grabbed his coat, Rachel's, and his mom's. "Where's Dad?" he bellowed.

"He's still at the office!" his mom called back.

Dad worked with a bunch of military types, so they had a great air-raid shelter at his office—but his absence still made Matt a little nervous.

He shook his head. Eric wouldn't get nervous. Eric would spring into action.

He shoved into his shirt and slipped on his boots.

"Are they here?" Rachel ran down the stairs in her nightgown, her thick braid swinging halfway down her back. "We have to hide!"

"Nobody's here," Matt said, and helped her into her coat. "It's just an air-raid siren."

Rachel's face was pale. She looked so scared that Matt grabbed her hand. Not because he liked holding hands, of course! But Eric had once held his hand during an air-raid drill, and it had worked. He'd felt safe.

"Don't worry," he told Rachel. "The shelter's right nearby. There's plenty of time."

She took a shaky breath and squeezed his hand. Then Chief barked, and his mother, only halfway inside her coat, threw open the door. "Children, run to the cathedral! I'll be along in a flash."

"We're supposed to stick together!" Matt said.

"You said if there's an air raid we need to stick together."

"I know, sweetie—but Mrs. Lloyd might need help."

Mrs. Lloyd lived next door, and she was pregnant. She was *very* pregnant.

"You remember where to go?" his mom asked.

"Sure," Matt said. "The shelter under the cathedral."

"Take care of Rachel."

"I *know*," he said. "C'mon, Chief!"

When he led Rachel outside, the air was cool on his cheeks. The rising-and-falling cry of the sirens sounded louder.

Chief ran ahead, then looked over his shoulder and barked, urging Matt to follow.

"We're coming!" Matt said.

A door slammed down the street. It sounded like a gunshot, and Rachel jerked to a halt and gasped something in Polish or Yiddish.

"C'mon!" Matt snapped, but when he looked at Rachel, he saw terror in her eyes. "Oh! Um . . ."

The siren shrilled, and Rachel stared down the street, her hand trembling in Matt's.

Matt asked himself what Eric would do. He'd probably give Matt a job. That would keep Matt busy, so he'd forget about being scared.

"Uh, tell Chief we're coming, Rachel. He'll believe you."

After a moment, she nodded. "We're coming, Chief!"

Chief lowered his chest to the ground and wagged his tail, like he wanted them to chase him.

Matt and Rachel followed him into the darkness. There were no lights from the buildings. The entire town—the entire *country*—was dark at night, every single night, so the German bombers couldn't find targets. There were no streetlights. Everyone draped thick "blackout" curtains over their windows. Even the ambulances had hooded headlights, to keep them invisible from above.

The buildings were spooky in the pitch-black, but the darkness meant they were still safe. Matt had read that German planes dropped flares to light up their targets so the next waves of bombers could attack them, using incendiary firebombs that burst into superhot flames and five-hundred-pound high-explosive bombs that detonated in terrible blasts.

"Stay calm!" an air-raid warden called. "If you don't have a shelter, head for the cathedral basement." Two dark figures rushed past nearby, while down the block people called to each other, rushing into the cool summer night and heading for shelter. The siren continued to wail.

Matt squeezed Rachel's hand and followed Chief to the end of the street—and that's when he heard them.

Engines.

Airplanes.

A wave of German bombers.

Matt's stomach ached, and his teeth chattered. He tightened his grip on Rachel's hand and followed Chief faster down the street. When a soft whistle sounded from the darkness, Chief gave a warning bark, raced ahead, then dashed back.

There were already bombs in the air! They were tumbling through the sky, coming closer every second.

What if they hit nearby?

What if they exploded on top of Matt and Rachel?

With a whuffle, Chief veered into a shortcut along a path behind a brick building. The whistling grew louder as Matt followed onto the next street, ran around the corner—

And froze.

The Canterbury Cathedral loomed atop the hill in front of him, glowing with a brilliant yellow-and-orange light. Stone towers rose into the sky, and weird shadows danced across the ornate walls. It was grand—like a fairy-tale cathedral.

Except at nighttime, in the middle of a war, Matt shouldn't have been able to see any details. The colorful glow was beautiful . . . and dangerous.

The shelter was underneath the cathedral, and the Germans were trying to destroy it!

CHAPTER 4

Chief felt the girl's little fingers curling into the fur on his neck. He wouldn't allow just any-one to grab his throat like that, but Rachel was only a pup.

Plus, she was scared.

Even more scared than usual. Chief could smell it.

Chief always took care of his pack. If that meant fighting or hunting, he'd fight or hunt. If it meant nuzzling a scared pup, he'd do that too.

The girl-pup startled at sudden sounds. She whimpered in her sleep. She was quiet and scared, but she was strong too. Chief smelled that in her.

The boy-pup was strong in a different way. Chief twitched his coat thoughtfully. Matt was not quiet, though: he reminded Chief of himself as a pup.

The mother and father were just old. Chief always tried to let them pretend they were in charge, but other than that, they could take care of themselves.

Chief missed the other member of his pack. The older boy had raised Chief. Eric. He was partly a father to Chief, partly a brother, and partly a pup.

The humans couldn't hear the loudest noises, they couldn't smell the strongest scents. They shivered in the wind and barely had any teeth at all.

They were so useless sometimes!

They needed a dog to look after them. That was okay, though. A pack always looked after each other. That's what made a pack a pack.

The rumbling of the iron birds in the night sky sounded louder, and the whistling of the fire-rocks made Chief growl deep in his throat. He prowled behind the boy-pup and girl-pup, urging them to go faster—but the girl-pup stopped at the sight of the flame-lit building.

She yipped in fear. The boy-pup smelled almost as scared, but he took a deep breath and said, "We need to head inside, Rachel. Like Mom said."

"We stick together?" the girl-pup asked.

"I couldn't get rid of you if I tried!" Matt said, and smiled at her.

She didn't smile back.

She stood frozen in place until Chief nudged her. Then she let Matt take her toward the line of older humans just . . . standing outside the big building. Waiting to get into the underground den that Chief smelled. But they were hardly moving!

He barked at Matt, telling him to push past the old people and get inside.

"Quiet, Chief," Matt said. "We're in the queue. You can't rush the English; they love waiting in line. We'll get there."

Two older females turned and beckoned to the kids. Rachel nervously stroked Chief's back as they joined the crowd. He smelled fear coming off her in waves and pressed closer.

Matt must've smelled her fear, too, because he spoke in a soothing purr. "I remember the first time Eric took me to the cathedral. I thought it'd be a musty old church. I asked if we couldn't just throw stones into the river instead."

"S-silly boy," Rachel said. "Throwing rocks at water."

Matt herded Rachel through the crowd toward the entrance. "Eric said the cathedral would really knock my socks off. And it did. My socks were completely knocked. I mean, all the stained glass and nooks and crannies and statues." He gestured toward the big stone building. "But do you know what's inside there now?"

Rachel shook her head. "The air-raid shelter?"

"Well, that's underground. But inside the normal sanctuary, I mean? The floor is covered in dirt. Huge mounds of dirt, like the biggest sandbox in the world. Heaped inside this ancient cathedral. I laughed when Mom showed me."

"Why all the dirt?" Rachel asked, her fear-smell fading.

Chief nudged Matt with his snout. He'd done well, soothing Rachel.

"That's what I asked!" Matt said, scratching behind Chief's ear. "Mom says it's to protect the air-raid shelter."

Rachel wrinkled her nose. "How does dirt protect the shelter?"

"Because the shelter is underground, beneath the cathedral floor. Which is now covered in truckloads of dirt, like ten thousand sandbags."

"So a bomb would have to blast through all that dirt before it reached the shelter?"

"Exactly!" Matt smiled. "And the shelter's really strong too. It's in an ancient crypt! Isn't that *aces*?"

"What is a crypt?"

Matt paused. "Oh, just like a really safe cellar. But the dirt on the floor overhead will protect it from bombs and stuff."

The roar of the iron birds rumbled from above. Too loud. Too close! Chief barked again and lunged forward, opening a path to lead Matt and Rachel through the crowd.

A shriller whistle sounded as a fire-rock plunged from the sky. Chief needed to get the kids inside. He needed to keep them safe!

CHAPTER 5

"**S**orry!" Matt told the people in the crowd as he followed a lunging Chief toward the crypt. "Sorry!"

The startled British faces around him looked angry at first—then they realized that Matt and Rachel were kids and hustled them toward the door.

"Shake a leg, Rachel!" Matt said.

She peered at him. "Shake my leg?"

"It means *hurry*!" he explained, pulling her forward.

The sound of the German airplanes faded when Matt and Rachel rushed inside the stone doorway. The adults pointed to a stairwell leading underground toward the crypt. Which wasn't actually just a deep cellar, like he'd told Rachel. It was more of an indoor cemetery. In the old days, they'd buried people there.

When Matt first heard about the crypt, he'd imagined cobwebs, skulls, and creepy old tombs. It wasn't like that at all. Instead, it was a huge rectangular room with rows of stubby stone columns. Lanterns cast a yellow glow on the dozens of people in the room. More arrived every minute, some carrying blankets and pillows and thermoses. One old man had even brought a sandwich.

At Matt's knee, Chief gazed at the sandwich and wagged his tail hopefully.

The old man didn't seem to mind, but Matt noticed other people giving Chief dirty looks. There hadn't been enough food for the *people* of Britain during the war years, much less for dogs. The government only allowed every family a couple of ounces of sugar and butter and cheese per week, and a few pounds of meat.

In fact, Matt had heard that dogs weren't really allowed in air-raid shelters. Nobody said anything to him, but he felt his cheeks warm. He wasn't about to leave Chief outside in the middle of a bombing.

"C'mon, Chief," Matt muttered.

He slunk toward a dark corner of the crypt where nobody would notice them. Rachel followed, of course.

"Where is your mother?" she asked, tugging nervously at her braid.

"She'll be here," Matt said, and leaned against a column to watch the entrance.

"It is not good to be away from the parents," Rachel said.

Matt almost made a dumb joke about not having to wash the dishes. But Rachel had left her parents behind when she'd come to England. Her parents and her older sisters. Her uncles and aunts and cousins—her home, her friends, her entire life.

She still had nightmares about saying good-bye. About leaving everyone she loved behind in

Nazi-controlled Europe. She'd probably give any-thing to hear her mother telling her to clean the table.

So Matt kept his mouth shut. And he felt sud-denly nervous, like Rachel's fear was catching.

Where was his own mother? She said she'd be right behind them, but she was nowhere in sight. They were supposed to stay together if the sirens sounded—that was their plan—and they'd already lost each other!

Matt chewed on his lower lip and stared at the door.

He tried to stay brave. He was twelve years old, after all, not some little kid. He'd traveled all the way from Minnesota, USA, across the ocean to England.

Plus, Eric always said Matt was tough—and he wasn't going to let Eric down.

Still, he kept searching the room, hoping that his mom was already in the crypt and that he'd missed her. Strange scrapes echoed, voices mur-mured, and lantern light flickered creepily.

When Chief nudged him with his furry head,

Matt felt a flash of hope. Maybe Chief had seen his mother! Matt rose onto his tiptoes and peered toward the door.

Someone was coming!

But when Matt caught a glimpse of the person through the crowd, he deflated. It wasn't his mother. Instead a bearded man in pajamas stepped into the shelter and shouted, "The bombers are getting closer!"

CHAPTER 6

A fearful hush fell across the shelter.

Matt's breath caught, and his fists clenched. What if a high-explosive bomb scored a direct hit on the cathedral? Would a bunch of extra dirt be enough to protect them?

But an instant later, the hush ended. Conversation returned. *Calm* returned, and an easy confidence spread through the room. One thing that Matt had noticed about the British, they weren't very good at panicking. *He* still felt a little panicky, though, trapped in a crypt during an air raid without his parents.

Chief nudged Matt again.

"What, boy?" Matt's worried gaze flicked downward. "You still can't have a sandwich."

Chief gave a short yip and looked intently at the door.

And to Matt's relief, his mother entered, helping Mrs. Lloyd into the shelter. Matt almost laughed in relief—and almost laughed again when he saw Mrs. Lloyd. She was wearing Matt's father's woolen hunting cap with ear flaps. His mom must've wanted to keep her head warm in the chilly June night.

"There she is!" he blurted, a little too happily. "Not that I was worried."

Rachel exhaled. "It is good she is here."

"Stay with Chief," he told Rachel, and trotted across the crypt.

He slipped between the columns to the small crowd around his mother. He squirmed through and found Mrs. Lloyd lying on one of the few bunks. Despite the cool crypt air, her face was glossy with sweat beneath his father's woolen hat.

A bunch of ladies stood around the bunk. One

of them was stringing up a clothesline to hang a curtain for privacy. Another chatted with a priest from the cathedral. Matt felt a spark of pride that his mother was the one holding Mrs. Lloyd's hand.

"Mom!" he said, squeezing forward.

"There you are, sweetie!" His mother shot him a distracted smile. "Find a place to settle in where you aren't in the way."

"Aren't you coming?" he asked. "We're supposed to stay together. That's the plan."

"I need to stay with Mrs. Lloyd right now."

Despite her pale face, Mrs. Lloyd smiled as she offered Matt the woolen hat. "I'm afraid I need to borrow your mother longer than I borrowed your father's hat."

"Um." Matt took the hat and looked past Mrs. Lloyd to his mother. "You told me a million times. 'If there's an air raid, stay together.' Now Dad's not even here, and you're—"

"Matt, please!" she said, a warning note in her voice. "Not now."

"Fine," he grumbled. It wasn't fair, but that

didn't surprise him. Nothing was fair when you were a kid.

"Thank you. Now you look after Rachel." Her gaze moved past Matt's shoulder. "And *you* look after Matt."

When he turned, he found Rachel at his elbow, chewing on the tip of her braid, with Chief standing beside her. Great. First his mother scolded him when *she* was the one ignoring the air-raid plan, then she didn't even say anything about Rachel wandering around.

One of the women gave Matt an armload of blankets and shooed him away.

He stalked toward the column in the corner. "I told you to stay there!" he told Rachel.

She didn't answer. She just tagged along like always.

"At least we have blankets," he said. "You can go back to sleep."

"I am not sleepy."

"Yeah?" he said. "Well, if I go to sleep, I'm sure you'll follow."

She tugged at her braid and fell silent again.

She looked small and young and miserable.

Matt felt bad for snapping at her, so he tried to change the subject. "Hey, you know what they call these raids?"

"Raids have a name?"

"Well, last year the Germans bombed London, right?"

"That was called 'the Blitz,'" Rachel said, though she pronounced it "bleetz."

"That's right. They dropped bombs on London every single day for three months. They destroyed a third of the city." Matt stopped at the column where they'd been earlier. "Well, the Brits started hitting back."

"Like Eric," she said. "Fighting the Japanese."

"Yeah, like Eric. So the Germans switched to these air raids in reprisal. In, um, payback. They call this the 'Baedeker Blitz.'"

Rachel wrinkled her nose. "What is a baydecker?"

"Baedeker. They're guidebooks, I guess. Like travel guides?"

"The Germans want to stop travel?"

"No, they want to break the Brits' spirits. They're targeting important buildings. Historical sites, things like that. The Nazis said they're going to bomb every city with a three-star rating in the Baedeker guides."

"And Canterbury has three stars?"

"We've got five," Matt told her, even though he wasn't sure if it was true. Still, he figured if they were getting bombed, they deserved as many stars as possible.

He spread the blankets beside the wall behind a column, in a quiet nook. He sat beside Rachel and patted the floor. "Down, Chief."

Instead of lying beside Matt, Chief nuzzled Rachel, then laid down beside *her*. Like he didn't even remember whose dog he was.

Matt scowled to himself and lifted the woolen hunting cap to his nose. It smelled of his father and of his *real* home, back in the States. Wood smoke and snowfall and pipe tobacco. With his father always working and Eric on a boat in the Pacific, Matt was trying to be the man of the family.

He didn't feel grown-up, though. He ju
tired and cranky and scared. All he wanted to
was curl up and cry. And the bombs hadn't evei
started falling around the shelter.

At least not yet.

CHAPTER 7

The girl-pup's breathing turned quieter. She wasn't asleep, but she was resting. Her skinny arm draped across Chief's shoulder. Meanwhile, the boy-pup watched his mother on the other side of the stone cave.

Chief saw Matt's sadness as clear as if the boy-pup had a tail to put between his legs. He was scared, and he wanted to be with his parents. But his father wasn't here, and his mother was helping a woman who would give birth to a human pup.

Chief knew that a newborn would come soon.

Not yet, though. He flared his nostrils and smelled sweat and soap in the stone cave. He smelled the scents of a hundred houses clinging to the clothing of the humans.

He smelled ash too. He heard the growl of the iron birds in the sky, dropping more fire-rocks on the city.

Voices echoed and crashed in the stone cave, but through the clamor, Chief heard a familiar patter of footsteps. He cocked his head to locate the sound.

There, at the entrance!

The father was entering the stone cave.

Chief woofed softly at Matt, and twisted his ears to show where he was listening.

"Dad!" Matt yipped, and scrambled to his feet.

Matt ran across the stone cave toward the father. Chief felt the boy-pup's gladness . . . then noticed how the father was standing. His shoulders were slumped, his head was down. He looked like he was suffering, even though Chief didn't smell any blood.

Chief's ears flattened. Something was wrong with the father.

The girl-pup noticed too. She whined and followed the boy toward the old ones. Her head-tail bobbed between her shoulders.

Chief slunk along behind her and Matt. Before they reached the old ones, the father hugged the mother and started crying.

"They sent the telegram to me at work," the father said. "It's Eric."

Chief's ears pricked at the sound "Eric" and at the grief in the father's voice. Something was *very* wrong.

"Oh no," the mother whimpered. "No, no."

The humans whimpered softly to each other. The mother stank of misery, of hopelessness.

"What?" Matt asked, stopping short. "What's wrong?"

His father made a noise like a wounded animal, and his mother knelt and took both her pups in her arms. She stroked their heads and talked quietly to them. Matt started shivering.

Chief whined and licked his hand.

Rachel smelled confused. She didn't understand what was wrong. She cried, though, feeling the mother's and father's fear and sorrow.

Chief heard the sound "Eric" again, and he made himself stay near the pups even though he wanted to pace, he wanted to prowl, he wanted to *hunt*. Something was wrong with the pack: he needed to find the threat and stop it.

But this wasn't the kind of threat you could sink your teeth into. This was worse. This was grief and loss. So Chief wedged himself between Rachel and Matt, so they could lean on him if they needed to.

Matt didn't lean. Instead, he wiped tears from his face and straightened up. His long-paws tightened into fists, and his fear turned into a blaze of anger.

"It's your fault!" he shouted at his parents. "You could've stopped him. You didn't have to let him go. It's *your* fault Eric is gone!"

The boy howled and snarled and ran away.

Chief's muscles bunched with urgency. He wanted to stay with the grieving pack—with Rachel and the old ones. But he *needed* to follow Matt. He needed to protect him!

CHAPTER 8

12:45 A.M.

Matt staggered across the crypt. Faces turned toward him. Arms reached for him. The clamor of hundreds of people pounded in his head.

Columns rose like stone guards. His eyes blurred with tears.

MISSING IN ACTION.

That's what the telegram had said.

THE SECRETARY OF WAR DESIRES

ME TO EXPRESS HIS DEEP REGRET
THAT YOUR SON, MARINE PRIVATE
ERIC DAWSON, HAS BEEN REPORTED
MISSING IN ACTION • • •

Eric was MIA. Missing in action.

Gone.

Vanished.

Matt stumbled and almost fell. He caught himself on the wall and just stood there, his forehead against the cool stone.

Eric was okay. He had to be. They'd find him again.

He was just missing. Not KIA. Not killed in action.

Missing.

Tears leaked out of Matt's eyes. He heard the *click-clack* of Chief's nails on the floor behind him and felt Chief's snout nuzzling his hand.

He couldn't even stand to look at Chief, not now. Chief didn't know what was happening. He didn't know the world was at war. He didn't know they were hiding from bombs. He didn't know Eric was gone.

The room spun around Matt. He couldn't take it. He couldn't just stand around in a crypt while Eric was missing somewhere in the Pacific, halfway around the world.

He needed to be alone.

Matt heard his father call his name, and he lurched toward an alcove in the shadows, away from the hustle and bustle of the main room. The alcove was dark and cool, but Matt's anger suddenly burned as bright and hot as an incendiary bomb.

"He didn't have to go!" Matt muttered, his voice echoing against the stone. "Not so soon. Why did he go? Why did they *let* him?"

If only Eric hadn't enlisted, he'd still be safe. They'd still be together. And—and even if he'd enlisted later, at least he wouldn't be MIA now.

Instead, he'd left Mom and Dad behind.

He'd left *Matt* behind.

Eyes stinging with tears, Matt stumbled into a flight of stairs. He kept running, like he was trying to escape the news, and found himself in a narrow stone hallway. Through a window, he saw the yellow-and-orange light of the Germans' glowing flares reflecting against the branches of a tree.

Then he caught sight of pale, stern faces staring down at him.

Cold, unforgiving faces. His heart clenched, and he jerked backward—then realized that the faces were just cathedral statues.

He took a slow breath . . . and heard a rumbling buzz. As he cocked his head, the noise turned into a mechanical growl—it was the German bombers, louder than before!

And closer than ever. They were directly overhead!

Matt panicked. He spun back toward the air-raid shelter, but when he squeezed through the door, the smell of dirt surrounded him. He'd run in the wrong direction!

He darted into the closest stairway and ran up a flight of stone stairs to a wide balcony.

He wasn't trying to reach the shelter anymore. He wasn't trying to escape the danger. He was trying to escape from that moment when his father had showed him the telegram.

Matt skidded to a halt in a chapel with rows

of stained-glass windows. He slumped against the wall, then slid down to the floor and pulled his knees to his chest.

Eric was still alive. Matt knew he was. He was probably washed ashore on a deserted Pacific island, building an SOS signal on the beach with rocks or logs. One day soon Matt would see him again, and they'd play ball and eat ice cream.

Matt squeezed his eyes shut. When he'd been six or seven years old, Eric had taken him to buy ice-cream cones on a hot summer day. The top scoop of Matt's cone fell off and smeared down his shirt. He'd cried. So Eric had given Matt his shirt, which was so big it fell to Matt's calves like a baggy dress. He hadn't cared that he'd looked silly. He'd been so proud to wear Eric's shirt he hadn't even minded dropping his ice cream.

Opening his eyes, Matt took a shaky breath. He needed to be strong. Eric would be fine. And Eric made Matt promise to take care of Chief, so that's exactly what he'd do.

Which meant he needed to get back to the shelter.

He rose unsteadily—and the *click-clack* of

claws on the stone floor almost made him laugh. He didn't need to find Chief. Chief had found him!

"Chief!" he called. "I'm in here!"

The *click-clack* came faster as Chief trotted closer. He barked twice, sharp warning barks, and started to run.

Matt felt a jolt of panic at the warning barks. Something was wrong! He started toward Chief and—

A bomb exploded outside.

The stained-glass windows shattered, and the surge of air felt like a slap on Matt's face. The sound deafened him. His fear made his knees buckle, and the blast slammed him to the ground.

Billows of dust blinded Matt, and an ache pounded in his head. He couldn't hear Chief anymore; he couldn't hear his own gasps and whimpers. He couldn't hear anything at all.

CHAPTER 9

When Matt ran into the corner of the stone cave, Chief hesitated beside the girl-pup and the old ones.

At least until he realized that the boy-pup *wasn't* in the corner. He'd left the cave through a different tunnel.

He was gone.

Chief broke free of the pack and dashed across the cave. He smelled a whiff of perfume, the tang of tears. He heard a wheezing breath, the crinkle of paper, the shuffle of a shoe against the floor.

He caught Matt's trail.

It led into a stairway. Chief followed, loping higher until he lost the scent in the overwhelming smell of freshly dug earth.

Chief put his nose to the ground. He ran in one direction, then the other.

There! He found the trail again and heard the iron birds flying closer in the sky. He heard the whistle of fire-rocks falling.

He ran toward Matt and scrambled around a corner, slipping on the smooth stone. He heard the boy-pup's breathing and smelled the salty damp of his sadness.

Matt yelled the sound that meant he needed help: "Chief!"

Chief ran closer, trying to reach Matt before the fire-rock hit the ground. He knew he couldn't win the race, but that didn't matter. The pup needed him. Muscles straining, he sped forward . . .

The fire-rock boomed.

The blast lifted Chief like a pair of massive jaws grabbing the scruff of his neck. It shook him and tossed him across the room. Glass fell and

shattered across the floor with tiny sharp teeth.

Chief crashed into a wooden bench and slumped limply.

His vision turned black—but he woke suddenly moments later. Maybe moments. He couldn't tell. The glass wasn't falling anymore. The iron bird was flying away, getting quieter.

And Matt was gone.

Still disoriented by the blast, Chief inhaled deeply. He needed to find the boy-pup, but a thousand new scents swirled in the air: scorched cloth and charred leaves and melting rubber.

Which way had the boy-pup run?

Either outside into the night, or higher in the old building. Surely even a human wasn't foolish enough to run higher, toward the iron birds!

Except Chief knew that humans didn't have any sense. That's why they needed dogs to look after them.

So he prowled carefully closer, sniffing deeply, alert for the slightest hint of Matt.

And a familiar smell tugged at him!

He turned suddenly and ran through the wreckage toward the door leading to the lawn.

Just there, in the doorway, he found the woolen hat that smelled of the father, of the older boy, of the pregnant woman—and of Matt. He must've come this way.

When Chief ran outside, the trail ended in the stink of the burning city: charred cloth and blistered paint. He growled in frustration, his ears pricking for the sound of Matt's voice, for his footsteps. Too many noises!

Maybe the boy-pup had run back to the den. The house. Chief would look for him there. And if he didn't find him?

He'd keep looking. When a pack member was in trouble, you never gave up.

CHAPTER 10

Matt's hearing returned with a low, aching hum. He scrambled to his feet, trembling. His ears hurt and his head pounded and—and where was Chief?

He must have been caught in the blast!

Still shaking, Matt took a breath and called, "Chief?"

He peered through the smoke and dust. He didn't see Chief anywhere. He whistled and called again but still didn't hear anything.

Then he saw the stairway leading upward. *Oh no.*

"Here, boy!" he called.

The stupid dog must've gotten spooked by the explosion and bolted upstairs.

Matt blinked at the stairway. He knew he should run for the shelter, but he wasn't about to lose Chief. He'd promised to look after Eric's dog, and that's exactly what he'd do.

So he took a deep breath and started toward the stairway.

Halfway there, he realized that he'd lost his father's woolen hat in the explosion. No time to look for it now, though. It didn't matter.

He started up the stairs. The stone was uneven, worn from centuries of use—and slippery. Matt almost fell twice before he reached the first door. He almost grabbed the knob, but realized that didn't make sense.

Chief was a smart dog, but not even he could operate a doorknob!

Matt climbed higher. Yellow light shone on the stone a minute before he came to an open door. The air smelled like a bonfire, and he heard men shouting roughly.

Matt peered through the door and found himself looking onto one of the cathedral's roofs. There must've been dozens of them, tucked between all the towers and spires. This one was only slightly angled, with high walls rising along two sides.

A man was standing in the open, beside a small mound on the roof. For a terrible moment, Matt thought the mound was Chief lying there.

Except no, it wasn't a dog. It was a low heap of . . . something.

Matt frowned and looked closer. He couldn't tell what it was. And what was the man *doing*? He was skinny and sort of rat-faced, and he looked suspicious to Matt. Was he making trouble? Was he working with the Germans?

Then Matt spotted two other men on the roof! What kind of people stood around on a cathedral roof during an air raid?

A knot of worry tightened in Matt's chest— then the rat-faced man glanced toward the door where he was standing.

Matt froze, afraid of being spotted. He didn't move, he didn't breathe. He focused on the sound of the wind buffeting the cathedral spires.

The rat-faced man didn't see Matt in the shadows, though.

Matt exhaled shakily. He'd tell the people in the shelter when he got back. But Chief wasn't here, so he'd keep on searching. He started to turn away, and a hand grabbed his arm.

"Yeee!" he yelped, almost jumping out of his skin.

When he spun, he didn't see a shadowy figure or a rat-faced man. No, he saw *Rachel* standing in the doorway. Following him, like always!

"Would you get lost!" he snapped at her.

"Oi!" a man shouted from the roof. "What're you kids doing?"

Matt turned back and found Rat Face staring at him, holding a big net. Big enough to catch a kid.

"Don't move!" the man snarled at them.

"I, um, we're looking for—" Matt couldn't say

"my dog!" "Um, the shelter! Sorry, bye!"

Rat Face took a step toward them. He started to say something . . . then stopped at a loud *CLATTER*. Something hard had slammed into the roof and now skittered through the shadows.

"A bomb!" Rachel gasped.

She was right. The German planes were trying to bomb the cathedral, and they'd dropped an incendiary—a firebomb—only twenty feet away. But it hadn't exploded. Not yet. Matt knew that some incendiary bombs didn't burst into flames immediately. Instead, it took a few seconds for the chemicals inside to mix together and ignite after dropping.

Only a few seconds, though! Matt stared in horror, waiting for the bomb to explode.

Instead, it rolled to a halt ten feet away—and Rat Face sprang into action.

He ran *toward* the bomb and threw his net on it.

Except it wasn't a net. It was a big square of burlap. That's what the heap was made of: burlap sacks, for handling bombs!

Matt's knees trembled. One second passed. Two seconds! He knew that inside the firebomb, the chemicals must be mixing together. He knew the bomb was about burst into superhot flames.

Still, Rat Face didn't falter. He grabbed the bomb with the burlap.

He raced to the side of the roof.

He threw the bomb off the cathedral.

A moment later, the bomb hit the grass—and burst into flames.

The fire blazed brightly, scorching the lawn, but it didn't burn the building. That's what the men were doing on the roof! They were fire-watchers, catching bombs before they ignited and throwing them over the edge.

Matt gazed in amazement at the man—and another bomb fell.

It clattered and rolled . . . and stopped between the man and the pile of burlap.

He wouldn't have time to run for another cloth. The bomb would start the cathedral burning!

Without pausing to think, Matt raced to the heap of burlap. He grabbed the top sheet and

whipped around toward Rat Face. How long before the bomb exploded? The other one had only taken a few seconds. How much time did Matt have left?

CHAPTER 11

The man on the roof yelled at Matt. He probably swore too, but Matt didn't hear the words.

With his heart beating fast enough to burst from his chest, Matt raced across the roof.

He stretched toward the man. The man snatched the burlap from Matt, shoved him toward the door, and darted at the bomb.

Matt stumbled. He looked over his shoulder once before he reached the door and caught a glimpse of the man standing at the edge of the roof, heaving the bomb into the darkness.

Flames glowed behind the firewatcher, and Matt didn't know how he'd ever thought the man looked rat-faced. At that moment he looked exactly like a movie hero or a monument of bravery.

Then Rachel grabbed Matt's hand and tugged him into the cathedral stairwell.

"We need to get back to the shelter," Matt said.

"Vee can't," Rachel told him, her accent thicker from fear. "Not yet."

"Of course we can! We need to—"

"I saw Chief," she said, "running into the city."

"Oh no!" Matt thought for a second as they clattered down the stairs. "You go back to the shelter. I'll find him."

Rachel didn't say anything. She just looked at him.

"C'mon, Rachel. *Please.*" Matt couldn't look after her and Chief at the same time. "Please go back to Mom and Dad."

She still didn't say anything. She was going to

tag along like always, and he couldn't stop her. He wanted to yell at her, but he knew that wouldn't help.

"Fine!" he blurted, exasperated. "Come with me then. Just . . . be careful."

She nodded and continued down the stairs. Matt followed her to the ground floor of the cathedral and then outside. They headed along a walkway with arches open to the night.

"Wait a second," Matt said, and listened for planes.

He didn't want anyone to throw a bomb off the cathedral roof, straight onto their heads. He didn't hear anything, though. He'd read that bombers came in waves—first one squadron of bombers, then a pause, then another squadron.

Maybe this was the quiet period between two waves. He knew the raid wasn't over completely; the sirens hadn't sounded the "all clear" yet.

He and Rachel ran across the lawn, darted past a tree with a huge knobby trunk—then stopped short. Matt gasped, and Rachel blurted something in Yiddish when they saw the city spread out at the bottom of the hill.

Entire streets were engulfed in flames. Tiny figures were silhouetted against the flames. A few cars rolled through the rubble-strewn streets, barely visible in the light of the fires. A single fire truck stood in a crossroads.

Matt swallowed. "Chief's down there somewhere. We—someone's going to come looking for us soon, to take us back to the shelter. We have to find Chief first!"

"Then we find him."

"Which way was he running?"

She pointed. "There, I think."

"Let's go." Matt started away. "Stay close."

To his surprise, Rachel actually giggled.

He didn't understand for a second, then he laughed. He was always yelling at her for following him, and now he wanted her to stay close.

They ran downhill, calling for Chief.

The poor dog. He needed Matt. How could a dog survive an air raid? Chief must be so confused and afraid. He didn't understand what was happening. He didn't know how to take care of himself.

The street was empty at first. Flames glowed

over the rooftops. An engine sounded, and Rachel's grip tightened on Matt's hand.

He pulled her into a doorframe for protection, but the engine wasn't a plane. It was a car. A dark-green sedan with a big grille and a woman behind the wheel.

"Oh!" he said. "She's ATS."

Rachel tugged on her braid. "Eighty what?"

"ATS," he said more clearly. "The women's branch of the British army."

The car rumbled over a scattering of bricks in the road, thrown there after a bomb struck a nearby wall.

"They are ambulance," Rachel said.

"Nah," Matt told her. "Ambulances are bigger and—" He stopped when he saw another woman in the back seat, helping an injured man. "Oh! You're right."

"Little ambulance," Rachel said.

"Yeah. I guess they're evacuating the wounded in staff cars." He realized that Rachel wouldn't know what that meant. "Er, which are officers' cars. Those ladies are the drivers."

"The wounded?" Rachel said, her eyes

widening. She didn't care about the cars, she cared about the people!

"Don't worry," Matt told her as the car rolled around the corner. "I'm sure we won't run across any trouble."

"Okay, if you are sure." She grabbed his arm. "Do you hear?"

"Hear what? The sirens? The bombers? The—"

"Hush!" she said.

He thought she was being silly, but he pretended to listen for a second. And that's when he heard it: a faint cry sounding from behind a half-fallen brick wall.

A quiet plea for help.

CHAPTER 12

1:11 A.M.

Chief prowled through ash-filled, rubble-strewn streets. The boy-pup needed him. How could a *human* survive all this trouble? Matt must be so confused and afraid. He didn't understand what was happening. He didn't know how to take care of himself.

The smoke stung Chief's eyes and clogged his nostrils. Too many scents. Burning wood, burning fabric. The greasy stench of charred rubber.

The crackle of the flames and the crumble of the buildings sounded louder now than everything except the sirens.

Chief slunk along the sidewalk outside the house. Faint scent trails branched from the front door. Old trails, but where was the boy-pup *now*?

A truck drove past. Chief watched carefully, then trotted toward the center of the city, the place most crowded with buildings.

Humans shouted and barked in the distance. Chief prowled along a street where flames crawled through the walls of the buildings. Maybe the boy-pup was with the other humans?

Chief didn't smell him, though. He didn't hear his voice.

He listened closely, and he heard something else. A few of the men *sounded* like his family. Their growls and barks reminded him of the way Matt and the old ones spoke—and mostly of Eric, the one who'd raised Chief.

They sounded familiar. They sounded like puppyhood, like home.

Chief trotted toward them. Ash fell like snow onto his fur. Hoses spread across the street like giant snakes as men sprayed water on the fires. Filthy puddles formed on the ground.

The two men with the familiar voices jogged toward the fire truck. "We've got to help the Brits!" one of them said.

"Remember what you told me before we went on leave?" the other man grumped. "'Let's visit Canterbury, it'll be relaxing . . .'"

"Hey, buddy!" the first man called to the firemen. "We're here to help. What do you need?"

"You're Americans?"

"That's right, US Army," the first man said. "We're on leave, but tell us what you need and we'll get to work."

"We're clearing houses. Ensuring nobody's still inside." The fireman gestured to a few houses. "See that lot? They've already been cleared. You two start at that door there."

Chief didn't understand the words or smell the boy-pup . . . but he did hear a faint scratching. A *scrrt, scrrt, scrrt* sounded through the clamor.

The noise came from a house with smoke billowing from the windows. *Scrrt, scrrt, scrrt.* Someone was alive in there.

Someone needed help.

Chief dashed forward, though the smoke. Past

a metal box. Over the hoses. Along the sidewalk. His eyes watered, and his nose burned. Embers fell on his back and charred his fur.

"What's that dog doing?" someone yelled. "He's running into the fire!"

"You, Yanks! Stop him!"

One of the men loomed in front of Chief. "C'mere, boy!"

Chief stopped. The man sounded *very* familiar. Just like Eric.

"C'mon, boy! We're the United States Army! If you can't trust us, who can you trust?"

Chief eyed the man, but his ears still swiveled, tracking the scratching coming from inside the burning house. *Scrrt, scrrt, scrrt.*

"He hears something inside!" the familiar-sounding man called.

"That house is clear!" another man shouted back.

"Okay, I'll grab him." The familiar man reached for Chief, but Chief easily pranced away. Humans were so slow. "Stay!" the man shouted at him. "Sit!"

Chief waited for the man to crouch down,

then raced past him and sped toward the fire.

He burst through the open door. Smoke burned his eyes. *Scrrt, scrrt, scrrt.* He scrambled into a room with little desks. Bright flames climbed one wall. The heat stung his nose, and he stayed close to a high counter that blocked the fire.

The scratching sounded louder.

Chief dashed into a back room. A heavy beam had fallen from the ceiling and smashed a row of cabinets. Wood paneling and metal bits scattered the floor.

In the middle of the wreckage, a narrow table was bowed under the weight of the beam. The remains of a broken cabinet surrounded it. But where was the person?

Scrrt, scrrt, scrrt. The scratching was coming from under the table!

Chief started digging at the smashed cabinet that was trapping the person beneath the table.

He didn't flinch from the heat or the embers scorching his ears and nose. He didn't smell the stinging fumes. He didn't notice the shattered glass jabbing his paws.

He just dug toward the *scrrt, scrrt, scrrt.*

"Hello?" a wavering voice said from under the table. "Is someone there?"

Chief barked and dug faster.

"I hear him!" the familiar voice called from inside the house. "Come here, boy! *Come*! Get out of there!"

Chief barked again. Smoke filled his lungs, but he didn't stop digging. He'd never stop digging, not while he still heard that *scrrt, scrrt, scrrt.*

The familiar man ran into the kitchen. "You stupid mutt, get your shaggy—"

"Hello?" the voice called from under the table.

"Holy Moses!" The man stopped in shock, then bellowed, "There's someone trapped! Get in here!"

The man crouched beside Chief, tugging at the shattered cupboard. He pulled and heaved as Chief dug. The cabinet shifted two inches, three inches . . .

More men ran into the back room. The humans yelped at each other, but Chief didn't listen. He kept digging, panting for breath in the smoke-filled room.

Crash!

The cupboard tore free. Two of the men crawled under the table and helped a fur-faced human onto his feet.

"Your dog . . ." The fur-faced human gasped, reaching toward Chief. "He saved me."

Chief raised his head to lick the man's hand . . . then staggered. The smoke seemed to squeeze the air from his lungs.

He panted faster but couldn't catch his breath. He felt weak and dizzy. He curled his tail under his belly, and his vision darkened.

CHAPTER 13

Matt darted closer to the half-fallen wall. He paused, listening for the cry for help.

"Can you hear anything?" he asked Rachel.

"I think it came from that way," she said, pointing past the wall.

They jogged to a cobbled drive that led into a dark courtyard. One half of the courtyard must've been a lawn before the war, but it was a vegetable garden now.

"Help!" the voice called again.

Matt jogged through the smoke and darkness,

and he spotted an old woman kneeling beside an old man who was lying on the ground.

For a terrible moment, Matt thought the man was dead. But no, he was holding the woman's hand tight.

"What happened?" Matt flushed for asking such a stupid question. He knew what happened; they got caught in an air raid! "I mean, do you need help?"

"Children!" the old woman snapped. "Get to a shelter at once!"

Matt and Rachel looked at each other. Matt knew that Rachel was thinking the same thing he was; they couldn't just leave this old couple lying here in the open.

"We will," he told her. "But we'll send help on the way."

Rachel looked at the old man. "Is he okay?"

"I'm afraid my husband can't move his leg," the old woman said, her voice sharp with fear. "However, you children have no such excuse, and must—"

Crrrrrk-slam!

Somewhere out of eyeshot, a roof collapsed.

Over the rooftops, dust and smoke swirled into the air. The fire glowed yellow on the clouds of ash. Matt looked toward the cathedral but couldn't see anything through all the smoke. He hoped his parents were okay.

"Little ambulance?" Rachel asked Matt.

"Definitely." He gazed around the dark courtyard. "Which way was it going?"

Rachel pointed. "Toward St. George Street. Toward the fire."

"Okay. You stay here in case they need anything, I'll run for the ATS ladies." Except he'd only taken three steps when he heard Rachel following him. He spun around. "Stay here!"

She shook her head.

"Would you listen to me for once?"

She tugged on her braid. "We stick together."

"Your sister's a good girl," the wounded man groaned. "Looking after her brother like that."

Matt scowled. The man thought *Rachel* was looking after *him*? He didn't say anything, though, because he was pretty sure you weren't supposed to yell at injured old men. He just jogged away, toward St. George Street.

Toward the fire.

"You've got to do what I say," he told Rachel. "We're in the middle of an air raid!"

"I will. I promise. If you say, I will do."

"So when I tell you to stay put, *stay put.*"

"Except not staying put."

"Rachel!" he snapped as they jogged along the middle of the street. "That's the only thing I need from you!"

She didn't say anything until they paused at the corner. "Would you stay put if Eric told you?"

"*Yes,*" Matt said. "Of course!"

"Oh," she said.

"So?"

"So in that case," she said. "I still will not."

"This isn't a game, Rachel! I'm not just being mean or—"

"There!" She pointed. "Ambulance!"

Hooded headlights cast dim light on the rubble-strewn street. A dark green sedan prowled into view. A massive dent on the hood caught the flickering flames, and scratches crisscrossed the car roof: it must've been hit by falling debris.

A young ATS woman sat behind the wheel,

but not the same one they'd seen earlier. There must've been a bunch of them driving down the dark, deadly streets, ferrying the wounded to the hospital.

Matt and Rachel waved their arms until the sedan stopped. "There's an old man!" Matt blurted. "He's got a broken leg or something!"

"Where's your mum?" the woman in the passenger seat asked. "Have you a shelter at home?"

"No, but we, um—"

"Vee saw the old man!" Rachel interrupted, her accent thickening. "He can't shake his leg."

The ATS woman blinked at her. "Pardon?"

"He's back that way," Matt said. "He needs help."

The ATS women looked at each other, then one said, "We'll find him. You run along to the nearest shelter. And take your sister."

"There's a shelter in the school," the other women told him. "You know where that is?"

Matt shook his head. "I'm not sure."

"I know," Rachel said, taking Matt's hand to lead him.

When the car started to drive off, Matt ran

alongside and shouted, "Wait, wait!"

The car slowed, and the driver looked through the window. "What's wrong?"

"Have you seen a dog? A big dog, running around lost?"

"Tonight? I can't imagine that any—" The sound of gunfire tore through the night, and the driver quieted.

"Oh no," Matt said, his stomach sinking as he looked again toward the smoke-obscured cathedral.

"That sound is good news, lad." The driver gave a satisfied grunt. "That's our boys! That's antiaircraft fire, taking the fight to the Nazis."

"And bad news as well," the other ATS woman said. "If they're firing, there's another wave of bombers on the way."

Sure enough, Matt heard the distant drone of bombers. His skin crawled, and Rachel muttered in Yiddish.

"Run to the shelter!" the ATS driver said. "Now! Hurry!"

CHAPTER 14

1:30 A.M.

Matt and Rachel rounded the corner at a run. The sky was gone. The moon and stars were gone. Nothing was visible overhead but the smoke that covered Canterbury, swallowing up even the cathedral steeple.

And the growl of the bombers sounded louder and louder!

"More planes!" Rachel said.

"Maybe that's just the roar of the fire," Matt said. "Or—or fire trucks."

"No." Rachel grabbed his hand. "More planes."

"Which way is the school?"

"Here," she said, pulling him along the sidewalk.

"I hope they've got a basement," he said. "Or a—"

The *BOOM* of a high-explosive bomb shattered the night.

Rubble spewed into the street from the end of the block. Windows shattered, walls burst. Twists of blackened metal pinged against cobblestones, and bits of charred cloth drifted in the air.

Rachel stumbled, shouting in fear.

Matt pulled her to her feet. His skin prickled with fear. His throat closed. The whistle of a falling bomb screeched in his ears.

He couldn't move. He couldn't think. All he could do was stand there holding Rachel's hand while she shivered and—

No! No, his sister needed him.

He needed to be strong for her, like Eric would've been for him.

He dragged Rachel backward. Glowing

embers billowed around him, the sparks prickling his exposed skin like mosquito bites. A chunk of splintery wood slammed into the ground ten feet away and scraped across the cobblestones.

Without warning, another explosion sounded behind them. Matt flinched and ran faster. Faster. Dirt flew over his head and stung the back of his neck. He ran until he couldn't tell if the noise was bombs or rescue workers or the pounding of his own heart.

Finally, he turned to Rachel. "Are you okay?"

Her cheeks were pale, and her eyes were big. She said something in Polish or Yiddish, her voice faint. Still, she squeezed his hand and tried to smile.

He tried to smile back.

Neither of them did a great job, but he still felt some of his fear fade. He scrambled onward, turned a corner—and a red-faced man with wild eyes spun to face them.

"Turn yourselves around!" the man shouted in a thick English accent. "Get back, away from Butchery Lane!"

Matt stumbled backward, not understanding.

"It's a firebreak! It's burning, the whole thing—"

A firebreak? Matt remembered Eric telling him about those. A firebreak was a cleared strip of land, with no bushes or trees—or anything flammable. It was wide enough that a fire couldn't cross it.

But Butchery Lane was a street in downtown Canterbury. What did the man mean it was a firebreak? Were they letting the whole street burn to the ground, so the fire couldn't spread into the rest of the city?

Matt didn't know. He didn't ask. He just blindly led Rachel through the smoke-filled streets. She kept repeating a singsong phrase under her voice, and he realized she was praying.

Bombs fell around them. Thick smoke changed the city into a nightmare. Matt heard the clatter of a bomb and saw a blaze of intense fire. His mind raced with fear: now the Germans were dropping both incendiary bombs *and* five-hundred-pound high-explosive bombs? The

incendiaries burst into super-hot flames, but the HE bombs blasted entire buildings into rubble.

As Matt stumbled away from the flames, a bone-shaking explosion almost knocked him to the ground!

He grabbed Rachel's hand and dashed into a side street. Smoke stung his eyes, and the dark city streets spread in front of him, strange and threatening.

Finally he and Rachel stumbled into a sprawling, shadowy city park with a big mound. After a moment, Matt recognized the area. "Oh! This is the park!"

Rachel wrinkled her nose. "Which park?"

"Where I tried to teach you baseball."

"The baseball is silly," Rachel said. She hadn't hit a single ball. She could barely hold the bat right.

Matt's fear faded a little at the familiar surroundings. He turned in a circle, getting his bearings. According to Eric, this had been a Roman cemetery almost two thousand years earlier. The old city walls ran along one side of the park. The bandstand had been torn down for scrap metal to help with the war, and some kind of military warehouse was dug into the wall nearby. Not a shelter, though. They still needed the school for that.

Now that he'd stopped running, Matt realized that he'd been hearing a rhythmic pounding for a while.

"I guess that's antiaircraft fire," he told Rachel. "Like the ATS woman said."

"Oh no," Rachel said. "More fire?"

"No, no! It's a good thing! It's the Brits shooting back at the bombers."

"The Brits," Rachel repeated, because she thought it was funny that the British were called "Brits" and the Americans were called "Yanks."

"That's right," he said, looking at the smoke-filled sky. "And do you hear that?"

"I hear a lot of *thats*."

"That new engine sound! I bet it's RAF night fighters finally come to blast a few holes in Jerry!"

"British fighter planes?"

"Yeah." Matt glanced down at Rachel. "They'll teach Fritz a lesson."

Rachel squeezed his hand and shot him a

quick, grateful look. She knew he was trying to distract her by using the terms "Jerry" and "Fritz" for the Germans.

"Now, um . . ." He frowned. "Which way is the school?"

Rachel pointed across the dark garden. "I think there."

"Okay, we'll run on three," Matt said. "You count."

Rachel nodded as Matt gripped her hand. "One, two . . . three!"

They raced from the park onto the street. As they ran toward the west, the glow of the fire got farther away. The sound of explosions sounded fainter, too, along with the shouting and sirens.

Matt exhaled in relief. Finally, they were getting away from the target area. But what about Chief? What about his parents? Were they still in the cathedral? If he knew them, they'd be on the streets looking for him and Rachel.

A car rolled through an intersection ahead of them, as more ATS women searched for the wounded. Two fire trucks with hooded lights sped along Castle Street behind them.

"I bet they're from other towns," Matt told Rachel. "Coming to help fight the fires."

Rachel tugged on her braid. "I'm a little twisted around."

"A little what?"

"Twisted around. I forget which way is the school."

"Oh!" he said. "You're a little *turned* around."

"No, I'm not!" she announced with a sudden smile. "Is this way!"

She jogged along the street, toward the school and Greyfriars gardens. Matt liked Greyfriars. He liked wandering along the narrow canal and walking the meandering paths. And he liked the view of the cathedral spires.

Matt peered at the sky above the rooftops, hoping to catch sight of the cathedral now. But he couldn't see any towers or spires through the smoke. He hoped his mom and dad were okay. He hoped that Chief had found his way back to them.

He must've. He was a smart dog. He was Eric's dog, and . . .

A wave of grief washed over him just as

suddenly as a wave of bombers. Matt didn't want to think about Eric.

He lowered his teary gaze—but not before spotting a dark shape swooping over the city.

His head sprung upward. "Look! There!"

"What?" Rachel asked. "I don't see."

The dark shape swirled and vanished over the rooftops, falling away from the burning streets, toward Greyfriars. "There was a . . . I don't know."

"Is only a few blocks to the school."

"I think it was a parachute!"

"You think from one of the English night fighters?"

Excitement kindled in Matt's heart. After running away from danger all night to save themselves, maybe they could finally run *toward* something, to help someone else. Maybe that's how Eric had felt about enlisting.

"I bet!" he told Rachel. "The pilot must've bailed out."

Rachel wrinkled her nose. "Like a bale of hay?"

"No, no! He must've parachuted out of the plane!" He grabbed Rachel's arm. "Come on, we've got to find him. We've got to check that he's okay!"

A cloud of smoke wafted down the street. Matt coughed and closed his stinging eyes—but only for a second. Then he started tugging Rachel through the choking smoke, tracking the dark shape toward where it must've fallen a few blocks away.

CHAPTER 15

In the smoke-filled back room, Chief's head spun. He struggled for breath as his vision grew darker. He smelled the bittersweet seep of gas and heard a snakelike hiss.

He whimpered a warning to the men carrying the fur-faced man away—then an explosion in a nearby room shook the walls.

Shelves cascaded onto the floor, and Chief collapsed amid the wreckage. He struggled for breath. He tried to rise onto his paws—and felt himself lifted into the arms of the first man, the one with the familiar voice.

The man smelled of sweat and countryside, with a hint of the tangy, metallic scent of blood. Chief forced his eyes open and saw ash smudging the man's face and a scratch bleeding on his cheek.

Still dizzy and weak, Chief licked the man's cut. Humans weren't very good at licking their wounds, so you needed to take care of that for them.

On the other paw, they were extremely good at carrying a dog out of a fiery building. The man brought him down the hallway, into the blast of heat and the glow of flames. Then the man staggered with him across the rubble-strewn floor, through the door. Onto the cool, wide-open street.

Fresh air filled Chief's lungs. He coughed, then struggled in the man's arms. He needed to feel the ground under his paws, to make sure he was okay.

"Is that better, boy?" the man asked, setting him on the pavement and kneeling in front of him.

Chief shook himself to chase the stink of smoke out of his fur. He tensed his shoulder muscles, he felt the strength in his legs. Much better.

"You look okay. What's your name, boy?" The man reached for the jingling collar that Chief wore to help his people find him. "Chief?"

Chief barked.

"Good boy, Chief," the man said, laying a gentle hand on his chest. "What a good boy."

"Hey, Landry," another man said. "You coming?"

"Not without Chief," the one called Landry said. "This dog's a natural."

An ominous grinding sounded from the building. Chief raised his hackles. The walls weren't going to stand for much longer.

"A natural what? Flea motel?"

"A natural search and rescue dog," Landry said.

Chief shifted impatiently. Landry kept yelping at his packmate like he couldn't tell that the building was about to collapse. Chief heard a deep creaking, then the crack of fire-weakened beams.

In a few heartbeats, the entire place would fall—and the humans were standing directly outside it, without a care in the world!

So Chief grabbed Landry's wrist in his teeth and backed him farther away.

"He's biting you!"

"He's not biting me. A German shepherd like this? If he bit me, he'd break my bones. No, he wants to show me something down the street." Landry's tone changed. "Don't you, Chief? Isn't that right?"

Chief pulled him another few steps.

"What is it, boy? What do you—"

With a *RUMBLE-CRASH*, the burning house fell in on itself. Flames washed onto the street. A wall toppled, shattering into a spray of rubble. A dust cloud rose around Chief and the men, who shouted and—finally!—ran from the danger.

"Well don't that beat all," the other man said, after they stopped down the block. "Maybe he *is* a natural."

"He's a whiz," Landry said, patting Chief's flank. "This dog is genuine army material."

Chief heard admiration in the man's smoke-roughened voice and peered up at his face. Maybe he wasn't smart enough to run from a collapsing building, but Chief liked him.

He reminded Chief of Eric.

CHAPTER 16

Matt and Rachel raced to the end of the street, chasing the fallen parachute. They clambered over a cement ridge that rose a few inches from the ground. The iron fence posts once planted in the cement had been removed for the war effort.

Grass grew on the other side of the ridge. A stone's throw in front of Matt, a few trees lofted overhead.

The air smelled of fresh water. The river ran along the base of those trees. It wasn't much of a river, actually. It was more of a canal, running smoothly between high walls. Matt liked it better than a regular, wide, unwalled river; it was more historical, almost like a moat.

"Do you see him?" Rachel asked.

Matt scanned the sky. "No."

"You are sure it was a parachute?"

"Either that or the biggest bat in the world." He followed a path closer to the river. "I guess it could've been the shadow of a plane in the smoke."

Rachel shivered. "There is no light to make shadow."

"Are you cold?" He looked at her, wrapping her arms around herself in her thin pajamas and slippers. "You look cold."

"You look cold too. I'm not going away!"

"I never said—"

"Hush," Rachel said.

"You hush!" Matt said.

"No, hush and *listen*. Do you hear that?"

"Hear what?" Matt cocked his head. *Flup. Flup-flup-flup.* "Oh! Something's flapping."

"Like a parachute?" Rachel asked.

Matt squinted into the darkness of the park. "Yeah."

"Or like the biggest bat in the world?"

"Let's find out," Matt said, and jogged toward the sound.

When he rounded a bush, he almost couldn't believe his eyes. He was right! A dark, ragged shape stretched overhead, tangled in the branches of a tree.

A black, flapping shape.

A parachute!

Cords and ropes stretched from the tree, across the ground, then disappeared.

What? That didn't make any sense.

Matt ran closer. "Oh!" he told Rachel. "The river!"

The parachute cords disappeared into the inky blackness of the canal.

"Hello?" Matt called. "Hello?"

"Here!" a man's voice replied weakly. "In here."

"Coming!" Matt said, and scrambled to the edge of the canal.

When he looked over, he found a man dangling at the end of the parachute ropes. Blood smeared his face beneath a soft leather helmet with built-in ear protectors. The river water covered his flight suit to his shoulders.

"You—you're a night fighter!" Matt said, still amazed. "You flew a Spitfire here to defend the city!"

The half-submerged, blood-streaked man peered up at Matt. "And you are the sight for the sore eyes."

. Matt almost admitted that he daydreamed about flying a Spitfire, but he remembered just in time that Spitfires weren't usually used for night fighting, anyway. Instead the Brits used "Beaufighters"—and Matt couldn't let his daydreams distract him now.

"Don't worry," he said. "We're here to help."

"Good, yes." The pilot groaned. "I could use a few helping hands."

Saying "a few helping hands" instead of "a helping hand" made Matt think of Rachel, and how she sometimes got English phrases wrong. Something was strange about the man's accent, but the British often used different words for things, like "lorry" instead of "truck" and "lift" instead of "elevator."

Matt crouched down to grab the parachute

cords. He pulled and yanked, but the pilot didn't budge. Rachel grabbed a handful of the cords behind Matt. They heaved together . . . and still couldn't pull the waterlogged man from the canal.

"He's too heavy," Matt told Rachel.

"I cannot free myself from these threads," the pilot said, his voice strained as he fought to stay above the water. "And if I slip, they will keep me from the swimming . . ."

"He'll drown," Rachel breathed.

"No, he won't," Matt said. "We won't let him."

CHAPTER 17

The parachute cords jerked in Matt's hands when the pilot shifted, trying to climb up the side of the canal. Matt braced himself and tugged. The cords didn't budge.

When he looked into the canal, he saw blood dripping into the pilot's eyes from a cut on his forehead. The tangling ropes kept him from getting a grip, and he slid deeper into the water!

"Hold on!" Matt wrapped the cords around his wrists. "Rachel, tie the other end to the tree!"

"There is too much . . . I don't know the word! Loose parts."

"Too much slack?"

She scuffled behind him. "I'll get a stick!"

"A what?"

Rachel darted away, disappearing into the shadows under the tree.

"What're you going to do with a *stick*?" Matt grunted as the parachute cord tugged at his arms. If he wasn't careful, he'd get pulled into the water too.

Rachel's voice floated from the darkness. "Tie the ropes around it."

"There's no time for that!" Matt leaned backward until he fell onto his butt. He wedged his heels against the stone lip of the canal. "Hang on!"

"I am hanging," the pilot said. "Believe me."

The parachute cords slowly pulled Matt closer to the canal. He strained with all his might and held fast. "Sorry!"

The pilot swore—but not in English.

"What—" Matt felt a chill on his skin. "What's that?"

"Er, nothing for youngster ears!"

Matt peered into the darkness. "I haven't heard your accent before."

"I am . . ." A splash sounded from the river. "Scottish."

"Oh!"

A grunt arose from the darkness. "Plus I am almost drowning."

"Yeah." Matt turned his head. "Rachel! Where are you?"

Her answer floated from the shadows. "I can't find a stick big enough."

Matt chewed his lower lip. He needed to do something fast. Something better than telling Rachel to stop looking for a stupid stick. The parachute cord dug into his wrists. His arms ached with the strain. His back burned, and his knees wobbled.

He needed Eric. He needed Chief.

He needed *help*.

The parachute cord bit into his skin. The ground chilled his legs through his pajamas. He took a breath and tried to ignore the pain.

He couldn't hold on for much longer, he couldn't—

"One minute!" Rachel said, behind him.

The cords jerked and wiggled in his grip. He dug in his heels and tightened his grip.

"Done!" Rachel finally said.

Matt glanced over his shoulder. She'd wriggled a stout branch between a bunch of the parachute cords, then spun it around. The cords had gathered together, looping around the branch. The parachute was still stuck in the tree, but now the cords had a branch shoving through them, like a reel on a fishing pole.

And as Rachel turned the branch over and over, the parachute cord looped around more tightly. When she wound the cords around the branch, it took up the slack in the ropes.

In a moment, Matt felt the cords tighten from behind him. He loosened his grip, and the pilot didn't plunge into the water.

"Hold on!" he yelled, scrambling to his feet. "We've got you!"

A faint splashing sounded from the canal.

Matt darted to Rachel, flapping his hands

to get rid of the ache. "Great job, Rachel, you smarty-pants!"

She peered at him. "I have clever underwear?"

"No, I mean—oh, forget it!"

Matt helped her spin the branch around and around, pulling the parachute cord tighter . . . and dragging the pilot from the water.

Inch by inch.

The tree branches bent toward the canal.

Twigs snapped.

The cord grew tighter, wrapping around the middle of the branch.

Pretty soon, the branch stopped spinning so easily. Matt and Rachel pulled and shoved and grunted, reeling the pilot higher.

Good!" the pilot called. "Only a little more. *Schnell, schnell!*"

Rachel gasped. "Drop him! Matt, drop him!"

"What? What's wrong?"

"Didn't you hear what he said?"

"That's just Scottish."

"It's *German*. He wasn't in a British night fighter. He was in a German bomber!"

CHAPTER 18

2 A.M.

Down the block from the collapsed house, Chief shook himself until he felt his strength return. He still stank of smoke—and of the biting scent of burned fur—but his ears were pricked and his teeth were sharp. Ready for anything.

The two men from the burning building jogged down the street ahead of him. The one named Landry snapped his fingers at Chief, which Chief knew meant that he'd need help again soon. So Chief ran alongside him, listening for trouble.

"What do you know about dogs, Landry?" the packmate said.

"My aunt's got a kennel," Landry told him. "Have you heard of the Dogs for Defense program?"

One of the men with the hoses asked, "Dogs for the fence?"

"*Defense*. Dogs for Defense."

"What's that?"

"A new program for training dogs to serve in the US military."

"Oh! You've got that thick American accent."

"I don't have an accent! You're the one with the accent."

The men barked laughter at each other like silly puppies, then pointed to various buildings and streets. The iron birds were flying closer overhead. Chief narrowed his eyes. He couldn't see through the smoke, but that didn't matter. He could track every one of the falling fire-rocks by sound alone.

"Chief!" the man named Landry said. "This way!"

Chief started to follow them—then stopped.

He'd caught scent of Matt and Rachel! He sniffed the smoky air.

"What're you smelling, boy?"

Chief inhaled again, but the scent faded. Where *were* they? A couple of furless human pups weren't safe in the fiery night, not without a dog to help them.

"Chief?"

Chief growled in frustration. He'd lost the scent. He paced back and forth for a moment, trying to find it again. It was gone, though, so he followed Landry into a block of flattened buildings where flames danced among the ruins. Puddles of water from the hoses collected between cobblestones. The stench of burning oil hurt Chief's nose.

He raised his ruff at the smell and followed along.

"Find!" Landry said to him.

Chief didn't know who "Find" was, so he watched the man.

"Find!" Landry repeated.

"What're you doing?" the other man asked. "He doesn't speak English."

"That's the word some rescue dogs are trained with," Landry said. "You play hide-and-seek with them as puppies. When they find you, you give them a treat. Over and over. Then someone else hides, and you tell them 'Find!' And you give them a treat when they find that person. It's standard training."

"Well, this one's looking at you like that Englishman. Doesn't understand a word."

"Chief," Landry said, crouching down, muzzle to muzzle. "You're a good boy."

Chief licked Landry's face again. That scratch of his needed attention.

Landry smiled. "You're the whiz around here. C'mon, boy. If you hear anything, you let me know."

Chief knew the man wanted something, but he didn't know what. Probably the man didn't know what he wanted either. Humans often didn't.

So when Landry started trotting down the street, Chief loped alongside him. Staying alert for any out-of-place smells or noises in the ruined buildings. Someone could be alive in there.

And nobody would know but him.

CHAPTER 19

Matt froze. "German? Are you sure?"

"Of course I am sure!" Rachel said, tugging at Matt's arm. "Let go!"

Matt kept hold of the branch. "We . . . we can't just drop him."

"We leave him here. We run to tell someone!"

"What if he drowns?"

Rachel stared at Matt. "You do not know who he is."

"Of course I know! He dropped bombs all over Canterbury, and—"

"He fights for murderers. For Nazis. To help them murder."

"Yeah, but . . . but he's just air crew. I mean, I hope they put him jail and throw away the key, but he's only a soldier."

"I am just a soldier," the pilot called, his voice softer. "You are right. I should not have lied."

"Why did you?"

"I am scared! I bailed out in the enemy territory. For me, this is the scariest moment of my life."

"Let's go, Matt!" Rachel urged.

Matt rubbed his face. What would Eric do? He couldn't tell. "I—I don't know . . ."

"I'm only a regular bloke," the pilot said. "I was drafted into the Luftwaffe. The German air force. I always loved airplanes, since I was your age."

"I . . ." Matt swallowed. "I like airplanes too."

"They trained me. They sent me on my very first bombing run . . . and I am shot from the sky. And worse, about to drown in a little stream."

"We can't let him drown." Matt tied the parachute cords around the branch to keep it in place.

"We need to get him out of there."

Rachel didn't say anything. She didn't even tug on her braid.

"Then we'll turn him in," Matt said. "But first we need to save his life."

Rachel just looked at him with her dark eyes.

"Fine," Matt said. "I'll do it myself."

He approached the water, and for once Rachel didn't follow him. Reeling in the parachute cord had brought the pilot—well, the *German*—to the very edge of the canal. If the man hadn't been wrapped in cord, he could've just pulled himself onto firm ground.

But the cords twined tightly around him. He was trapped.

He looked up at Matt with pleading eyes. "I give you my word. I will surrender myself to a soldier."

The German smelled of canal water and machine oil when Matt knelt beside him. "Okay."

"Pull me up."

Matt yanked and tugged. He grabbed a handful of the German's flight suit and heaved until finally the German squirmed onto the ground.

"Ah!" the German said. "Thank you."

"Yeah, um . . ." Matt didn't know what to say. "Is your head okay?"

"Only a scratch." With shaking hands, the German unstrapped his parachute harness. "Ah. Much better."

"So I guess we should find someone . . ."

"What are the chances, eh? To fly across the Channel and land here?" The German looked around. "A pretty city, Canterbury."

"Yeah, I guess."

The German removed his helmet. "And this is a quiet little corner."

"It's, um, a park."

"I count myself lucky that I did not fall into the downtown."

"Yeah, it's on fire." Matt didn't say, "Because you were dropping bombs on it."

"And here we are. Nobody knows I am here, except my two . . . how do you say? Someone who rescues a person."

"Um, a rescuer?"

"A savior! My two saviors." The German looked around. "If I hide my chute and change my clothes? Well, then, perhaps nobody will capture me. Perhaps I'll stay free."

A dagger of fear stabbed Matt's heart. "Except you gave your word about turning yourself in."

"Of course!" The German raised his hands as if he were surrendering. "Of course, I am just thinking out loud."

"So I guess we should—"

"One question," the German interrupted. "Do you know if there is an English saying about how much a promise is worth in wartime?"

The fear throbbed in Matt's chest. "Um, no."

"Well, boy . . ." When the German shifted, a combat knife gleamed in his right hand. "It is not worth much."

"You promised—"

The German grabbed Matt's arm and raised the blade. "I cannot let you tell anyone that I am here."

"Rachel!" Matt yelled, trying to break free. "Run!"

CHAPTER 20

"Here!" Landry's packmate shouted. "Bring the dog here!"

"C'mon, Chief," Landry said. "Here, boy."

Chief ignored him for a moment, standing atop a heap of overturned earth and charred wood. He'd caught Matt's scent again, somewhere in the distance, along with a whiff of grass and river water. . . .

Then the wind shifted, and all Chief smelled were bitter fumes and the guts of fallen buildings.

"Chief!" Landry shouted again. "Come!"

Chief darted down into the road. The man needed him. He flashed around a cluster of firemen and stopped beside Landry. He didn't hear any special threat. He smelled blistering metal and charred plastic, but he didn't sense any looming danger.

"Over here," the first man said, standing outside a brick building. "I heard something inside this movie theater."

Landry jogged to the man. "Where exactly?"

"I don't know," the man said. "I can't hear it anymore."

"C'mere, boy," Landry said, calling Chief into the building. "Find. *Find*, Chief."

Chief trotted into the ruins of a big den with rows of chairs and a high ceiling with holes blasted through it. The air smelled of cigarette smoke even more than fire smoke. The creak and clatter of settling debris sounded faintly from the far corner.

"A high-explosive bomb hit," the man told Landry. "I thought I heard something while we were clearing the building."

Landry looked at Chief.

Chief looked at Landry.

"Well," Landry told the man. "You didn't."

"How do you know? Make him check!"

"He already checked," Landry said. "He checked before he set foot inside."

"Are you sure?"

"Have you ever heard of a dog named Jet?" Landry asked, heading outside. "He's a German shepherd like Chief here. With maybe a little collie in him too."

Chief looked up at the sound of his name. Landry didn't seem to need any help, though, so he paused on the sidewalk to listen to the rest of the street.

"Jet's an English dog," Landry told the man. "They say he rescued a hundred people during the Blitz, when the Germans bombed London."

"A hundred people! You're pulling my leg."

"Maybe even more. Before that, he worked for a year guarding airfields, but search and rescue is in his blood. Most dogs—most animals, well, most *everyone*—is scared of fire. But Jet? He'd run into burning buildings to save people. He'd run through the fire."

"Like your dog did," the man say.

"He's not my dog," Landry said, resting a hand on Chief's ruff. "But that's right. That's how I knew he was special. Jet's handler has to hold him back to keep him from running into the flames to save people."

"Whoa, that's some kind of brave."

"Yeah. Jet once raced into a factory full of poison smoke. His nose is so good he found the one survivor in the entire place."

"You think Chief's like that?"

"Like I told you," Landry said. "He's a natural. He's—"

"Running off," the man said, from behind Chief as he loped toward a sudden gust of the metallic smell of blood.

Why did humans spend so much time yipping to each other? Couldn't they hear the far-off whistles through the smoke? Couldn't they smell the human fear-scent wafting from down the block?

Chief scrambled over a pile of rubble. A sharp metal edge ripped out a hunk of his fur but didn't cut his skin. He barked for Landry and the other man to hurry.

"I'm coming!" Landry yelled. "I've only got two legs."

Chief rounded a corner and found two women helping an injured man. He trotted closer and sniffed the air. He smelled more injured people. The women already knew about them, though. He could tell because of the scent trails.

"Hello?" Landry called to the women. "US Army here! Do you need help?"

"Not as much as they do," one woman said, pointing to the injured people.

"Oh!" Landry looked from the wounded people back to the women. "You're ATS. I thought you stayed in shelters during raids."

"You're Americans," the woman said. "I thought you stayed in cowboy hats."

Landry laughed and helped the women tend the wounded people. Chief watched approvingly for a moment, then cocked his head as a far-off whistle sounded sharper and closer.

Chief started to bark a warning, then caught the faintest whiff of Rachel. Where was she? He inhaled deeply. He smelled Matt, too, and a musky dampness. Not too far—

The whistling grew louder, dragging his attention back to his surroundings. A shrill, deadly sound. Falling directly toward this street.

Fire-rocks were going to hit Landry and the women!

CHAPTER 21

Matt tried to pull away, but the German's grip was too tight. The man's eyes narrowed. Blood oozed down his cheek, and water dripped from his flight suit.

"W-we saved your life!" Matt said.

"For which I thank you." The German raised his voice. "Girl! Show yourself! Come here, or your brother will be sorry!"

Matt tried to kick the German but missed. "Run, Rachel!"

"Enough!" The German shook him roughly.

"I don't have time to waste on—"

Thunk.

The German blinked at Matt.

He released his grip and swayed.

Matt ripped free from the man's loosening grip and saw Rachel standing behind him. Holding the thick branch like a baseball bat. Just like Matt had taught her.

She'd clubbed him in the head.

When Rachel pulled back for another swing, the German spun toward her! He swore and knocked the branch from her hands.

Matt tried to kick him again—and this time he succeeded.

The German, still tangled in the cords, stumbled a few steps.

"Run!" Matt shouted to Rachel. "C'mon, c'mon, *c'mon!*"

He dashed past the German, grabbed Rachel's wrist, and raced into the darkness.

A tree loomed.

Bushes tugged at his pajama legs.

Footsteps sounded behind them. A sort of shuffling drag as the German limped. But still moving fast. Too fast.

The German was gaining on them!

A wall loomed in front of Matt. He yanked Rachel to one side and lunged through a doorway into an alley.

He couldn't tell which way to go. He was too scared to focus, too scared to think.

He ran blindly ahead. Were they on Beer Cart Lane? St. Margaret's Street? He didn't know, he couldn't tell.

Sirens and shouts filled the air. Engines and explosions and smoke. More bombs were dropping! More bombs than ever.

Another wave of German bombers flew overhead, dropping hundreds of incendiary and high-explosive bombs. Yet the loudest things were Matt's pounding heartbeat . . . and the scuff of footsteps behind them.

He and Rachel sped around a corner, they raced across a street. Matt pulled Rachel into the thicker shadows of a building and risked a peek over his shoulder.

He didn't see the German. The streets looked deserted and—

Shuffle-drag, shuffle-drag.

There!

The German prowled forward. His knife gleamed in the reflected light of a fire.

"We need to find soldiers!" Matt pulled Rachel faster down the street. "Or firemen."

"Then we should run *toward* the flames." Rachel's braid flapped wildly around her shoulders. "That is where they'll be."

"That's the worst idea I've ever heard!"

"So what should we do?"

"Run toward the flames!" Matt said, stumbling into an intersection. "Like you said!"

The terrifying whistle of falling bombs sounded all around and above them. Every street looked like a minefield. If they took one wrong turn . . .

"It's another wave of bombing," Matt said. "The biggest one yet!"

"Where is the fire?" Rachel asked, blinking at the rooftops.

After taking a nervous glance behind them, Matt peered into the smoky sky.

An orange glow gleamed on the thick smoke

suffocating Canterbury. But where was the glow brightest? Matt couldn't tell. He looked for the cathedral steeple, but he couldn't even see the roofs of the buildings surrounding them. He hoped his parents were still in the shelter, still safe, and that Chief was—

Shuffle-drag, shuffle-drag. The sound of the German's limping footsteps came from a cloud of dust and smoke billowing down a nearby street.

Matt's breath caught—and the rhythm changed. *Shuffle-shuffle, shuffle-shuffle.* The German had spotted them! He was closing in!

Terror pricked at Matt's skin. "This way!" he gasped, fleeing across the intersection with Rachel.

An ambulance pulled into view down the block. A dingy pool of light spilled from the hooded headlights.

"Help!" Matt screamed.

"Over here!" Rachel yelled.

His mind reeling in fear, Matt raced forward, shouting and waving, but the driver didn't see or hear him. The ambulance turned the corner and vanished into the smoke.

Matt and Rachel ran after the ambulance, trying to catch it, but they couldn't keep up. Weaving around the rubble covering the street, they raced for safety—away from the German.

Matt listened for the shuffling limp, but he heard a shrill whistle instead.

There was a clatter on the rooftops.

A scraping sound, then a *clunk*.

An incendiary firebomb had fallen nearby!

CHAPTER 22

"The bomb is in front of us!" Rachel said. "There, on the sidewalk!"

"Where? Are you sure?"

"It's right there, Matt!"

"We can't turn around! Jerry's behind us and—"

"It's *right there*!"

Rachel shoved Matt backward. He almost fell, then caught his balance. He didn't see the bomb, so he couldn't tell which way to run!

Through his panic-stricken eyes, the street

seemed to turn into a maze of fire and death—and he froze.

Then Rachel tugged Matt's hand, and he unfroze. He felt a flash of relief as he followed her. He didn't always *need* to know what to do. Sometimes he could rely on his friends.

As they raced back along the smoke-filled street, a flare of light burned suddenly behind them when the firebomb ignited. Heat smacked the back of Matt's neck.

He ran until the heat faded, then glanced at Rachel. "I guess it was right there."

"Are you *sure*?" she asked.

He snorted. "Where is he? We need to—"

Shuffle-drag, shuffle-drag! From the smoke and darkness in front of them, the German trotted closer.

"Listen!" Rachel said.

"I hear him! He's coming—"

"Not him," she said. "Voices!"

Then Matt heard them too. Men calling to each other in the next street, men with English accents. Civil defense workers or firemen. Men who would save them!

He and Rachel sprinted toward the intersection. They just needed to get around the corner before the German got to them. Then they could run for the men who'd help them.

They just needed to beat the German in this deadly race.

Matt ran faster than he'd ever run. Except Rachel was smaller and younger. In a few steps, he'd shot ahead of her. He slowed down until he was running beside her. "C'mon, Rach! We're almost there! Just another twenty feet and—"

The German burst from the shadows, looming between them and the voices. "That is far enough!"

Rachel and Matt jerked to a halt. Rachel whimpered in Yiddish while Matt's stomach tied into knots.

"Th-they know we're here," Matt told the German. "They're coming for us."

The German limped at them from the corner. His knife swayed in his fist.

"Did you learn that from me?" he asked Matt. "How to lie like that?"

"They're coming!" Matt insisted, moving to

the side to get around the German. "My—my brother's there! He's a fireman, he knows we're—"

Despite his limp, the German sprang between them and the corner. "Your brother? I do not think so."

When he scuffled closer, Matt and Rachel backed fearfully away. Fearfully and *slowly*. The German was bigger than they were, and he moved faster. If they ran, he'd catch them.

"I think . . ." The German wiped blood from his face with his sleeve. "Yes, we must go somewhere private."

"Help!" Matt shouted. "Somebody help us!"

"Like that little street." The German pointed his knife at an alley. "*Schnell*, move!"

"Help!" Rachel yelled.

"Chief!" Matt shouted. "*Chief!*"

"Nobody can hear you," the German said, herding them into the narrow alley. "Not through all this tumult."

"Chief!" Rachel shouted.

"There is nowhere left to run," the German said.

Matt swallowed and backed away. "If you . . .

if you do anything to us, they'll know you're here."

"You are just two foolish young children," the man said. "Caught in an air raid. Nobody will look twice."

"Help!" Rachel screamed.

"There is no help," the man said, limping forward.

The orange glow of fire touched the smoke above the city, but the alley itself was as dark as a nightmare. Matt felt tears in his eyes. He wanted to cry. For himself, for Rachel. For Eric. For his parents.

He swallowed instead. He put one arm protectively in front of Rachel and backed closer to the end of the alley.

The dead end.

A brick wall rose behind them, two stories high.

"Help!" Rachel yelled again.

"It is time to be quiet," the German said, stalking closer. "As quiet as the grave."

"Chief!" Matt shouted. *"Chief!"*

CHAPTER 23

2:23 A.M.

Chief's ears pricked, tracking the whistling sound through the air. One of the fire-rocks would land right where Landry and the women were standing!

And somehow they didn't know. They couldn't hear. *Humans!*

Chief sprang forward and barked at them.

"Goodness!" one of the women said. "What does he want?"

"He hears someone in the buildings," Landry

said. "Chief, find!"

Chief barked again. *Move, move!*

"What is it, boy?" Landry asked.

"Is he part wolf?" the other woman said. "He's a trifle . . . fierce."

"Don't worry," Landry said. "He won't hurt you or—"

The whistling grew louder. Closer. Chief raised his ruff and started growling, deep in his throat.

"Er," Landry said. "I think."

Chief laid his ears flat against his head and growled at the women. A fire-rock hit on the other side of the buildings. Then another one, closer. But the humans still didn't notice.

Chief growled louder and slunk at the woman, low and sleek.

Still holding the man on the stretcher, the women backed quickly away from his bared teeth. They weren't stupid.

Landry crouched down. "What's *wrong*, boy?"

The shrill whistles of the fire-rocks were speeding at them. This wasn't the time for yipping! This was the time for action.

So Chief leaped at Landry and knocked him to the ground.

"Hey!" Landry shouted, rolling away. "Bad dog!"

Chief nipped his leg and nipped his arm.

Landry kept rolling, and the women with the injured man kept backing away. Chief raised his gaze from Landry and bared his teeth at them until they moved behind the car.

"What is he doing?" the woman said. "What's wrong with him?"

When Chief growled at her, Landry shoved him away and tried to stand. He steadied himself—

And Chief jumped on top of him, as hard as he could.

Landry fell with an "Oof!"

"He's attacking!" one of the women yelled. "He's run mad! Watch out, he—"

The fire-rock slammed into the ground where they'd been standing moments before. The blast exploded into Chief's side and flung him off Landry.

His ears rang painfully, and his vision blurred.

The smell of brick dust assaulted his nostrils—and he thought he heard Matt's voice calling, "Chief, help!"

The sky swirled above Chief, and he couldn't tell what he'd heard over the throbbing in his ears.

The scents dulled, and the buildings seemed to wobble.

"He—he saved you," one of the women said, after the dust had settled.

"He saved us all," the other woman said.

Landry knelt beside Chief and touched his side gently. "Chief? Chief. I've got you. I've got you. *Shh*. What a good boy. What a good, *good* boy."

Chief licked his hand.

"I'll never doubt you again, boy," Landry said. "Not ever."

"How bad is it?" one of the women asked.

Landry's fingers touched Chief's coat here and there, as soft as butterflies. "I think he's okay. Thank God. He got the wind knocked out of him, that's all."

The world still wobbled around Chief, though. And had he really heard Matt calling for him? He thought he'd heard Rachel too. Except he must've imagined the two pups yelling for him, because now everything sounded muffled and far away.

Chief tried to stand. His legs were too weak. Landry held him tight and said his name, over and over.

Chief smelled the relief on Landry. He smelled affection. He listened closer, but he couldn't hear Matt or Rachel. He couldn't hear anything.

CHAPTER 24

The German stalked closer, his knife swaying like a snake.

Matt backed to the end of the alley, keeping Rachel behind him until she hit the wall. A dark niche opened to Matt's right, and a pile of shattered bricks stood to his left. A bomb must've smashed one of the surrounding buildings.

There was nowhere to run.

The German pointed his blade at Rachel, and fear almost stopped Matt's heart.

His knees wobbled, and his throat clenched.

Still, he knew what Eric would do if he were here. He knew what Eric would do if someone threatened *Matt* with a knife.

With a fearful whimper, Matt stepped toward the German—and shoved Rachel into the dark niche beside them.

He was trying to protect her, trying to keep her away from the German.

Except instead of hitting the wall and stopping, she kept going. She tripped over a plank on the floor and yelped.

Not a plank, a *door*. A door that had been ripped from its hinges by the bombing and thrown to the ground.

Rachel stumbled through the open doorway and vanished inside the big square building.

She yelled Matt's name.

The German cursed and lunged.

But in a flash, Matt followed Rachel.

He shot across the wobbling door. He lost his balance and sprawled to the rubble-filled floor of the building—but he didn't stop moving.

He crawled frantically forward, down a long corridor that led deeper into the space. Rachel appeared from the gloomy darkness and helped him to stand.

The German lost his balance on the shattered door behind them. He swore as he fell with a crash. He was bigger and heavier than a kid; he thrashed and struggled instead of just hopping back onto his feet.

Matt and Rachel ran farther into the dark corridor. Matt's mouth tasted of dust and ash. His pajama shirt was damp and speckled with burn marks from embers.

Rachel pulled him past a pile of crates and two closed doors. Then the corridor ended in a pile of debris.

A wall of wood and concrete must have blasted through from the next room. The dullest glimmering of light brushed shattered glass and scorched cloth.

"Can we climb over?" Matt asked.

Rachel peered into the darkness. "I do not think so."

"Quick." Matt spun around, turning toward the German. He groped in the pitch-dark for Rachel's hand, then led her back the way they'd come. "Hurry!"

He tried the first door. It was locked.

The German coughed nearby, invisible in the gloom. His boots scuffed through the debris on the floor. Ten feet away. Five.

Matt froze, holding Rachel's hand.

Neither of them spoke. Neither of them breathed.

The limping scuffle sounded closer.

Closer.

Then the German stopped. Just two feet from them. Matt could smell cigarettes and canal water.

The *shuffle-drag* moved past them, heading for the pile of debris filling the corridor.

Moving mouse-quiet, Matt crept closer to the opening to the alley. Once they got back to the street, they could run for help!

He tiptoed one step.

Then another.

Then his foot landed on a loose bit of concrete

or twisted metal. The scrape sounded loud in the dark corridor.

"Ha!" the German said, from the darkness. "I thought I—"

Matt lunged for the knob of the second door. He turned it desperately and flung the door open!

He burst through, pulling Rachel along with him, and slammed the door behind them.

When he turned, he found himself inside a movie theater.

Rows of chairs faced the stage . . . except for the ones torn and toppled by a blast. A balcony rose along one wall. The faint white rectangle of the screen seemed to hover in the darkness. A wide gash opened in the ceiling high above, and the orange glow of fire raging outside seeped through, giving a tinge of light.

Not enough to keep Matt from slamming his shin twice before finding the aisle between the chairs.

"Crawl!" he whispered to Rachel, falling to his hands and knees.

The door slammed open behind them. The German stepped inside.

Shuffle-drag.

Shuffle-drag.

Matt and Rachel crawled between the chairs. Across the wreckage-covered floor toward the wall. Under the balcony, the movie theater seemed to darken.

Shuffle-drag, shuffle-drag.

Matt's breathing sounded loud and harsh. He crawled behind Rachel until she reached the wall.

Rachel put her hand on his arm and whispered. "There is no way out. Just wall."

The *shuffle-drag* sounded closer, and Matt prayed that the German couldn't see them. But when he peered into the half-ruined movie theater, the first thing he saw was the glint of the German's eyes.

Looking directly at him.

"You ran the good race," the German said, prowling between the chairs to stand over Matt. "But now you have reached the finish."

CHAPTER 25

Matt scooted backward against Rachel, trying to get away from the German.

He retreated until he couldn't move any farther. He felt Rachel's breath on the back of his neck. He saw the German standing above him, silhouetted by the dim light that seeped through the hole in the ceiling.

The German drew back his knife. Matt raised his arm—

A *SMASH-clatter-clatter* sounded in the balcony above them.

"Huh," the German grunted.

Matt peeked between his arms, and a noise tore through the theater. So loud that it that felt like a thousand firecrackers going off. Too loud for an incendiary firebomb. It was a high-explosive bomb detonating on the roof above them!

The blast blew through the ceiling and smashed balcony chairs into splinters. A rain of wood chunks pelted the theater. Bits of wood and plaster fell around Matt and Rachel and bounced off the German's shoulders.

Rachel clung to Matt, and he gripped her arms tightly in a terrified daze. He couldn't think. He couldn't move . . . and a terrible *crack* sounded overhead.

The edge of the balcony swung down toward them.

The German dodged, barely avoiding getting smashed. He dove away from Matt and Rachel, racing for the exit, while Matt gaped in shock.

The balcony stopped falling five feet overhead. It hung from a dozen half-shattered planks directly above Matt and Rachel. Dust swirled in the dim orange light, bent metal struts groaned.

And then, with the snapping of wood and the moan of railings, the balcony started to collapse completely.

"Rachel!" Matt yelled, shoving her away from the danger zone.

She scrambled away—

And a chunk of balcony slammed down.

Pain flared in Matt's legs, and dust clogged his nose. At first he saw nothing but blackness. He heard nothing except the crash, still echoing in his mind. Yet as the dust cloud from the bomb settled, his vision cleared. With another section of the ceiling blasted away, more orange light seeped into the room.

From behind him, Matt heard Rachel crying and calling his name.

"He's gone!" he said, without looking at her. "I think he's gone."

His leg ached as he shifted—and he found himself staring at the remaining section of the broken balcony, dangling above him. If that one fell, they'd be in trouble. Well, in even more trouble.

Matt swallowed a mouthful of dust and ash

and peered quickly across the theater. The German was gone. Either he figured that Matt and Rachel were dead in the crash, or he was afraid the building was going to fall on him.

Which made sense. The whole place could collapse at any moment.

Matt pushed himself onto his knees.

Creak!

The section of balcony above him swayed and creaked. He needed to run! He needed to escape!

He reached for Rachel . . . but she wasn't there.

Instead, the fallen bit of balcony covered the corner of the theater between him and the wall.

"Rachel?" he yelled, frantic with fear. "Rachel, say something! Are you there? Can you hear—"

A little voice came from beneath the collapsed balcony. "Matt!"

Matt almost fainted in relief. "Are you okay?"

"Stuck . . . ," Rachel said.

Matt rolled to his side. Pain throbbed in his leg, but he reached along the fallen balcony until he found a small opening. "Rachel?"

The darkness shifted beneath the rubble. "Matt?"

"I'm right here." He poked his arm into the opening. "I'm here."

A soft hand curled around his wrist. "Are you hurt?"

"I'm fine," he said, not looking at his leg. "How about you?"

"Not even a scratch," she said, her voice trembling. "Except I'm stuck. I can't get out."

He looked at the rubble separating them. There was way too much for him to move. Plus, what if he tried to dig Rachel out and everything collapsed on her?

"Don't worry," he said, trying not to let his fear sound in his voice. "We'll find a way."

She didn't speak for a moment. Then she tried to make a joke. "You finally get your wish. If you leave, I can't tag along with you."

"I'm not going anywhere. You were right all along. We need to stick together."

A sniffle came from the darkness.

"You're the bravest kid I know," Matt said. "Boy howdy! You socked a Nazi with a stick!"

"Like Eric," she said.

"Just like Eric," Matt said, feeling tears prick

his eyes. "You and me, we're a team."

"Yes but . . . you must run before the roof falls."

"I'm not leaving without you. You're my sister. We stick together."

Rachel squeezed his hand. After a minute, she said, "I know I will never see them again. My mother and father. My sisters. My family."

"Maybe you—"

"I will never see them again, Matt," she said, and the tone in her voice silenced him completely.

Another silence fell, and this time he squeezed her hand.

"I will never see them again," she repeated, "and I cannot lose another family. You have to go. Run for help."

"I won't leave you."

"Come back with help!" she said. "Find help and come back."

"I'm not leaving you, Rachel. I don't care what—"

Creak.

Crash!

The noise burst from above Matt. When he looked upward, the final section of balcony seemed to fall at him in slow motion.

Pipes skewed into the air. Sparks flew, and wooden beams tore.

And with a *slam* the balcony crashed down around Matt. It didn't hit him, but it surrounded him. The dim orange light turned pitch-black.

Matt groped with his hands and his injured legs, and he couldn't feel a way out.

Now he was trapped too.

CHAPTER 26

Even after Chief shook the ringing from his ears, the car's engine sounded dull as the women drove away. The whistle of fire-rocks still shrilled, but not too close.

The scent of fresh blood felt like a sharp tang in Chief's nose. He sniffed the area where the injured people had been. No, that's not what he was smelling.

He turned his head to Landry, who knelt beside him.

"Good boy," Landry was still saying. "You're a real champ."

Chief nudged the human's shoulder, which was damp with blood.

"Ow! Oh!" Landry tugged at his shirt. "When did that happen?"

Chief tried to knock away Landry's hand, to give the wound a few healthful licks. Landry didn't let him, though. That was fine. Chief didn't insist. Sometimes you needed to lick your own wounds.

Landry probed his shoulder. "It's just a scratch. Still, you should've told me a few minutes ago. That pretty ATS girl could've bandaged me."

The wound smelled okay, so Chief turned and loped back toward the area with the ruined buildings. That's where people needed help. And it's also the direction from which he thought he'd heard the girl-pup and boy-pup.

"Okay, okay," Landry said, trotting beside him. "Slow down, four legs."

When they reached the street, Chief sniffed for people inside the buildings. He pricked his ears to listen, too, but the world still sounded far away. As he cocked his head, the up-and-down machine yowling changed into a loud howl.

"It's the all-clear siren!" another man told Landry. "Hey—you're bleeding."

"I caught a splinter."

"Sit down. Let's get you patched up."

"I can't, I've got to patrol with Chief. The raid's over, but his work is just starting."

"Patrol after you're bandaged, soldier!" the man said. "That's not a request. Give the dog to one of your buddies."

So Landry tied a rope to Chief's collar and handed the other end to another man. Chief eyed the man dubiously. He probably wasn't as well trained as Landry. Still, as long as he knew how to follow a leash, he'd be okay.

While another human started wrapping Landry's wound, Chief led his new man along the street. The smoke grew thicker even though the iron birds were gone.

And a hint of sweat and fear wafted from beneath a pile of rubble.

CHAPTER 27

Bombs fell outside. Sirens screamed.

Matt curled onto his side and hugged his knees. He'd lost Eric. He'd lost Chief. He'd lost his parents, and he hadn't even kept Rachel safe. Instead, he'd gotten her trapped in a bombed-out building.

He blinked back tears as he listened to Rachel cry. Maybe he cried too.

Finally the noise quieted. Both the tears and the bombs.

"Do you think the raid is over?" Rachel said

into the darkness.

"Either that or there are more waves coming."

"There can't be! When will it stop? When will— Oh!"

"What?"

"I heard people!" Rachel took a breath. "Help! Help!"

"We're in the movie theater!" Matt yelled, even though he didn't hear anyone. "We're trapped!"

"Help! Anyone!"

They yelled and yelled, but nobody answered. Nobody heard.

"It's no good," Matt said, his throat aching. "The balcony's padded. It's muffling our voices."

"'Muffling' isn't a word," Rachel said.

"It is too."

"English is silly," she said. "Muffling."

Matt smiled in the darkness. "It's softening our voices."

"Maybe we should . . . Do you remember what Eric taught us? About Morse code?"

"Brilliant!" Matt said. "We can tap out an SOS!"

"That's the signal for help?"

"Yeah," Matt said. "It goes 'dot-dot-dot, dash-dash-dash, dot-dot-dot.'"

"I remember now!"

"Do you have anything to tap with?" Matt reached in the darkness, wincing at a twinge of pain in his knee. "There's a pipe here. And a . . . I think it's a chair leg or something."

"I have a piece of lamp." Rachel made a long scraping noise on the other side of the balcony. "Like that."

Matt tapped the chair leg against the pipe. *Clunk, clunk, clunk. Clunk, clunk, clunk. Clunk, clunk, clunk.* "That sounds like dot-dot-dot, dot-dot-dot, dot-dot-dot."

"Start over again."

Matt tapped the chair leg. *Clunk, clunk, clunk. Cl—*

Scraaape, came from Rachel's section under the balcony. *Scraaape. Scraaape.*

Clunk, clunk, clunk, Matt tapped. *Clunk, clunk, clunk.*

Scraaape. Scraaape. Scraaape.

Clunk, clunk, clunk.

"Maybe the balcony is moffling this too," Rachel said.

"Muffling," Matt corrected.

Rachel giggled. "I am teasing!"

"We're trapped in a bombed building, and you're making jokes?"

"Only a very bad joke," she said. *Scraaape. Scraaape. Scraaape.*

"That's okay then." Matt smiled in the darkness and tapped the pipe. "I hope my folks are okay."

"And Chief."

"I'm sure he's fine. He's tough. He's Eric's dog. Nothing bad can . . ." Matt trailed off when he remembered that Eric was MIA. "Can happen to him."

Neither of them spoke while he tapped and Rachel scraped out SOS-SOS-SOS.

"You should not have yelled at your parents," Rachel eventually said. "Back in the shelter. You should not have yelled."

"They shouldn't have let Eric join the army

so early! They should've kept him with us. With the family. At home. We need him." Matt's tears came more easily this time. "I . . . miss him. All the time."

"If I had my parents, I would never yell at them."

"If you had a brother, you would." *Clunk, clunk, clunk.* "You'd yell at your parents if they let him leave and he went missing."

She didn't say anything. She just went *scraaape, scraaape, scraaape,* and Matt realized that she'd give anything just to have parents to yell at.

"Anyway, you *do* have a brother," Matt said. "Me."

She stopped scraping. Matt heard her move on the other side of the fallen balcony, like she'd turned to look at him.

"What would you do if *I* went MIA?" he asked her.

"I would yell," Rachel said.

"Good," he said.

"Except not— Oh! Oh, do you hear?"

Matt cocked his head in the darkness and

heard a single long blare of the sirens. "That's the all-clear sign! The raid's over!"

"There are people nearby too," she said.

Sure enough, faint shouts sounded from the street outside the theater.

"There's nobody in there," a man's voice said.

"The movie theater's clear?" another voice said.

"Hello?" Matt called. "Hello?"

"We're trapped!" Rachel shouted in her accented voice. "Help!"

The men didn't hear them.

"We already checked in there," the first man said. "Move out."

"We're in here!" Matt shouted at the top of his lungs.

The voices faded away . . . then Matt heard a distant bark.

"Is that Chief?" Rachel asked.

"Chief!" Matt shouted. "Chief! We're in here!"

Two sharp barks.

"Chief!" Rachel yelled. "Chief!"

"What is that mutt doing?" a voice said. "We've got a situation around the corner. Get a wiggle on!"

Matt and Rachel screamed and shouted, but the men's voices grew fainter and fainter.

Until they all disappeared—even Chief's.

And Matt and Rachel were alone again.

CHAPTER 28

3 A.M.

Chief dragged the man toward the ruined building. The man was so slow! And clumsy. He kept pulling in the wrong direction.

Chief gripped the ground with his claws and tugged until he pulled the man toward the building. Toward Matt.

A few other men were walking past. "We've already checked the movie theater. Search somewhere else."

Matt's voice sounded faintly from inside the building—and a whisper of Rachel's voice.

The humans didn't hear, so he barked louder.

"This way, Chief!" the man said.

Chief lunged toward the doors of the building.

"What is that mutt doing?" another man said. "We've got a situation around the corner. Move him along!"

Chief barked and barked.

"Silly dog just wants to watch a movie," the man said.

Together the two men started dragging Chief away from the building. Chief hunkered down and pulled, but he couldn't budge two men at once. Not without biting them, and Eric had taught him not to bite.

"Hey!" Landry ran toward Chief with his unfinished bandage flapping. "Can't you hear him?"

"He's trying to get into the theater," the other men said. "There's nobody there."

"There is if Chief thinks so," Landry said.

"The dog cleared it himself earlier. You believe someone ran *into* a bombed building?"

Landry looked at Chief. He looked at the men. Then he untied the leash and said, "I believe

whatever this dog tells me."

Chief raced toward the building with Landry stumbling along behind him. A pile of debris filled the front door. Chief paced. How could they get inside?

"Around back," Landry said.

"Private Landry!" another man yelled. "Stand down! We need that dog around the cor—"

"Someone needs our help right here!"

"Can *you* hear them? We don't take orders from a mutt."

"No, I—" Landry quieted.

Clunk, clunk, clunk.

Scraaape. Scraaape. Scraaape.

Clunk, clunk, clunk.

"Yes. Yes, I can."

"That's an SOS," the other man said. "The fleabag is right! Someone's buried in the rubble!"

CHAPTER 29

When Matt heard Chief barking again, he wiped the tears from his eyes. "He's coming back."

"Chief?" Rachel asked.

"I knew he'd come back. I knew it."

Still, Matt tapped louder for a few minutes, and Rachel scraped harder as the sound of rummaging through rubble came from outside.

"Hello?" a man called.

"Hi! Hello!" Matt and Rachel yelled. "We're in here!"

Chief barked.

"Chief!" Matt shouted.

Three more barks sounded, sharper and louder.

"Good boy!" Matt yelled.

"Good bear!" Rachel yelled.

Matt sensed that the man was squatting down next to the rubble. "You know Chief?"

"He's my brother's dog!" Matt said.

"He's really something," the man called, as the sound of rummaging continued outside. "He heard your SOS. That's pretty spiffy, a dog who understands Morse code."

That was a really stupid joke, almost as bad as Rachel's. Still, Matt smiled—mostly from relief.

"What're your names?" the man asked.

"I'm Matt," Matt said. "My sister is Rachel."

Chief barked.

"I'm Landry. Private Landry of the US Army. We'll have you out of there in a few minutes." His voice seemed to deepen. "Is anyone else in there? Anyone hurt?"

"No," Matt said. "We're okay."

"Matt's hurt," Rachel said.

Matt wrinkled his nose. How did Rachel know about that? "My leg's a little banged up is all. Um, are you American?"

"I am!" Private Landry said.

"So'm I! What're you doing here?"

"I could ask you the same question! You chose a bad time to catch the double feature."

A scrape and clatter sounded as rescuers shifted the rubble, trying to get to Matt and Rachel. The noise sent a shiver of fear into Matt's heart, and he heard Rachel gasp.

"What's happening?" Matt asked.

"This is going to take a few minutes," Private Landry said. "Don't worry, I'm not going anywhere. I've got a scratch, and now I'm stuck here getting bandaged."

"Good," Rachel said, her voice a little shaky. "You stay here."

"It would've been worse than a scratch if not for Chief," Private Landry said. "He saved me. He's a whiz of a rescue dog."

"Rescue dog?"

"He's a natural," Private Landry said, and

launched into a story about Chief's adventures that night.

Matt figured that the American soldier was just talking to keep him and Rachel calm, but he didn't mind. He liked it, actually. And it really was keeping him and Rachel calm, despite the throbbing pain in his leg and the grinding of the rubble being cleared.

"Have you heard of Dogs for Defense?" Private Landry asked.

Matt shook his head in the darkness. "I don't think so."

"It started earlier this year. Dog breeders and trainers joined together to train guard dogs for the War Department."

A metallic groan sounded, and the balcony trembled two feet above Matt's head. He almost yelped—he almost burst into tears—but he needed to stay strong for Rachel. So he only whimpered and said a silent prayer.

"The army doesn't even have a place to keep all those dogs," Private Landry continued, "forget about training them. So dozens of private kennels around the country are volunteering to house and train them. That's how I heard. My aunt owns a kennel."

"You are a trainer of dogs?" Rachel asked.

"My aunt is," Landry said, and the balcony shifted again. "Most of the army dogs are donated from private families, but the training program is moving pretty slowly so far. That's why Chief is so remarkable."

"Because he's so quick?" Matt asked, trying to keep his voice steady as he eyed the balcony.

"Yeah. He reminds me of a dog I heard about on the front lines. This dog's platoon got cut off from base. They were out there all alone, under heavy fire, with no way to ask for help against the Germans."

"Against Nazis," Rachel said.

Landry gave a little laugh. "That's right. So the soldiers attached a phone cable to the dog's collar, and he ran through enemy territory, dodging gunfire and shells until he reached the base. The platoon used the cable to call for backup, and they survived, all on account of that dog."

"That's amazing!" Matt said.

"Yeah. Like Chief here."

Chief barked.

"That's right, boy," Landry said, before raising his voice again. "He doesn't run from fire or fumes. He doesn't run from *bombs*. He knows if someone's trapped, and he'll fight for them. He's some kind of hero, this dog. All he cares about is saving lives."

"My brother . . ." Matt took a breath. "My brother, Eric, trained him."

"Then he's a hero too. Chief is the kind of dog the army needs. He's a real soldier dog. If he—"

Chief barked again, more urgently. Was he warning them? Was the building about to collapse?

"Hey, wat—" Matt started to shout at them to be careful—and all in a rush, a pile of rubble shifted. "Chief, no!"

CHAPTER 30

Matt's stomach dropped. His breath caught. Was the building falling on him and Rachel even as rescuers tried to dig them free?

Then a gap formed in the rubble. Faint light gleamed from outside, and cool smoky air billowed around Matt. The rescuers had done it! They'd dug a way out!

"C'mon, kid," a man's gruff voice said. "Movie's over."

"Where's Rachel?" Matt asked. "You need to help Ra—"

"I'm right here!" Rachel said from in front of him. She'd been trapped against the building's wall, so they'd reached her first.

"Oh!" Matt exhaled in relief.

Matt crawled toward the light, following Rachel's feet. Pain throbbed in his leg, and rubble scraped him through his pajamas.

A pair of strong hands lifted Rachel from the rubble, and then the gruff voice murmured to her, "You're safe, lass. We've got you now."

Matt squirmed forward, and another man hefted Matt from the rubble. This one had a bandaged shoulder and a warm smile. A rope-leash looped around his wrist and dangled on the floor. "I'm Bert Landry."

"Matt," Matt said. "Matt Dawson."

The gruff man asked Matt, "So is Chief your dog?"

"Or are you Chief's boy?" Landry asked, bringing Matt to the wreckage-strewn street.

Matt smiled. "A little bit of both, I guess."

"Well, he's—"

Two paws landed on Matt's chest, and a wet tongue licked his face. "Chief!" he cried. "I was so

worried about you!"

Chief licked Matt twice more. Then Matt got a face full of wagging tail as Chief turned to lick Rachel.

"Chiefy!" Rachel said, and fell to her knees to give Chief a hug.

Matt coughed from the smoke and dust as he looked at the people who'd rescued them. A couple of American GIs stood nearby, and Matt recognized a familiar sedan: the ATS women were there too. And British firemen and air-raid wardens and civil defense workers were scattered in the street beyond them.

The destroyed street.

Through the thick smoke still pouring from blazing fires, Matt saw that half of the buildings had been completely flattened. The sight made him a little faint, and he grabbed hold of Landry's arm to keep from falling.

"I know, kid," Landry said. "You got lucky."

"Tell them," Rachel told Matt. "Tell them about the pilot."

"What pilot?" Landry asked.

Matt took a breath to collect his thoughts. "Well, we were running for the shelter in the school when we saw—"

"Matt!" a familiar voice shouted. "Rachel! Thank God!"

Matt turned to find his father running wildly toward him and Rachel, his face smudged with ash and his clothes filthy like he'd been digging in the rubble. Which judging from his tear-streaked cheeks was exactly what he'd been doing: searching the rubble, trying to find Matt and Rachel.

Then another figure appeared behind his dad.

Matt never thought he'd see his mom racing across a rubble-strewn street in her nightgown, her robe flapping like a cloak. He never thought he'd see that look on her face either; her relief at finding him and Rachel alive couldn't hide the terror she'd been feeling.

Matt's father took him and Rachel in his arms, squeezed them in a tight hug. Pain bloomed in Matt's leg, but he couldn't stop smiling anyway.

His mother touched his face and kissed Rachel's head, then wrapped all three of them in her arms. She kept saying how worried she'd been, and how happy she was, while his father just squeezed him and Rachel and wept.

"Mr. and Mrs. Dawson, I'm Private Landry of the United States Army." The American soldier stood beside them, with Chief at his heels. "I'm wondering if—"

"He's the one who found us!" Matt said.

"Actually . . ." Landry put a hand on Chief's head. "Chief is the one who found them. I wanted to ask if we could borrow him for the rest of the night. There are still people trapped."

"Borrow Chief?" Matt's father said.

"He's a natural-born search and rescue dog," Landry said. "He found your kids. Found four other people too. He saved my life."

"Goodness!" Matt's mother said. "Well, of course. Anything to help."

"He's not the only one who helped," a man with an English accent said, stepping closer.

For a moment, Matt didn't recognize him. Then he realized it was the rat-faced man—that is, the *hero*—from the cathedral roof.

"Your kids helped clear the roof," the man said.

"The cathedral roof?" Matt's father asked.

"They must have had quite a busy night," an ATS woman told the man. "Because these are the same children who led us to an injured couple."

Matt's mom squeezed him and Rachel even harder. "Looks like Chief isn't the only hero in the family."

Rachel tugged at her braid, and Matt flushed. Landry crouched to tie his makeshift leash to Chief's collar.

Firemen shouted. An ambulance picked its way down the street. Matt's exhausted gaze dragged over a man in a smock wandering from the smashed dentist's office as a horse and cart helped clear the wreckage and—

Shuffle-drag. Shuffle-drag.

Matt's blood chilled. That noise. It was the limping German pilot.

"Matt!" Rachel whispered.

Shuffle-drag.

"Where is he?" Matt asked, scanning the smoky street.

Rachel pointed with a trembling finger toward the man in the dentist's smock. Matt barely recognized the German without his flight suit, but the limp was the same, and the waterlogged boots.

"Hey!" Matt yelled. "That man—*him*—he's a German! He's a bomber!"

CHAPTER 31

"*C*hief!" Matt bellowed. *"Fetch!"*

Chief heard more than fear in Matt's voice. He heard anger.

His hackles raised, and he stood guard between Matt and Rachel. Where was the threat? The humans yapped uselessly at each other while Matt and Rachel flailed their arms.

Chief pricked his ears and . . . *there*! Footsteps! Running away. Fleeing fast between buildings— and leaving a strange scent trail. The smell of river water and engine oil and something else. Violence and . . . and *Matt*.

The man had Matt's scent on him.

A growl of fury rumbled in Chief's throat. He flashed forward. Landry wasn't stupid; he released the leash and followed Chief.

Chief's legs blurred, his muzzle lifted in a snarl. His ears pinpointed the fleeing man, and he chased him through the smoke and the rubble.

His heart pounded with the hunt. Landry and the other men followed, blocks behind.

The prey's scent changed. The man was afraid. Good.

The man scrambled into a wide-open space with a hard floor. He spun to face Chief, and a long metal tooth grew from one of his hands. Sharper than any dog's tooth.

The man crouched, raising the metal tooth—

A distant part of Chief's mind told him to wait for his pack. Wait for the men. Circle the prey-man and wait.

But a bigger part still smelled Matt's anger.

Chief didn't hesitate. He didn't break his stride. He flattened his ears and bared his teeth and ran directly at the man.

He leaped for his throat.

The metal tooth bit into Chief's side.

He felt the burn of a wound, but he didn't yelp or cringe. Instead, he slammed the man backward.

The man fell with a grunt, cracking his head on the ground.

Chief rolled and stood and bit the man's arm, the one holding the metal tooth. He shook his head like breaking a prey animal's neck, and the tooth flew. It clattered against the ground in the shadows.

Chief's side still burned, but he didn't care. He bunched his legs for another leap.

"Please!" The man dragged himself away from Chief. "Call him off, call him off!"

"Chief!" Landry ran into the open space. "Down. Down, Chief!"

Chief stalked the man, ignoring Landry's yipping.

"Call your dog off!" the prey-man wept. "Please, *bitte*! *Bitte nicht!*"

Chief didn't understand the yipping, but he approved of the sudden hardness in Landry's

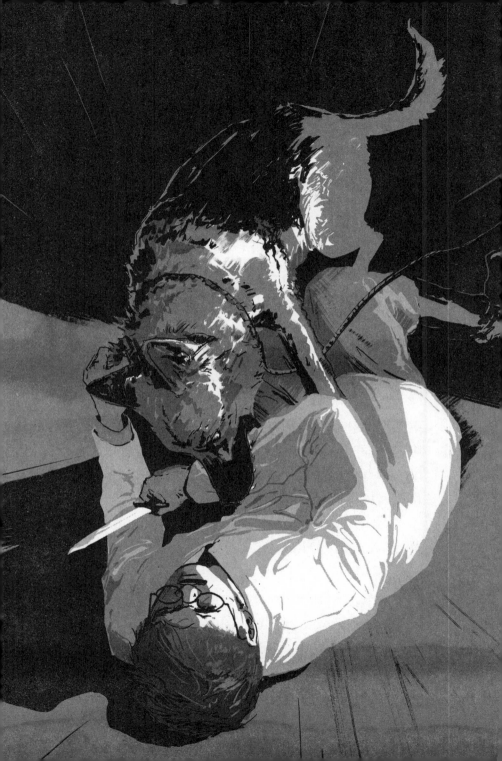

posture. The sudden wolfishness. The prey-man was an enemy.

"It is true!" the man yipped. "I surrender! The boy is right! I am a Luftwaffe bombardier."

"Well, Mr. Bombardier," Landry said, his voice smooth with threat. "If I were you, I'd keep very still."

The prey-man went motionless—except for his frightened panting.

Chief bared his teeth and eyed the man's throat. Blood soaked the fur on Chief's side. He ignored the weakness in his left leg and watched the man. Looking for any sign of defiance.

Chief felt woozy, but he stayed watchful, ready to pounce. The prey-man didn't move. Not until the rest of Landry's pack came. As Chief's leg started trembling, they dragged the prey-man to his feet and shoved him away.

"You really are a doozy," Landry told Chief. "I'd say you're the cat's meow, but I don't want to insult—"

Chief flopped to the ground, exhausted from the long night and the slash on his side.

"You're bleeding!" Landry sat beside Chief, looking at his cut. "You're hurt!"

Chief rested his head on Landry's leg, and darkness came.

CHAPTER 32

For days after the raid, smoke hung in the air above Canterbury, smelling to Matt like melted rubber and charred wood. Eight hundred buildings lay in ruins, and over five thousand more were damaged. Almost fifty people had died in the night.

But the steeple of the Canterbury Cathedral still rose above the haze.

The Nazis had wanted to destroy the cathedral. They'd wanted to break the spirit of their enemy.

They'd failed.

Hundreds of fire trucks had gathered to fight the flames during and after the raids. Civilians and soldiers banded together to help each other while firewatchers patrolling the roofs and gutters threw incendiary bombs to safety.

The cathedral still stood tall, though it bore the scars of the attack: shattered windows, a crumbling wall, and scorched lawns.

Farther down the hill, Matt crept along the hallway in his house.

Stealthy. Silent. And a little sad.

He paused outside the kitchen door and listened.

He made a face when he heard murmuring inside. He took a breath for courage, then turned the knob very slowly.

If Chief had been around, he would've noticed Matt. His ears would've pricked, and his tail would've thumped a few times. But as it was, nobody saw Matt open the door an inch and peer inside.

His mom sat with Mrs. Lloyd at the table. And the newborn baby—the noisy, red-faced infant—slept in Mrs. Lloyd's arms. Actually sleeping, for once. The baby screamed so loudly at night that Matt heard her from next door.

He called her "the Siren."

But Rachel, for some reason, found the baby adorable. She was standing next to Mrs. Lloyd right now, gazing at the little monster with misty eyes.

"Pssssst!" Matt said, staying quiet so he wouldn't risk waking the Siren.

"Yes, Matt?" his mother said in her regular voice.

"Shh! Don't wake her!" Matt looked to Rachel and whispered, "Are you coming?"

Rachel touched the baby's swaddled foot. "Is it already time?"

"Shh! Yes. *C'mon.*"

"Okay, okay." Rachel followed him into the hallway. "You are always wanting me to tag along."

"Very funny."

"Every time I turn around, there you are," she said. "A shadow."

"Shake a leg already," he told her.

She giggled and followed him outside. They

tromped through the streets—keeping away from the ruined ones—toward the park.

When they got there, they found Private Landry throwing a stick for Chief.

Chief flashed between the trees, moving smooth and strong. His coat was glossy despite the shaved patch where a vet had stitched his cut. He didn't seem to notice Matt and Rachel, except one of his ears swiveled toward them before he pounced on the stick.

Matt smiled. He liked knowing that Chief knew he was there, that Chief always kept track of him.

"Rachel, Matt!" Private Landry called. "I can't believe how fast Chief has recovered. You've taken really good care of him."

"That's nothing." Matt looked to Rachel. "Are you ready?"

She nodded and told Private Landry, "Count to a hundred. Then tell Chief to 'find.'"

Private Landry gaped at Rachel and Matt. "You've been training him?"

"One!" Matt said, jogging toward the other end of the park. "Two!"

Rachel ran beside him. "Three!"

They scrambled around a vegetable garden and through a thicket, then veered onto a path. *Thirty-five, thirty-six.*

The path curved toward the river, which smelled of geese and pond. *Fifty-seven, fifty-eight.*

Matt stopped beneath a tree and interwove his fingers. Rachel put one foot in his hands, and he boosted her onto a thick branch.

"Eighty-five," she whispered, as Matt clambered beside her. "Eighty-six . . ."

They counted the rest silently. Hiding in the tree. Quiet and still.

In the distance, Landry shouted, "Chief! Find!"

Matt held his breath. He and Rachel had trained Chief every day since the vet said he could run. And every day, Chief found the person hiding almost immediately. Then he'd look at them like they were stupid for getting lost again.

Except they'd never tried this with anyone *else* saying "find." What if Chief didn't understand? What if—

Paws rustled through fallen leaves, and a sharp bark sounded.

Chief's bright eyes watched them. Matt imagined him thinking, "How did you get lost up in a *tree*? Silly humans."

Chief barked again.

"I'm coming, I'm coming!" Landry called from farther in the park.

"Matt?" Rachel put her hand on Matt's arm. "Are you sure about this?"

"Yeah." He swallowed a lump in his throat. "It's what Eric would want."

"Yes, but what do *you* want?"

Matt felt tears in his eyes. "I understand now. I know why my parents let Eric enlist. There are things you can't ignore. Battles you can't run from. Sometimes you have to fight. Sometimes you have to give everything you've got. And Chief?"

Chief barked.

"He's not a pet, he's a soldier." Matt looked down. "A soldier dog."

When Landry jogged into sight, Matt dropped from the tree. Then he fell to his knees. He felt tears on his cheeks as he spread his arms to Chief.

Chief knew how he felt. Chief always knew. He stepped into Matt's hug and rubbed his head against Matt's chin. His fur was warm and soft.

Matt heard Rachel and Landry talking to each other, but he just held Chief and cried. After what felt like a long time, he kissed Chief's head and stood. Wiping the tears from his eyes, he reached into his shirt and pulled out the clump of cloth he'd stuffed there.

"This is for Chief," he said, giving it to Landry. "It's my pillowcase. So wherever he goes, it'll always smell like home."

Matt knew he'd cry when Chief left to join Dogs for Defense, but he also knew it was the right thing to do. For him, for Chief. And for Eric.

He felt bad about saying goodbye, and at the same time he felt good about his decision. He kept sniffling, though. And he didn't even mind when Rachel took his hand. He didn't have Chief anymore, but he wasn't alone.

Matt and Rachel walked home in silence.

Until, three doors down from their house, they heard a shriek.

"There goes the Siren again," Matt grumped.

Except it wasn't the baby crying with hunger or a wet diaper.

It was his mother, screaming with joy.

She burst from the front door waving a telegram and shouted, "They found him! They found Eric! He's okay, he's alive!"

Relief and joy exploded in Matt's heart, brighter than any bomb.

He whooped and hugged Rachel. When he spun her in circles, her braid flapped wildly, and her laughter rang out. The Canterbury air didn't stink of melted rubber and charred wood to Matt. Not anymore.

Now it smelled of hope.

DID DOGS LIKE CHIEF REALLY SERVE DURING WORLD WAR II?

Yup! When the war broke out, many Americans wanted to help—including the furry ones. Families across the country donated their dogs to a group called Dogs for Defense, who trained the brave pups to do important military tasks.

In boot camp, canine trainees learned to search for folks lost in fires and under rubble, carry cables and supplies, and alert their handlers to enemy sneak attacks. They were taught to respond to spoken commands like "FIND!" and "ATTACK!"

The character of Chief was inspired by two of WWII's bravest soldier dogs, Chips and Jet!

CHIPS

US ARMY HERO DOG

NATIONALITY: AMERICAN

BREED: GERMAN SHEPHERD-COLLIE-SIBERIAN HUSKY MIX

JOB: SENTRY DOG

STRENGTHS: BRAVERY, SPEED, LOYALTY

TRAINING: WAR DOG TRAINING CENTER IN VIRGINIA

STATIONED: EUROPE AND NORTH AFRICA

HEROIC MOMENT: RUNNING INTO MACHINE GUN FIRE AND JUMPING INTO AN ENEMY BUNKER IN ITALY TO PROTECT HIS SQUAD

HONORS: PDSA DICKIN MEDAL, BRITAIN'S HIGHEST HONOR FOR DOGS.

JET

NATIONALITY: BRITISH

BREED: GERMAN SHEPHERD

JOB: SEARCH AND RESCUE

STRENGTHS: BRAVERY, INTELLIGENCE, GRIT

TRAINING: GLOUCESTER WAR DOGS SCHOOL

STATIONED: LONDON

HEROIC MOMENT: SAVED MORE THAN 150 PEOPLE FROM BOMBED BUILDINGS DURING THE LONDON BLITZ

HONORS: RSPCA MEDALLION OF VALOUR AND THE PDSA DICKIN MEDAL

TOP TEN SOLDIER DOG STATS:

1. 40,000 American dogs were volunteered for the war effort.

2. The US Army used 10,000 of these patriotic pets over the course of the war.

3. The main jobs for World War II soldier dogs were sentry dogs, patrol dogs, messengers, search-and-rescue dogs, and mine-detection dogs.

4. Seven breeds were eventually accepted as the best soldier dogs: German shepherd, Belgian sheepdog, Doberman pinscher, collie, Siberian husky, malamute, and Eskimo dog.

5. Boot camp for dog soldiers lasted just as long as it did for human soldiers—eight to twelve weeks.

6. A dog's sense of smell is forty times more sensitive than a human's—making them great for search and rescue missions and sniffing out landmines and bombs!

7. A German shepherd can bite down with 238 pounds per square inch of force—that's twice as powerful as a human bite, and with sharper teeth!

8. Dogs can run at speeds of up to 30 mph.

9. The army trained dogs for use in all branches of the military.

10. Soldier dogs in training could only spend time with and be fed by their handlers, so they'd learn to tell the difference between friends and enemies.

TIMELINE OF

December 8 to December 10, 1941
First Battle of Guam: Japanese forces capture the Pacific Island

September 1, 1939
Germany invades Poland; war breaks out in Europe

December 8, 1941
US enters war

December 7, 1941
Attack on Pearl Harbor

May 1941
End of London Blitz

1938   1939   1940   1941

December 1, 1938
First Kindertransport leaves Berlin

May 14, 1940
Last Kindertransport leaves Netherlands

September 1940
London Blitz begins

September 1940
US government begins the draft

WORLD WAR II

September 2, 1945
V-J Day (Victory in Japan),
Japanese sign surrender agreement

August 14, 1945
Japanese forces surrender

August 9, 1945
Atomic bomb dropped on Nagasaki

August 6, 1945
Atomic bomb dropped on Hiroshima

September 1943
Italian forces surrender

May 8, 1945
V-E Day (Victory in Europe)

May 7, 1945
German forces surrender

1942   1943   1944   1945

January 1942
First American troops
arrive in Britain; Dogs
for Defense program is
founded

April 1942 to June 1942
Baedeker Blitz

June 1, 1942
Canterbury Blitz

July 1942
US government commits
to use of trained war dogs

August 1942
US begins work on atomic
bomb

June 6, 1944
D-Day at Normandy in
France

July 21, 1944 to
August 8, 1944
Second Battle of Guam: US
takes control from Japan

August 25, 1944
Paris is freed from German
control

Q&A ABOUT AIR RAIDS

Q. What's a blitz? Isn't that a football thing?

A. Yes, but it meant something else in World War II. "Blitz" is short for "blitzkrieg," the German word for "lightning war." During the London Blitz in 1941, German forces dropped bombs on Britain's capital every single day for three months and destroyed a third of the city. Tens of thousands of people died in these attacks, and the Luftwaffe (the German air force) dropped over 41,000 tons of bombs—that's almost a hundred MILLION pounds of bombs! (41K × 2K = 82 million)

Q. What kinds of planes did the German forces use in their attacks?

A. The Luftwaffe used several different kinds of planes for their blitzkrieg bombing—including the Heinkel, Messerschmitt, and Junkers (pronounced "yoonkers"). Each plane was used for a different kind of attack, including long-distance, nighttime, or heavy artillery.

Q. What's the difference between firebombs and incendiary bombs?

A. During the Canterbury Blitz, German bombardiers dropped two different kinds of bombs. Five-hundred-pound high-explosive firebombs burst into flames right away and were intended to blow up buildings. Incendiary bombs were used to start fires. Sometimes the chemicals inside them took a few seconds to mix together and ignite after dropping—giving the firewatchers time to throw them off the roof of the cathedral!

Q. So fire was a big threat during an air raid?

A. Yes! Volunteer firewatchers and firefighters played a huge role in protecting cities during an air raid—but sometimes the fires grew out of control! In the Canterbury Blitz, a street called Butchery Lane was used as a firebreak—a strip of open space that prevents a fire from spreading. Lucky for Canterbury, it worked! While one side of the street was destroyed in the Blitz, the other survived relatively unharmed.

Q. How did people fight back?

A. The Royal Air Force fought back in planes like the Spitfire and Beaufighter. The Spitfire was the most common British fighter plane. It seated only one pilot and was light and easy to steer through dogfights. Beaufighters were bigger, which meant they could carry more weapons and were often used in nighttime battles during the air raids. The British also used antiaircraft missiles to shoot down German planes from the ground.

Q&A ABOUT THE CANTERBURY BLITZ

Q. What was so special about the Canterbury Blitz?

A. The Canterbury Blitz was one part of a series of German attacks called the Baedeker Blitz. Germany didn't just want to win the war, it wanted to break the British spirit by destroying important historical sites in England. So the German military picked up a copy of the popular Baedeker travel guide and chose the most popular landmarks to attack. Canterbury became a target because the cathedral was built in the 1070s and many British people loved to vacation in this small coastal city.

TOP CANTERBURY BLITZ STATS:

1. Bombs began dropping on June 1, 1942, around midnight.

2. German planes dropped 130 high-explosive bombs.

3. Most of the bombs missed the historic eight-hundred-year-old cathedral because a breeze blew the flares off-target.

4. Eight hundred other buildings in Canterbury were destroyed and more than six thousand damaged.

5. More than a hundred people were injured, and forty-three died.

6. Most of the kids in Canterbury had already been evacuated through Operation Pied Piper, which began on September 1, 1939.

7. Air raids like the Canterbury Blitz came in waves—first one squadron of bombers, then a pause, then another squadron.

8. Most air-raid shelters were in the basements of homes, office buildings, and factories—and even deep within subway stations! But the main shelter in Canterbury was in the crypt beneath the cathedral.

9. Canterbury was attacked AGAIN throughout the war—135 separate raids total!

10. A total of 10,445 bombs were dropped during all the raids.

11. In the raids, 731 homes and 296 other buildings in the city were destroyed, and 115 people were killed.

12. The Canterbury Cathedral still stands.

MORE QUESTIONS ABOUT WORLD WAR II

Q. How did ATS help the war effort?

A. Keeping England safe was a team effort. Aside from groups like the air-raid wardens and firewatchers, ATS—short for Auxiliary Territorial Services—played a big role. The ATS was the women's branch of the British Army, and although they weren't allowed to serve in combat, they filled lots of important roles from communication to first aid, intelligence, military police, and radar operators. By the time the war was over, 190,000 British women had served.

Q. What was the Kindertransport?

A. "Kinder" means children in German. In this book, Rachel comes to live with Matt's family as part of the Kindertransport, a British program that saved around ten thousand Jewish kids from the Nazis. After it became clear to Great Britain that the Nazis had terrible plans for the Jewish people living in Germany and the surrounding countries, the British government found foster families for

Jewish children under the age of seventeen. The sad truth was that many of these children never saw their families again.

Q. Did the US Army and British troops really use Morse code in World War II?

A. They sure did! Morse code is the system that represents the letters of the alphabet with dots and dashes; it was invented by Samuel Morse in 1844. You had to know it to be a pilot, and it was also used for navigating at sea. Morse code was especially important to both sides in World War II because it allowed secret encrypted messages to be sent almost instantly between planes, ships, and land. In this book, Matt and Rachel use the Morse code SOS to call for help.

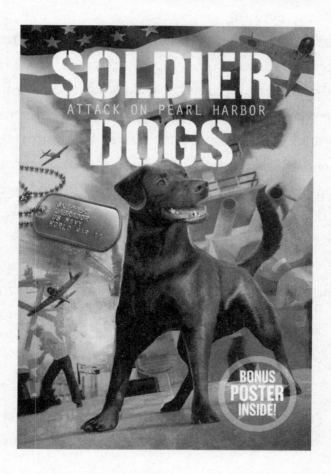

The attack came out of nowhere.

No warning, no declaration of war, no siren, before the enemy descended on the US naval base at Pearl Harbor in a wave of fire, panic, and destruction.

All across the island of Oahu, unsuspecting Americans were enjoying a perfect Hawaiian Saturday morning in what was as close to paradise on earth as one could get. Warm sunlight shone between the leaves of gently swaying palm trees. Stores and restaurants opened in preparation for a day of weekend shoppers. Hula music played softly on radios in windows and cars as coffee brewed and breakfast sizzled in pans. On the decks of the vessels of Battleship Row, a group of eight military battleships in port at the harbor, sailors were finishing up breakfasts, playing a little early catch on deck, or getting ready for a weekend's shore leave with their wives and families.

Then, the roar of plane engines.

The crackle of machine gun fire. The thunder of bombs exploding. The thud of torpedoes slamming into ship hulls beneath the rocking waves.

America was being attacked.

That was all anyone knew.

On the deck of the USS *West Virginia*, Joseph Dean, eleven years old, son of the ship's head cook, had no idea the planes raining gunfire and destruction on him and his friends were from the Empire of Japan. He didn't know that the aircraft carriers from which those planes had taken off had left Japan ten days earlier with plans to destroy Pearl Harbor. He didn't know the small black packages dropping off them were armor-piercing bombs. And he had no way of knowing that the nearby USS *Arizona* had just taken on a full 1.5 million gallons of fuel in preparation for a trip to the mainland.

All Joe knew was that Skipper, his new dog, had sensed something. She'd started barking at the edge of the ship, losing her cool in a way he'd never seen before. It had spooked them all—a warning of something they didn't understand.

A warning that came too late.

Joe saw as the planes appeared overhead. They swooped aggressively low over the ships along the Row, bathing them in bullets and bombs. Suddenly, Joe was dodging bullets and smelling smoke, and then—

BOOM!

A wall of white-hot air slammed into Joe. He flew through the air and landed on his back.

Joe sat up, dazed and hurt. Stunned, he could only watch as the *Arizona* was cut in half by a massive explosion. The ship's belly was like an opening into the pit from one of his grandmother's Bible stories, a raging fire that filled the sky with oily black smoke. As Joe tried to regain his bearings, the twenty-nine-ton battleship began to sink to the bottom of the harbor over only ten minutes, the deafening blast taking with it over a thousand American lives.

As Joe stared on in horror, Skipper appeared in front of him. She barked and barked, trying to rouse him to action. Terrified and confused, Joe threw his arms around her neck and hugged her for dear life.

"Oh, Skipper," he cried, his body shaking against hers, "what's going on? Who's attacking us, girl? How did this happen?"